ENTERING INTO REST

SELF, WORLD, AND TIME

Ethics as Theology 1

AN INDUCTION

FINDING AND SEEKING

Ethics as Theology 2

ENTERING INTO REST

Ethics as Theology 3

Entering into Rest

• •

Ethics as Theology 3

Oliver O'Donovan

WILLIAM B. EERDMANS PUBLISHING COMPANY
GRAND RAPIDS, MICHIGAN

Wm. B. Eerdmans Publishing Co.
2140 Oak Industrial Drive N.E., Grand Rapids, Michigan 49505
www.eerdmans.com

© 2017 Oliver O'Donovan
All rights reserved
Published 2017
Printed in the United States of America

23 22 21 20 19 18 17   1 2 3 4 5 6 7

ISBN 978-0-8028-7359-0

Library of Congress Cataloging-in-Publication Data

Names: O'Donovan, Oliver, author.
Title: Entering into rest / Oliver O'Donovan.
Description: Grand Rapids : Eerdmans Publishing Co., 2017. | Series: Ethics as theology ; 3 |
    Includes bibliographical references and index.
Identifiers: LCCN 2016050275 | ISBN 9780802873590 (pbk. : alk. paper)
Subjects: LCSH: Religion and ethics. | Ethics. | Christian ethics. | Theology. |
    Philosophical theology.
Classification: LCC BJ47 .O46 2017 | DDC 241—dc23
    LC record available at https://lccn.loc.gov/2016050275

Contents

Preface	vii
1. The Sovereignty of Love	1
The Inverted Triad	1
The Foundationalizing of Love	9
The Future of Love	14
Cooperation	19
2. Ends of Action	24
De finibus	24
Further and Latter Ends	31
Judgment	40
3. Communication	45
Ends and Community	45
The Common Good	53
Two Cities	59
The Sin against Community	65
4. Sanctification	72
A Dogmatic Preamble	72
Thanksgiving	79
Perfection	85
Social Transformation	93

5. The Communication of Work — 102
   - Body, Soul, and Spirit — 102
   - Work and Existence — 107
   - Labor, Society, and Self-Realization — 111
   - The Wrongs of Work — 121
   - The Sanctification of Work — 127

6. The Communication of Friendship — 135
   - Coexistence — 135
   - The Commitment of Friendship — 138
   - The Wrongs of Hostility — 147
   - The Sanctification of Friendship — 153

7. The Communication of Meaning — 163
   - Meaning and Reality — 163
   - Narrative and Description — 170
   - Theology, Ethics, and Narrative — 174
   - The Wrongs of Falsehood — 183
   - The Sanctification of Meaning — 192

8. The Endurance of Love — 200
   - The Bewilderment of Love — 200
   - Suffering — 202
   - Death — 207
   - The Sanctification of Temporality — 214
   - The Eternity of Love — 225

Index of Names and Subjects

Index of Scripture References

Preface

Ethics as Theology began with an "induction" into Christian Ethics, *Self, World, and Time,* which was concerned with the study of Ethics itself as an ordered reflection on moral thinking and on its place within the life of faith. In *Finding and Seeking* the focus shifted from the study of moral thinking to moral thinking itself and explored its progress from the original consciousness of agency, to the world as the structure of value, and to the time that determines the moment of decision. With this third volume the exploration turns from the progress of moral thinking to its object, the forward horizon with which moral thinking engages. Broadly speaking, the two aspects of our exploration correspond to the classical discussions *de officiis*, "on duties," and *de finibus*, "on ends of action." If this study in Theological Ethics may presume to render any service to wider philosophical undertakings with Ethics, it may be by reminding philosophy of its own legacy in this important ancient distinction. The moral experience on which Ethics reflects is necessarily two-directional, involving consciousness of responsibility, on the one hand, and goals to be pursued, on the other. But the habit of modern programs for a tidier Ethics has been to ground everything on one or the other aspect of this double experience, "deontology" or "teleology," which is why modern programs are one-legged, casting around for a crutch to support them.

What is implied for Ethics by this transition from one focus of attention to the other? Ethics, when it understands itself correctly, follows and interprets moral reason, without trying to take over its role in thinking towards concrete decision and action. Moral reason is both reflective and deliberative, while Ethics is always reflective, even when the object of its reflections is deliberation. But it may reflect on moral reason formally, observing its logic and discipline, and it may reflect more materially, observing its objects and goals. It has a task that may be referred to, unsatisfactorily but intelligibly enough, as "deontology," accounting for the logic by which a responsible moral decision is reached, and a task that may be referred to as "teleology." And when Ethics takes up the latter task, it takes a step closer to the point of view of the deliberating agent, not ceasing to reflect and interpret, but reflecting from inside, as it were, and looking out with the agent's eyes on the future horizon and what it offers to action.

Once the formal parallel has been acknowledged, it must be said at once that Christian Ethics understands its deontology and teleology very differently from classical ethics. Our *de officiis* has taken us through the three theological virtues of faith, love, and hope, though it goes without saying that this distinctively Pauline way is not the only possible one, and we have remained in constant conversation with other themes. No quarter has been given in these volumes to a methodological monism that champions virtue ethics, command ethics, imitation ethics, or even an ethic of love, against all rivals. The last thing that could benefit Theological Ethics at this point would be yet another reduction of the moral message of the Christian Gospel to a single word, or even to three words. In particular, the moral psychology of Jesus of Nazareth, with its strong focus on the dialectic between the inner heart and the outer performance, is a reference point that professional moral theologians too easily overlook. Our *de finibus* now gives us a view of the climax of the Pauline triad in the sovereignty of love. Again, there could be other possible starting points; the Sermon on the Mount suggests itself, framed as it is by declarations of the moral significance of the ultimate future, for the teleology of classical ethics is drawn, in a Christian context, inexorably into the magnetic field of eschatology. I entertain the fantasy that, were I to begin this enterprise again, I might take my starting point from the teaching of Jesus. Those pastors and preachers of the church who cling to the Sunday Gospel with a sure instinct for where safety lies are in this respect wiser than their teachers! I hope, at any rate, that the time will come when moral theologians may dare to make Jesus their point of reference without being suspected, or guilty, of a "low" Christology. The patristic church, Augustine, the Reformers, and even the scholastics learned constantly from Jesus how to reframe the questions their intellectual world presented to them. We should be able to do as much.

It is an author's greatest privilege in offering a new work to the public to acknowledge his debts, and his greatest embarrassment to discover that

Preface

they are too many to be acknowledged. Every page has been carefully read through by Joan Lockwood O'Donovan; sections have enjoyed the benefit of comment and advice from Christoph Raedel, Kevin Vanhoozer, Bernd Wannenwetsch, and Tom Wright. Parts have been presented in more or less preparatory form at the University of Saint Andrews, the University of Edinburgh, the Institut Catholique de Paris, the University of Chicago, the annual meeting of the Society for the Study of Christian Ethics, the 2014 Lumen Christi Institute Conference on Economics and Catholic Social Thought in Chicago, the Kirby Laing Institute for Christian Ethics at Tyndale House in Cambridge, the Lupina Centre at Regis College, Toronto, and the Archbishop of York's Colloquium on Social Issues at Bishopthorpe, and they have been greatly improved by discussions they received there. To my friends at Eerdmans, whose support has encouraged me since the appearance of *Resurrection and Moral Order* in 1986, I am, as always, in debt. My thanks are due also to Andrew Errington for help with the proofs and indexes. But these acknowledgments only scratch the surface. In every thought we are the beneficiaries of those who have done such work before us, and every footnote records some help the author has received from what another has written. If justice were to be done to it all, the world could not contain all the footnotes that would be written.

CHAPTER 1

The Sovereignty of Love

The Inverted Triad

At the conclusion of the famous thirteenth chapter of his First Letter to the Corinthians, Paul takes a triad of virtues that was familiar to him and his readers in the form "faith, love, and hope" and rearranges it: "now there remain faith, hope, and love, these three."[1] And as though to draw attention to what he has done, he adds: "The greatest of them is love." What did he mean by doing this? That question has been on the horizon of our explorations throughout the two previous volumes of *Ethics as Theology*.

We cannot simply exclude the suggestion that he might have meant nothing, and that it is no more than a ploy of rhetorical variation. The most conscientious of commentators have had little to say about it.[2] The force of that suggestion, however, can be reduced by tracing a logic at work in Paul's reflections on the moral life which makes good sense of the shift of focus in the inverted triad. The sequence in which faith is followed by love, and love by hope, reaches its conclusion in action. Paul conceived it as representing the shape of the Christian life—baptism, church membership, and endurance. In *Finding and Seeking* we traced the same shape beneath the surface of common human moral thought, as responsibility, attention to the world, and deliberation. But applied either way, its horizon is action and life in the

---

1. For the tally of occurrences see *Self, World, and Time*, pp. 98-99.
2. It is overlooked, for example, in the extensive Commentary of Anthony C. Thiselton, *The First Epistle to the Corinthians*, New International Greek Testament Commentary (Grand Rapids: Eerdmans, 2000), pp. 1071-74, where the discussion of this verse is otherwise as comprehensive as could be imagined.

1

world. Action and life in the world have no ending; they are perennial. But rearranged in another sequence, faith, hope, and love open up to a further horizon, that of accomplishment, the satisfaction of moral agency in its end. It is the horizon of a second reflection, a point of rest on the far side of deliberation to which practical reason may look as its goal, not alien to practice or superseding practice, but pushing its horizon back to the accomplishment that life itself is offered.

Questions that Paul confronted in the course of his Corinthian correspondence drew his thought along two converging lines: the life of the church, and the expectation of the end. The first was prompted by the uncomfortable experience of a dysfunctional and conflicted church, the second by one feature of that conflict, the competitive prizing of exceptional personal vocations. In the first line of thought Paul developed his case for the self-restraining, deferential character of life in community; in the second he contrasted the limited historical usefulness of particular vocations with the eschatological finality of moral perfection. "Love" was the category upon which the two lines of thought converged.

At the center of the thirteenth chapter, then, we find a series of characterizations of love as deference. Love's "patience" (for it now presupposes hope), and love's "generosity" are explored both negatively and positively: not jealous, not boastful, not self-important, not dishonorable, not self-seeking, not quickly riled, not keeping count of evils, not gloating over wrongs, but also truth-loving, tolerant, faithful, hopeful, and persistent (1 Cor. 13:4–6). Astonishingly, it has been possible to read this famous chapter in a way that bypasses these characterizations. In its most memorable musical interpretation, the fourth of Brahms's *Four Serious Songs*, they are omitted, with striking effect. The dying composer, using Paul's words to bid farewell to his art, celebrates the delicate inspiration at the heart of musical utterance in contrast to the showmanship surrounding it, but never acknowledges that music-making, most of all arts, requires the close attention of each performer to the others. Paul's account of love, by contrast, is less interested in utterance (of which he has heard too much from his Corinthian correspondents) than in mutual identification.

Negative or positive, these features of love move round a well-described circle: restraint of competitive self-assertion, acceptance of others' activities and initiatives, flexibility in waiting upon them, and readiness to give them time and space. They describe a moment when the urgent need to act is postponed in the interests of others' actions. This is a practical disposition, not one of inert passivity, but one of self-restraint rather than initiative, affirmative encouragement rather than competition. It is not that the sphere of action has been left behind for contemplation; rather, inaction has been drawn into the scope of the active disposition, which now extends its scope to include the activities of other people. The gifts we ourselves have been given, the living of the life we ourselves have been called to live, open up to an end of action enriched by others' gifts and others' lives. Jonathan Edwards captured this active-passive disposition in the expression "consent to being," a virtuous disposition which involved, as he explained it, both benevolence and "complacence," satisfaction in the benevolence of another.[3] We shall speak simply of "resting in" others' labors.

So when love is taken from its median position and relocated at the summit of the triad, it is a statement about the finality of community. But it is also a statement about the end of time, for love is now placed on the far side of hope, the virtue that "anchors" the endurance of time in a future of promise. An Ethics that had never heard tell of such a future could only end tentatively, in an uncertain hope of endurance for any further goal there may or may not be. Hope acquires its assurance with the word, "The time is fulfilled, and the Kingdom of God has drawn near" (Mark 1:15). Yet though anchored to this promise, hope cannot draw the Kingdom near enough to be talked of and experienced, for hope lives only in the dark. An Ethics that concluded in hope would be apophatic, gesturing towards a goal of which it could not speak. The same evangelical logic that brings assurance to hope, then, also implies that hope cannot pronounce the last word in Ethics. The Gospel confirms, but also reorders, practical reason. The Kingdom's drawing-near offers agency a provisional view of the final point of rest. Failure to reach that point would leave Ethics, with however great an emphasis on hope, a backslider from evangelical joy.

The drawing-near of the Kingdom is a reality that has first to be announced. It is not merely *teleological*, projected forward by the logic of moral experience, but *eschatological*. Ethics must be told of it, and then learn to refer to it in terms of moral reason. But the moral reference is possible only if the Kingdom, which lies beyond the goods of world and time, can somehow be represented within the goods of world and time. How may that be? Paul's answer to this question, achieved through his shift of focus, is to bring back a second time and in a new way, what Ethics has already known: love.

---

3. Jonathan Edwards, "Dissertation on the Nature of True Virtue," in *Complete Works*, vol. 8, *Ethical Writings*, ed. Paul Ramsey (New Haven: Yale University Press, 1988), especially pp. 539-49.

Love's *métier* is a world of meaning and goodness. Love is focused on an object, finding its rest in an objective world, not simply in its own exercise. God could have responded to the moral loss of mankind by making new worlds of which mankind was not part; instead, he has restored the world of which we are part, making it hospitable to our purposive action. The logic of Paul's inverted triad, then, is the logic of salvation and eschatology: no eschaton could be a Kingdom of God *for us*, if it were not also a redemption and recovery of the created work of God that we are. As we are offered love as the climactic moment in our moral thinking, concluding, ordering, and making sense of what has gone before, we know it as familiar, and yet we have never encountered it before *like this*. To discover the sovereignty of love is to discover created good given as a foretaste of the Kingdom of God, as the future appearing in a present familiarity, the past reappearing with a new message of what God will do.

Love's sovereignty is discovered beyond hope by an agent who has accomplished deliberate and purposive action and can include that experience in the good he or she is now given to love. That is to say, it is a reflective love, not simply an enjoyment. The good on which love feeds is the good of what God has done for and through love itself. We love our own love, Augustine liked to say—knowing well enough the ambiguity of that phrase, for his earliest experiences of love-of-love were those of an obsessive youthful eroticism, where love's capacity to dote on itself trapped it in subjective isolation. But there came a moment of redemption, when among the wonders of God in the world he could see what God had done in and through the loves he had quickened in Augustine, now part and parcel of a life in community. The self that could be grateful for this was an objectified and social self, encountering itself reflectively in history and society, understanding how every gift it possessed was given through, and exercised for, others. In a context that is neither simply the eschaton *tout court*, but is more broadly "eschatological," announcing God's future, the experience of redemption includes the representation of ourselves to ourselves as living wholly with, for, and in dependence upon, one another.

And so at the end of a hope that sprang out of love we have not taken one step beyond love. To put it in terms native to Saint John, the command of love is both "an old command, which you had at the beginning" and "a new command" (1 John 2:7–8). If hope, the last step of practical reason, narrows deliberation to the moment of opportunity and adventure, love now leads out into a world, not the final world of the Kingdom of God but a genuine anticipation of it, many agents living and acting with one common agency.

There is, for Saint Paul, a "communion of the Holy Spirit" (2 Cor. 13:13), a practical reasoning that is done together, "acting together and thinking as one" (Phil. 2:2). Community alone can tell us of the universal order yet to arrive. The point to which the thirteenth chapter of 1 Corinthians brings us is delight in, and acceptance of, others' accomplishments, a most perfect fulfilling of agency within a greater agency communicated by one to another. The perfect use of an opportunity to act is to give someone else an opportunity to act; the most perfect praise for what God has done is to find satisfaction in what he can do in and through others.

The "partial," which Paul insists is ultimately to give place to the "perfect," consists of performances that differ: the capacity for speech and understanding, for ecstasy, for service, and so on, all with varied and contrasting expressions. The "more excellent way" of love, on the other hand, to which he directs his readers, not as an ultimate but as a present possibility (12:31), leaves these distinctive gifts and accomplishments behind. God-given they may be, but they become less important; they are to be put in their places, taught to function cooperatively rather than competitively. The more excellent way involves restraint, not only in pursuit of *material interests* (which may be demanded already by the elementary claims of justice) but in pursuit of *independent action*, even action that renounces private interests and serves others. "If I give my body to be burned and have not love . . ." (13:3). For if, after all, there is nothing anyone else can *do with* my sacrificial self-immolation, it has failed of the real end, which was to enable and empower the community. Love is not "self-forgetfulness," such as was cried up by the moralists of a century ago, for self-recollection is indispensible to agency, and so to self-restraint, too. But together with our agency we may hold in view the co-agency of those who live and act alongside us, and as we learn to recognize the role our acts may have in cooperating with theirs, we find our occasions of action situated within the wider scope of a common action. To act that another may act well: that is to seek an end which carries the assurance of God's Kingdom within it. It is a crown God would set upon our ends, more spectacular than our works could have won for themselves.

Paul's name for it is simply "love" (*agapē*). On the impossibility of founding a "distinctive New Testament concept" of love on the use of this Greek word, enough has been said, and more than enough.[4] But the English language, following a distinction in Latin and the Romance languages, preserved until recently a special name for the more excellent way, and called

4. Cf. *Finding and Seeking*, pp. 120-26.

it "charity." Terminological baggage hastily discarded as excess weight not uncommonly proves to have enshrined important insights: love as charity was a second moment of balanced and reflective fulfillment, freed of the urgent pressure to act somehow; it had passed beyond decision, with its inevitable "for" and "against" that divide the world up into what we must support and what we must oppose. Yet it is also appropriate to call all forms of love by a single name. The Greek of the New Testament does so; *agapē* simply translates the Hebrew *ahabah*, "love." "Charity" is not something *other* than the focused love-of-the-world that allows faith and hope to bring human action to birth; it is the same love, but extended further, through another level of reflection.

At the climax of his contrast between the provisional gifts and the sovereign love Paul finds it necessary to reintroduce the virtues of faith and hope, not among the gifts to be superseded, but joined with the love that is to remain: "As it is, there remain . . . these three." Commentators have puzzled over the inclusion of faith and hope in the economy of what endures. But Paul's sense is clear: the three are bound up together as mutually implicating elements of moral reason. That love must go beyond faith and hope does not mean that it must displace them. Human beings are created to act and to rest, and if moral reason leading to action is then to lead further to rest, that rest must always be won through the dynamic of moral reason and action. What it might be to love without a self forged actively in faith and hope is something for angels to look into. It might be to *be* an angel, or it might be to be God. But for human beings love's rest is predicated on active faith and hope. The logic of love's sovereignty, then, is something like the logic of God's trinitarian being. The Son's service and the Spirit's witness have their object in the glory of the Father, but nothing in that service and witness is secondary to the divine being. If, in the famous metaphor of Irenaeus, the Son and the Spirit are the "two hands" of the Father, faith and hope may be thought of as the two hands of love, giving it an enacted concrete presence, without which it would be purely an idea, ineffably sweet and pathetically unreal, as so often it appears in the various forms of love-monism.

On one later occasion Paul returns to his rearranged triad of virtues. The fifth chapter of the Letter to the Romans introduces faith, hope, and love in that order, though with a fuller development of the logic that connects them, and a clearer relation to that other logic, that of the primary sequence in which they were differently arranged. The discussion having focused on the leading role of faith and its object, Paul proceeds with a summary statement of what faith accomplishes: "Justified, then, on the basis of our faith, we have peace with God through our Lord Jesus Christ." We might have expected a statement like that of Galatians 5:6, about faith's working out through love, but on this occasion the appearance of love is deferred till later. "Peace with God" serves as its placeholder: a positive relation is established to the government of the world, an admission to the regime of God's goodness, an "access to the grace in which we stand" (5:2). From this peace, as from the love which ensued directly from faith in the earlier sequence, we go forward to the "hope of God's glory," the assured hold on the future that makes active purposes conceivable in time. Hope is then elaborated to explain, as we have learned to expect, that it produces patient endurance: "Not only assured (of God's glory), but drawing assurance from our sufferings, too" (5:3). And then, when the deferred reference to love finally arrives, it arrives as a guarantee offered to hope: "Hope will not disappoint, since God's love is poured out in our hearts by the Holy Spirit that is given us" (5:5). Love offers the final validation of moral reason; that is the significance of its relocation at the climax. It answers the larger question, which Ethics can pose but cannot answer, about the validity of moral reason in the world, the question referred to by philosophers as "Why bother being good?" It introduces love not as a demand, but as a present reality, a sure sign of the presence of the divine, reflectively completing and evoking hope, an eschatological anticipation made real by the presence of the Holy Spirit.

Paul then supports this position with a duplicated *a fortiori* argument from God's past acts to their future completion: "For already, while we were still weak, Christ died for the ungodly . . . so that justified by his blood, there can be no doubt that we shall be saved by him from the (coming) wrath!" (5:6–9). Again: "If in our enmity we were reconciled to God by his Son's death, how much more, now that we are reconciled, shall we have salvation in his life! More than 'shall', indeed! We are assured of God through our Lord Jesus Christ, who is the means of our present reconciliation" (5:10–11).[5] The tenses in this passage are of crucial importance. There are past tenses, future tenses, and ("more than 'shall'") present tenses, and if faith has its object in the *past* acts of God, the death and resurrection of Christ, and hope has its in the *future* judgment and salvation to be wrought through Christ, the tense of love is the present tense, representing what we possess and know already, in this time of love's "pouring out." Love's "now" is a viewpoint which can take cognizance of all time, comprehending the arc in one sweep, spanning the gap that divides the accomplished from the still-to-

---

5. "More than 'shall', indeed!" is an interpretation of the elliptical οὐ μόνον δέ, ἀλλὰ.

be-accomplished, and situating the present situation, with its experience of the Holy Spirit and its practical tasks of service and endurance, in between those two temporal poles. For this is a *second* reflection of love, not merely upon the world God has redeemed, but upon the temporal moment of our salvation, emerging from and proceeding towards the purposes of God in time. No differentiation is made at this point between the love God has for us and the love we have for God, but the two comprise one reality. It is God who has communicated his love to us and elicited ours for him, and that is what "pouring out" implies.

What, then, has Paul achieved by his inversion of the triad, faith, love, and hope? He has indicated, first, an *eschatological extension* of practical reason, an extension implied by the drawing near of the Kingdom of God. To conceive of an end of action is no novelty; that idea is native to practical reason, and even the idea of a final end is not entirely alien to it. But the end is where natural practical reason finds itself exposed and unsure of its ground, in need of a disclosure to bring to light what it is groping after. In that disclosure is given back what natural practical reason "had" in its abstract ideality, and conferred what it "could not have" apart from promise. The destiny of practical existence is governed by the logic of the resurrection: restoring the world, and opening up a world made new.

Second, implied in this eschatological extension is an *ecclesiological orientation* of practical reason. Nineteenth-century moralists, torn between the direction set by Kant and the direction set by Hegel, sometimes assumed that what was new about Christian moral reason was its emphasis on the individual, the "personality," and that the orientation to community was the hallmark of antique pagan ethics.[6] Behind this assumption lay Aristotle's conception of the polis as the context where human action is satisfied, a conception vigorously reinstated by Hegel. This opposition overlooked the essential difference between the polis and the church. Augustine knew that the overcoming of pagan ethics involved a movement in precisely the opposite direction. Christian moral reason differed from antique moral reason in understanding community not as the *context* for practical satisfaction, but as the essential *content* of it.[7] It achieved its overcoming of the polis, in

---

6. For example, H. L. Martensen, *Christliche Ethik I. Allgemeiner Theil*, Deutsche Ausgabe (Gotha: Besser, 1878), pp. 71–78.

7. *City of God* 19.5: "*Quod autem socialem vitam volunt esse sapientis, nos multo amplius adprobamus*," which should be interpreted: "Now we turn to the view that 'the wise man's life is social', which we can support—much more strongly, indeed, than they do!" For the interpretation of this critical text, see my article, "Augustine's *City of God* XIX and Western Political

other words, not by elevating the individual subject over the community, but by accepting community in a commanding position among the moral purposes of agency, a change made possible by the re-foundation of community in Christ.

The Foundationalizing of Love

The sovereignty of love, then, is bound up with the bestowal of the Holy Spirit, the decisive pledge within history of our last end. Augustine would interpret the opening words of Psalm 122, "I was glad when they said unto me . . ." as a celebration of the "ascent" of love to the City of God. Christian moral reason, then, comes to rest in love as its provisional end, anticipating the hope of final communion. Love is not its first stage, but its last stage. Yet there is a long Western tradition of supporting the *finality* of love in moral reasoning by taking it back to a *foundational priority*. The sources of the tradition can be found in the earlier thought of Augustine, and it occupies a central place in Thomas. For this tradition the answer to the question "to what final end may we act?" must be the same as the answer to the question, "how do we first come to act?"

What is that second question about? We need to be clear that it is a real question, and that the tradition was right to propose an answer to it. It may seem that there is no question and no answer, since human agency is simply given, and talk of the priority of love explains nothing, but merely reiterates that we are agents. And it is true that we cannot be other than agents, and true that we cannot be agents without loving something. Yet how our agency is modeled will determine whatever success we may have in exercising it. Imagining it as like this or as like that, we cultivate it well or badly, or fail to cultivate it at all. We see agency as central to our identity, or we treat it as an external determination that we can marginalize. Do we act simply by force of habit, and come to ourselves only when we cease to act and begin to reflect? Are we meaningfully self-directive, or are we primarily receptors of experience? These questions take us to the heart of the meaning of "moral" as opposed to "aesthetic" judgment, and no one can reflect on these alternatives for long without appreciating that they are very real.[8]

Thought," in Oliver O'Donovan and Joan Lockwood O'Donovan, *Bonds of Imperfection* (Grand Rapids: Eerdmans, 2004), pp. 48–72.

8. Ramón Fernandez, in his essay of the 1920s comparing Proust and Newman on "the

A mid-twentieth-century work by Gérard Gilleman from the school of "transcendental Thomism" illustrates the culmination of this tradition.[9] Gilleman's determination that there is indeed a fundamental ground of active self-disposition, and that we become ourselves only by going out of ourselves, is proof of his seriousness as a moral theologian. But he is also a serious metaphysician, grounding self-disposition in what is of ultimate weight in the hierarchy of being, namely, divine love. Without too much controversy and with qualifications to be noted, we may characterize his model as broadly Neoplatonic. Love (in place of "the One") issues forth into other moral categories and returns to itself; it is the generative category of all moral reason and the ordering goal of all moral reason. Moral reason is thus conceived as self-expressive and circular, not forward-moving and developing. It is also conceived as *divine* self-expression, operating in and through human action. Building on the "thirst of beings for Being," the dynamic movement of moral redemption in history is wholly framed within the ecstatic and self-gathering movement of being. Our own being, Gilleman tells us, is a tendency, and this most "profound spiritual tendency" is love, mediated in moral actions and virtues through which it reaches out by way of concrete "moral objects" to wider "total objects," and ultimately to the "first object," the universal good.[10] Every concrete object of action, even the most contained and focused, is engaged by the *fundamental* subject and transparent to the *ultimate* object. "In the Christian," Gilleman can then add as an afterthought, this love, elevated by the gift of grace, is "charity."[11]

We should not conclude from Gilleman's talk of love's "elevation" and "progress" that the "primacy" of love is constituted eschatologically. When love is perfected as charity and comes to rest in God, it is a return of simplicity to simplicity, a confirmation of the *first* movement of our being. It is "nothing other than the exercise of our being," our spiritual being as active, living unity proper to it. We are essentially self-identical, though not isolated, since our only true self is that to which "we cannot be present without being present to God and other people."[12] Progress, then, is "passage from

---

guarantee of sentiments and the intermittencies of the heart," reads Proust as the example of one who "gives up on living, and concentrates wholly on the cultivation of the intelligence." *Messages* (1926); reprinted in Ramon Fernandez, *Newman* (Paris: Ad Solem, 2010), p. 47.

9. Gérard Gilleman, *Le Primat de la Charité en Théologie Morale* (Brussels and Paris: de Brouwer, 1952).

10. Gilleman, *Le Primat de la Charité*, pp. 69, 101.

11. Gilleman, *Le Primat de la Charité*, p. 148.

12. Gilleman, *Le Primat de la Charité*, pp. 129, 141.

the relative to the absolute," through the dispersal of the concrete back to the universal, while in concrete moral acts the demands of love "penetrate" the domain of the multiple, forming a "passageway for the biological to be spiritualised." There is self-transcendence, but it is intellectual; it is not the historical transcendence of end over beginning.[13]

There can be strengths in a Thomism conscious of its Neoplatonic heritage. The mutual interpenetration of cognition and affection is preserved, as is the openness of concrete intention to a wider context and horizon. Yet it is evident that whatever help these metaphysical reflections offer to Ethics, they cannot fulfill the promise of Gilleman's title, which was to offer a "moral theology." Though the theological decencies are preserved—there is salvation in God-as-Being, giving us "to be himself," and there is Trinitarian irradiation of love—they are evacuated of meaning by the sheer absence of history. Nothing has happened, or ever will—nothing, at any rate, that involves divine love. The drama of salvation is reduced to the perennial tension of simplicity and diversity; the only conflict, the "frontier battle" of action, is not between sin and righteousness or world and God, but between universality and multiplicity.[14]

And not *moral* theology, either, though a sympathetic reading will appreciate the attempt to escape from the demoralized equivocations of a love-monism that thinks all will be well so long as our actions express the immediate subjective demand of love. To this "expressivist" account ("situationist" to its protagonists) Gilleman replies by lifting love above the level of moral criteria and placing it in the ontological structure of the person. Rather than letting an appeal to love settle every practical question, love is taken off the stage of human action and is placed beneath it to provide architectural support for whatever drama happens to be playing. As a foundational tendency love is safely out of reach of improper demands for simple solutions. The agent who, in a moment of "apparent" conflict, wonders whether to tell a lie for love's sake is firmly told that this is a misunderstanding: love does not enter into the dialectic of decision as an advocate for one or another position.[15] Yet it is also out of reach, unfortunately, of the use moral theology traditionally made of it, which was to exercise a hermeneutic role in coordinating and interpreting moral norms. And Gilleman does not want to let that tradition go, which results in a certain amount of vacillation,

---

13. Gilleman, *Le Primat de la Charité*, pp. 91, 89.
14. Gilleman, *Le Primat de la Charité*, p. 89.
15. Gilleman, *Le Primat de la Charité*, p. 171.

at one moment referring moral reason to the objective categorizations of moral law and virtue, at another reintroducing love as a positive control, even trumping manifest duties.[16]

This uncertainty suggests that foundational status was the wrong way to refute the situationist appeal to love. The "primacy" of love, as Gilleman located it, was simply pre-moral, a universal psychological category, not a moral event. Gilleman's love is expressed as faithfully by Robinson Crusoe on his desert island as by anything that happens in community, and, more damaging still, it is no less in evidence in the showy performances of the Corinthian pneumatics than in the quiet practices of deference Paul advocates. The moral theologian has allowed himself to become a psychologist, talking about "confused" impulses and their potential, well guided, to flower in creativity—a thought with its own value in its own place, but addressing no moral questions about what it is required of us to do. The "primacy of love" thus speaks for our most comfortable experiences of ourselves, not of our challenges or goals. And because Love is the name of God, it speaks for a seductive sense of original affinity with God, as though everything we did were some kind of divine emanation. The New Testament does, indeed, speak of "participation in the divine being," but frames it in the language of promise and the knowledge of Christ, and at the climax of a painstaking progress through a sequence of moral virtues beginning with faith and concluding with love (2 Peter 1:4-8).

Action and the good: the whole way we conceive of the relation of these two terms is changed when we appreciate that faith, rather than love, is the root of action. To illustrate the point we may set faith and love beside another pair of terms, not to the fore of Gilleman's presentation of his doctrine but always in the wings: desire and attraction.[17] The good exercises an attractive, centripetal force. To experience desire is to fall within the field of its attraction and be subject to it. Though the place of desire in love has often been suspect—Nygren's "Eros" was merely a revival of common medieval anxieties about *amor concupiscentiae*—there is no reason to be suspicious of it. It is one of the most natural and useful emotions in the practical repertoire of human beings, and plays an important part in leading moral reflection forward to deliberation. (Though it is not alone; irritation and anger are at

---

16. In speaking of our age as one that has lost sight of the value of the person, Gilleman concludes with the question (*Le Primat de la Charité*, p. 310): "What can restore its true worth to the menaced person, if not love?"

17. See especially Gilleman, *Le Primat de la Charité*, pp. 103-24.

least as effective in this respect.) But if desire is one answer to the question, "how do we incline from reflective admiration to deliberative hope?" it is no sufficient answer to the question, "how do we come to be agents?" Desire is love experienced in a certain manner, as a sense of want. If desire is thought to be the sole engine of human agency, agency is understood to be driven solely by want.

There is a seductive appeal in the negative/positive polarity, which Plato calls *penia* and *poros*, poverty and plenty, love in want complemented by love in fullness. It seems to offer two things: a dynamism in the conversion of one to the other which accounts for active motion, and an overarching concept of love embracing both, which allows the motion to be circular, returning to where it began. But as an account of agency it fails in two matching ways.

(i) On the one hand, one cannot desire without desiring something *in the world*. There may, of course, be "nameless" desires, desires for we-know-not-what, but these, too, require a sense of the world as lacking something, a sense of the world's goods as given but unrealized or incomplete. When we desire some unknown thing, other people can make helpful suggestions as to what that thing might be. Knowledge of the world and the goods it contains is always presupposed. To make desire *primary and original* to agency, then, is to do one of two things. It is either to collude with the view that our agency is simply thrown up by the world, so that we are not agents in the image of God, but merely re-agents in the image of worldly stimuli. The drama of desire and the good is thus lined up with instinctual needs and satisfactions in animal life. Alternatively it is to make desire an *a priori* transcendental, originally *apart from* the world and antedating worldly experience as a fundamental of being, like a sleeping beauty waiting for the good to break through from the world to kiss it into active existence. But that is to part company with the distinctive emotional experience of desire (different from, and sometimes in conflict with, other distinctive emotional experiences such as contentment, sorrow, or listlessness), and to reassign the name "desire" to a metaphysical model of agency itself. And about this proceeding there is a theological argument to be had, which turns on how creation and creatureliness may be understood.

(ii) On the other hand, one cannot be *drawn* by desire for the good unless the good draws in one direction only, not tugging us apart. The account of action as desire responding to attraction requires a stable and effective focus. It is thus associated with the view that our actions have always one single good in view, a "motive." Motives differ from one concrete action to the next, but any one action is supposed to have just one motive, which defines it decisively as the kind of action it is. It is remarkable how strong a hold this simplification has on the common moral imagination, though experience seems to falsify it almost every time. The actions we are used to performing tend to be accompanied by a rich and expansive set of anticipations: not only clinching the business deal but getting rich, living happily ever after, being loved by one's friends, etc., etc. Though a single-motive act may not be impossible, it would surely be something quite peculiarly obsessive.

In sum, if we model active life on the progress of desire to satisfaction as an expression of an inner dynamic of love, we subject it to a monistic and negative love that leaves no room for the sovereignty the theological tradition has upheld. Love as the "perfecting bond," ordering and bringing to coherence a set of other moral principles and norms, love as the "greatest" of the three virtues of agency that have universal and perennial significance, disappear from sight. To call love sovereign is to locate it at the summit of moral reasoning, drawing its elements together in a moment of accomplishment and rest. At that point love is not admiration or desire, but something that exceeds both of them, which we shall call, simply for the sake of giving it a name, "devotion," the love that rests finally in its object and is wholly fulfilled in it.

The Future of Love

If love is an eternal return to the beginning, we can speak of it as an all-encompassing totality, but we cannot speak of it as sovereign. To be sovereign, love must be able to command moral reason, and to do that it has to stand at the end to which moral reason is turned. To be supreme in the last place, love must concede the opening moves to another virtue, that of faith, to which Augustine directed his attention especially in his later years.[18] Unlike love, faith is not a designation of the divine being. It corresponds to the creaturely character of human agency, summoned into being in response to the Creator's call in analogy to the Creator's agency, not in original participation of it. Faith is the agency of the creature called forth by God's agency; it is our bearing of the image of God, which is not an evocation or an echo, but an answer we are given to make to God's initiative.

18. Augustine, *Enchiridion* 1.5: "*Cum autem initio fidei quae per dilectionem operatur, imbuta mens fuerit, tendit bene vivendo etiam ad speciem pervenire, ubi est sanctis et perfectis cordibus nota ineffabilis pulchritudo, cujus plena visio est summa felicitas. Hoc est nimirum quod requiris, quid primum, quid ultimum teneatur: inchoari fide, perfici specie. Haec etiam totius definitionis est summa.*"

The Sovereignty of Love

In support of this contention we summon a witness from among our contemporaries, who has shown no less resolve than Gilleman to take morality and social existence back to their metaphysical roots, and who shares with him a worry about the influence of Scotism on modernity and a confidence in the power of analogy. Yet in contrast to Gilleman's ontotheological system John Milbank's metaphysical project of living "beyond secular reason" demonstrates a genuine evangelical impulse. A defense of his first book against its critics drew him into a presentation of the theological virtues, insisting on the priority of faith and hope, which, as ecstatic affects, could engage the cognitive leap beyond a reason conceived as self-evidence.[19] Beginning from three great evangelical overcomers of false universality, Luther, Pascal, and Kierkegaard, Milbank identifies the question dividing the postmodernist project as that of how "difference" is to be interpreted. The "Black Enlightenment" took the Enlightenment's confidence in reason to its inevitable conclusion: difference was the only universal that could confidently be asserted. That way lay nihilism. Christians understand difference differently, as a deferral of the universal in a peaceful and harmonious analogy of goodness. This requires an epistemology that is serious about the affections, and in characterizing faith and hope as affective "moods" (a term that may sound rather weak, if we do not have the Heideggerian background in mind), Milbank intends to expand the idea of cognition to encompass the capacity of the affections to reach beyond the flatly factual. Hope is a persistent element in our experience of time, and it depends upon a faith that "trusts in the unknown." Together, they reach ecstatically beyond the scope of measurable rational certainty, to discern the ultimate reality of the personal and to find a life-giving analogy between the measured and the unmeasurable. Only when led by faith and hope can love find its place as the "actual reception" of the mysterious unknown, imparted provisionally in an existing community, which is, of course, not the self-governing, self-confirming civil community, but the church, "not an institution but an event of dissemination," repeating the occurrence of divine love within the world.[20]

Alongside the evangelical trio from which Milbank takes his cue in this admirable essay, we may detect the influence of another figure, more representative of the Catholic tradition that Milbank avows, namely J. H.

---

19. John Milbank, "Theological Transgression," in *The Future of Love* (London: SCM, 2009), pp. 145–74.

20. Milbank, "Theological Transgression," p. 166. He adds that the church is "commanded by signs rather than people" and is thus "defined by its surplus over itself."

Newman. Milbank elsewhere devotes a close and critical review to the theory of knowledge in Newman's *Essay towards a Grammar of Assent*, judging it ambiguously poised: on the one side, a synoptic epistemology characteristic of the best medieval realism and phenomenology, on the other, the "conventional empiricism" of the "all too English" tradition of Locke and Hume.[21] And he draws attention to what goes wrong when the latter influence gains the upper hand in Newman: "In this case real assent is not really taking that "leap" which alone affirms the binding of the psychological with the ontological, but rather is simply affirming a sure train of inference as so nearly certain that it can be taken truly as such."[22] Whatever its divagations, however, *The Grammar* undoubtedly intended to assert the "leap." Its theme was the active and preemptive character of faith as a form of reason that advances on antecedent grounds, without waiting for final proof. The work's two parts, one concerned with "assent," the other with "inference," address what it means to be convinced of a truth and persuaded by an argument. In each case there is a point at which the agent *goes beyond* the evidence or the argument, a "surplus" of reason over proof which belongs to the active character of knowledge as such.[23] "Assent" is not simply being "compelled" by evidence, but positively deciding on it, and so contributes to the constitution of the believer's own life.[24] "Inference," similarly, is purely conditional, of the form, "if φ, then χ," until, with the exercise of what Newman calls "the illative sense" (Aristotle's *phronēsis*), we embrace the conclusion, so that it becomes *our* knowledge.[25] If nobody embraces it, it is not knowledge at all.

The apologetic aim of the *Grammar* was the all-important one of recovering a sufficiently generous conception of reason to accommodate rational grounds of presumption drawn from the thinker's past experience and understanding. Humans who think have histories, experiences, cultures, and, above all, reflective self-knowledge, all of which give rational reinforcement

---

21. Milbank, "What Is Living and What Is Dead in Newman's *Grammar of Assent*," in *The Future of Love*, pp. 36–59.

22. Milbank, "What Is Living," p. 52.

23. Or, in the form Newman recovered it from Locke, "surplusage"; Newman, *Essay on the Grammar of Assent* (London: Longmans Green, 1870), p. 163.

24. Newman, *Grammar*, pp. 90–91: "Belief . . . leads the way to actions of every kind, to the establishment of principles and the formation of character, and is thus again intimately connected with what is individual and personal."

25. Newman, *Grammar*, p. 172: "Inference is always inference; even if demonstrative, it is still conditional; it establishes an incontrovertible conclusion on the condition of incontrovertible premises."

to each new element they acquire and integrate into their stock of belief and knowledge. In defending this subjective authority, Newman declined to consider the question of how truth-in-the-world is objectively validated. He therefore ran the risk that the agent-mind would seem to occupy *both sides* of the knowing relation, as both subject and object, creating the world out of himself. That was the conclusion Ramón Fernandez thought he saw Newman heading for, and applauded: "faith itself becoming the real and actual past on which reason can exercise its definitions and judgments."[26] That was not Newman's meaning, but to have filled out his treatment of belief/faith in the *Grammar* Newman would have had to write about how a true object of belief could *make itself known*. And that would have required the introduction of a word strikingly absent from *Grammar*, which is "love."

Newman did, in fact, write a brief sketch along these lines. The origins of *Grammar* lie in his Oxford *University Sermons* of thirty years before, where we find many of the leading features of the later theory in outline.[27] Following the sermons that expound faith there is a sermon called "Love the Safeguard of Faith against Superstition," which intended to describe a "principle" to occupy the critical role often assigned to Reason, "some safeguard of Faith . . . some corrective principle which will secure it from running (as it were) to seed."[28] It bears many indications of hasty composition and irresolution on important issues, and not least unsatisfactory is his continued vacillation as to whether "love" is the right term to convey his meaning. But "love" was imposed by the scholastic phrase *fides caritate formata* and by the Pauline text, Galatians 5:6, "faith working through love," and where Newman expounds these two *loci*, what he has to say is very striking. Love is the way we recognize truth, and is evoked by the approach of the beloved. It is summed up in an arresting choice of text from John 10:4: "The sheep follow him, for they know his voice."

The phrase *fides caritate formata* was an object of suspicion with the Reformers. It was interpreted as referring to an Aristotelian "formal cause," the cause that determines the *essence* of any thing. So Luther insisted that it was not love, but Christ, who was the formal cause—a bold *prise de position* that was decisive for Protestant theology for a century afterwards, even with

---

26. Fernandez, *Newman*, p. 94: "La croyance ajoute à la connaissance, dépasse l'expérience, invente, crée . . . Pourquoi les 'grounds of inference' ne peuvent-ils être 'exhibited'? Parce qu'ils n'existent pas encore. . . . Qu'est-ce que l'événement qui confirme la foi? C'est cette foi elle-même réalisée, actualisée, devenue ce passé que la raison peut définir et juger."

27. Newman, *University Sermons* (London: SPCK, 1970), pp. 176–311.

28. Newman, *University Sermons*, p. 233.

such ecumenical figures as Hooker and Grotius. The phrase, moreover, was associated with a penitential theory that made the sinner's forgiveness depend not only on faith but also on a moral disposition. For the Reformers, its danger was what we may call "justification by love," the directing of God's gracious favor to a prior moral-psychological state of readiness for grace. Faith, in that case, could not be *living*, but could only be a preparation for life still to be breathed into it by love. At the heart of this problem lay the scholastic assumption that faith was essentially cognitive, and that active and affective impulses all originated with love.[29] Reverse this, as Newman did, and make faith active and love cognitive, then faith "formed" becomes simply well-informed faith, a living impulse given clear cognitive direction. Resistant to the Reformers on so much, Newman vindicated them on the essential point. For Newman, faith is the active, love the cognitive grasp. Faith "acts, because it is Faith; but the direction, firmness and consistency, and precision of its acts, it gains from Love."[30] Like Lazarus, we might say, Faith, summoned to live again, stumbles out from the tomb bound in bandages, and must be unbound in order to welcome a world of familiar faces, among them the face of him whose voice had reached him in the dark.

It is asserted that "God is love" (1 John 4:8). To take that seriously is to conclude that "love" is not a known quantity in the world, not anything from the root of our being that could be *turned towards* God, not anything we could think of *falling back upon* as a ground of our being in the world. And the knowledge of love, like the knowledge of God himself, lies on the future horizon, a promised disclosure of which we can only be partly in possession. And here is the importance of Milbank's readiness to contend for the *future* of love. Time, and the situation of moral reason within the passage of time, is what makes the difference between Milbank and the love-monism of Gilleman, whose primatial love is seeking what Milbank will criticize as a "secure space within time"—which must be not one moment later than the sixth day of Creation! If God has given himself in history, love, too, is given in history, and its sovereignty is the moral reality named by the expression "rule of God." That the Kingdom of love is eternal, disclosed rather than constructed, is the conclusion drawn by speculative faith from the eternity of God himself.

29. An excursus on *theologia scholastica* in Luther's late *Commentary on Galatians*, criticizing the designation of charity as "formal righteousness," touches precisely these two points: faith is necessarily vital, "not an idle quality or empty husk in the heart . . . until charity come and quicken it . . . but a firm consent," and faith lacks a cognitive dimension, since it is an "obscure knowledge, or rather darkness which seeth nothing" (*WA* 40 1.228).

30. Newman, *University Sermons*, p. 250.

But we can only grasp it as future, for practical reason faces the future. The eternity of God is offered for our affirmation in the act of worship, which, as Milbank finely writes, "is to let time pass as praise, and hope to receive it back through further arrivals, finally the arrival of eternity."[31]

Cooperation

Though standing on the far side of hope, charity is in no position to make an end of hope, since so long as we are situated in time, it does not exhaust the content of promise. "There remain . . . these three," while a promise is still to be held onto. Our rest in community can be no more than *provisional* rest, given in token of the promised final rest. Because the promise still lies ahead, we hope still, and in hope we return to deliberation, confident of finding in community the authoritative form of our own further acts. Our works are to be a part of a whole work, a work that is not ours, primarily, nor someone else's, nor many other people's, but God's, working within his redeemed creation. Others' works, too, are included in this great work, and to contemplate the works of witness others are given to perform may afford us a delight beyond any satisfaction we may find in our own works. An author—let us say, of a work of theology, or of a poem—may sigh with satisfaction on turning back to read a classic of the genre, a sermon of Augustine or a sonnet of Donne, finding a perfection there which will never be reached in anything of his or her own. Yet this satisfaction is also an affirmation of the author's own work. It proves that the genre is capable of great communication, and that contributing to it, however modestly, is doing something real, participating in a great enterprise. As we see fine works of witness performed by others, we are content to know that our own works are no more than a small part of what God has in hand. Freed from the suffocating illusion that the success of the universe depends on our own endeavors, we are allowed to conceive ourselves as "co-operators" (*synergoi*) in a common service of the work of God, and to know that is finer than being on our own. That conception is not solely reflective; it introduces a new element into our moral deliberations, which we may adapt cooperatively to the actions of others. The provisional "rest from" work envisaged in the New Covenant is a rest in the church; yet as we find our acts taken up into the acts of God's people, we do not lose sight of them as our own acts. They are given back to us, to discover ourselves

---

31. Milbank, "Theological Transgression," p. 172.

more completely empowered in this corporate agency than we ever were as agents in isolation.

If in the exercise of our freedom we fail to see a neighbor as created for freedom to act, too, or see his freedom only negatively as a "right" that sets limits upon our freedom to act, we lack the moral vision to conceive of community. We persist in assigning ourselves the role of providence, disposing all things for the best, making things go well for a neighbor who is incapable of doing them well by himself. The universalized rhetoric of "care," commending love by evoking the neighbor's dependency and impotence, contributes gratifyingly to our self-importance. Another train of thought, apparently quite different from care, turns in the same direction, namely, that of the neighbor's autonomous agency. If we cannot take the neighbor's destiny over and organize it, we will "respectfully" leave him to his own devices. His agency appears to us undetermined and undeterminable, inscrutable and unreceptive of our ambitions to serve it. So the neighbor retreats to become "the other," not sharing in co-humanity with us, not destined for fellowship with us, not designed for God's service in God's image. These two mistakes, one bossy and managerial, the other reserved and distant, actually turn out to be one and the same. Managerialism turns to *laissez-faire* the moment we introduce the skeptical thought that other people's interests in happiness are unknown to us other than in the form of an explicit demand they make on us. *Laissez-faire* turns back to managerialism as soon as we think we can confidently identify interests we can attribute to them (freedom from pain, maximization of choice, etc.), whether they actually demand them or not. The two poles of this back-and-forth between bossiness and withdrawal share the same defective conception of agency as untrammelled independence. They do not reckon with the fact that God has given us a freedom *for one another's* freedom. Paul's striking call, "For freedom God has set you free; stand firm, and do not submit again to the yoke of service!" (Gal. 5:1)—was addressed *to a community*. When we misconceive our freedom-in-relation as a freedom of self-sufficient autonomous universes, servitude is precisely what community degenerates into. The human calling to be free in mutual service is lost, and service becomes a yoke, a necessary but negative constraint upon a freedom which we think we could enjoy much more in independence.

It is a theme to which the apostle returns often. In Philippians 2:2–5 he describes the pattern of unity as demanding *humility* on the part of each participant. What is the content of "humility," and how are we supposed to "think of each other" in order to practice it? In a phrase that has been peculiarly vulnerable to zero-sum interpretations, Paul requires us to think of others as "above" ourselves. The translation "better than," favored in the English translation tradition, yields no sense. What could it mean to think of others (*all* others, not just some, and *all* the time!) as "better than" ourselves? The inevitable implication was drawn by the fourteenth-century Platonist poet Bianco da Siena: it meant a permanent disposition of self-denigration and self-hatred. In Littledale's popular English translation, "true lowliness of heart . . . o'er its own shortcomings weeps with loathing."[32] "Loathing" is not only repellent, but irrelevant to the apostle's sense. We may sometimes have shortcomings to weep over, sometimes successes to rejoice in, but humility can be exercised in both those conditions, and not only in the first of them. It is a virtue of restraint and deference, a discipline of allowing space for others to take practical initiatives.

The climax of the dogmatic expositions of the Letter to the Romans is immediately followed by the appeal "to present your bodies as a living sacrifice" (Rom. 12:1). This call to action—that is the import of the reference to "bodies" as physical instruments for God's purposes—is developed not in terms of what his readers should do, but in terms of how they should think. The "renewed mind" of moral reflection is to transform deliberation, giving "discernment" of "what it is God wills." Whereupon the apostle, happily unaware of generations of editors and commentators who will interrupt the flow of his thought with an intrusive paragraph-break, proceeds at once to develop the idea by demanding that they "think about thinking judiciously" (12:3).[33] The subsequent sentences are thick with variants of the verb *phronein*, of all Greek verbs for "think" the one most especially used of practical reason. Paul's interest lies in how his readers may think on lines appropriate to the practical service of each—not judgments of value, which would be common to them all, but concrete deliberations differentiated by the variety of gifts and offices. Thinking will be "judicious" to the extent that it reflects the particular "measure of faith" allotted by God to each, the ability to discover an individual gift of service within a certain function (prophecy, pastoral ministry, teaching, encouragement, charitable giving, and so on) each exercising the distinctive gift in confidence, evincing the faith of agency precisely in relation to that service. The simile of the parts

---

32. Bianco da Siena, *Laudi Spirituali*, 35 (Lucca: Giusti, 1851), p. 93: "*Odie se stesso sempre in ogni canto.*"

33. English translators take the bulldozers to the delicate phrase φρονεῖν εἰς τὸ σωφρονεῖν, which is Paul's expression for a second reflection on moral thinking itself. Most successful among the modern versions, perhaps, is the New English Bible: "think your way to a sober estimate."

of the body, used several times in Paul's writing and each time to slightly different effect, here emphasizes diversity. Each is to follow a course *unlike* that of others. Not being "conformed to the shape of this age" does not mean being conformed to some other uniform standard; it means "discerning what God's will is," i.e., concretely, for the task of service required of this agent now.

This healthily particular line of practical thinking may be imperiled by something Paul calls "overthinking" (*huperphronein*). Translators and commentators agree, again, in interpreting this as over-valuation of the self and its capacities. Again, it makes better contextual sense to see it as an exaggerated idea *of the task*, the special gift which can become, if allowed, an all-absorbing and total preoccupation, casting a shadow over the corporate life of the body. Each person's faith must appropriate just that service that God has assigned, not underestimating it in the light of commonplace worldly values, but not overestimating it either, for the overestimate will fail to see how the Spirit who gives this opportunity to one, gives other opportunities to others. Getting on with the task with enthusiasm is not consistent with casting doubtful glances sideways, wondering whether one's role is as much appreciated as it should be, or is of more importance than the next person's. It means recognizing the importance of others' tasks, since we and they are equally essential to the whole and to each other; it also means believing in our own vocation, the simple fact that *this* is the Spirit's gift *to us*, a sufficient ground to give ourselves wholly to it without wanting to boost ourselves by belittling other tasks.

The list of gifts in Romans 12 concludes (in verse 9) with a simple demand: "love must be without pretense." "Love," the last word on gifts and tasks, is not itself a gift or a task. It is a claim made on all gifts and tasks by the community of action, the whole within which the particular gifts and tasks are given their work. Does this authorize the conclusion that unity is the overriding imperative, and that the needs of the institution must restrain the Spirit-given freedoms of individual action? Not at all, for it is *love* that must have the last word, and an imposed unity can never command the authority of love. Institutions may sometimes hijack the language of communication and cooperation to impose conformity, but imposed conformity and free cooperation are two quite different things. The authority of love lies in its reflectivity, its inseparable association with what we can conceive and admire. "Love without pretense" has avoided pretense by appreciating the good that God is doing for and in the community, and by giving its wholehearted assent to being part of it. When we see that possibility realized, we know that God will redeem his creation. And we are invited to see it first, not exclusively but representatively, in the church.

A few brief theses about the scope of practical reason will pave the way from this introductory reflection on the sovereignty of love to the chapters that follow. Practical reason terminates in the decision to act; that is the defining line that distinguishes practical from theoretical thought, and it therefore defines the limits of Ethics, too. But a decision to act is formed in relation to a context in the world, which includes not only the existing situation and its antecedents, but the horizon of anticipation that bounds the agent's view of the act projected. No one can deliberate without anticipation playing a part, as we have argued already.[34] The problem with the old adage, *fiat iustitia et pereat mundus*, is its failure to recognize this point. While it is perfectly right to insist on doing the right thing come what may, the *discernment* of the right thing depends, among other things, on careful anticipation of what is likely to come of it. If the world perishes when I do justice, I had better not be taken by surprise, at least! If I am, it was not justice that I did. But we can state more precisely how anticipation enters the process of deliberation, from three different angles: (*a*) in order to envisage our action correctly, we must envisage its accomplishment as an event within the world; (*b*) in order to envisage it as an event in the world, we must envisage it as accessible to the general observation and knowledge of others; (*c*) in order to envisage it as an event we ourselves have brought about, we must situate it as a moment in the narrative of the self. Each of these angles corresponds to a need of moral reason: (*a*) the need of a purpose to be attained in the act; (*b*) the need of an assent to the act which confirms its character; (*c*) the need of a narrative within which the self can discern its agency. In the next three chapters we take up these three in turn, exploring the ends of action, communication as an end, and the sanctification of the agent.

---

34. *Finding and Seeking*, pp. 150-59.

CHAPTER 2

Ends of Action

De finibus

In a traditional phrase derived from classical antiquity we speak of the "end of an action."[1] If we understand what we say when we use this phrase, we mean something *to which* the action is directed, but which does not lie *beyond* the action. The end of action is what we *intend by* our action, not something else that we may intend, or hope, or anticipate will *follow from* our action. It gives our exertion its purpose. It is not, then, a consequence. We decide upon the ends of our action, but we do not decide upon the consequences that will follow them. We are immediately responsible for our ends, but the consequences can, at most, be anticipated, desired, or feared. Though we may be responsible for failing to anticipate something, not even the most clear-sighted anticipation can make things happen or not happen. Neither is it a "motive," as that term is commonly understood, i.e., as a further and more broadly defined aspiration which helps justify a particular act, e.g., "harmonious working relationships" as a motive for conceding some claim we might properly have insisted on. The end is particular to the action; our concession may have in view the end of settling the one quarrel, but further and more general goals are not ends *of that action*. My "motive" for traveling to the Mediterranean may be my health; my "end" is simply to

---

1. Philosophically, antiquity was interested in generic ends of human active existence rather than in concrete ends of actions, which were taken for granted. Cicero's *De finibus bonorum et malorum*, which evoked commentary both from Ambrose and Augustine, was concerned with different views of what human activity as a whole should aim to realize.

be in the Mediterranean. In common parlance (here, as often, misleading) we speak of the end as the "reason" for acting. Ends are indeed reasons, but not all reasons are ends. Ends are always precise, always forward-looking; reasons may sometimes be diffuse and broadly conceived, and are often backward-looking. I may declare war because an invasion has taken place or I may declare war to prevent an invasion, and either can sensibly be called my "reason"; the *end* of declaring war, on the other hand, is neither the invasion nor the non-occurrence of the invasion, but simply the state of war which I bring about by my declaration.

The end, we might say, is the action itself from the point of view of what it purposes. It is the state of affairs envisaged, determining the exertion as an act with a purpose. Action is exertion to a purpose—exertion, on the one hand, because it is an event and not merely an idea, but purposed, on the other, because it is not a *mere* event, but an event shaped in conformity to an idea. The "end" of action is not the exertion, but the idea, the "object" as framed in the mind. As such, it is an anticipation, an imagined future state of affairs with things as they *will* be when we *shall have* acted. There are performances such as blowing one's nose or eating, in which the object—nose blown, food eaten—is hardly distinct from the blowing and the eating. But these performances barely rise above life-sustaining functions, and lack the differentiated structure typical of *deliberate* actions. It is precisely in anticipating the object, *as distinct from* the exertion, that we can deliberate seriously about reasons for doing one thing rather than another.

An anticipation carries no guarantee of truth. The end we envisage may fail to be realized as an outcome. We can picture a state of affairs in which justice will be done, and succeed only in punishing the innocent. We can anticipate the truth of some matter being made plain to see, yet our explanations may only add to the confusion. Ends may be realized or unrealized in action. They may also be wrong as well as right, and some failures to realize our ends are simply fortunate, as when we plot the death of an enemy, who then escapes us. But even if ends are wrongly framed or unsuccessful, they will, if *clearly* framed, have a certain coherence as anticipations of how the world *may* come to look. Sometimes they are not clearly framed, in which case no possible outcome could realize what was intended, since there was no definite state of affairs that *was* intended. (At the time when Quebec's independence from Canada was much discussed, it was said by some wit that what the Quebeckers really wanted was "an independent Quebec at the heart of a strong Canada.") The end of action is not a posit, not a decision, not an invention of the one who purposes to realize it; it is a foresight, tentative but apparently possible, of the world as it shall be when we have done what we purpose, and of ourselves as we shall be when we have done it. The end is a possible future held in the mind to give definition to an exertion. It is exposed to the risk of miscalculation and falsification, but those risks, after all, are always present to human action. To realize ourselves as agents, we must brave the dangers of deception and disappointment that beset all anticipations. There are, as we have said, other reasons for acting than the confident anticipation of a likely future.

The end of action is a possible future, but a determinate one, given shape and clarity by the process of deliberation. It does not acquire shape and clarity without deliberation. One weakness of the notorious "rational choice theory" of the economists is that it envisages the agent imposing a "preference" upon a range of possible futures, or "outcomes," a class of entities that does not in fact exist. The object is discerned as an eligible possibility only when it is formed as an end of action, and not before that. It is not one of a range of predetermined possibilities, but is clarified within a field of *indeterminate* possibility. There is no median stage, no class of possibilities determined as equi-possible, equi-eligible, and equi-determinate without any one of them having yet been resolved upon. We may, of course, sometimes organize a complicated deliberation in two stages: we draw up a short-list of qualified candidates first, and then select our appointee out of it. But there is nothing ontologically revealing about this technique; it does not tell us what action is, all the time and in every case. If there is a number of likely possibilities, we employ it, and if there is not, we don't bother. The more correct description of the deliberative process is that we *narrow our view* of the field of possibility until we achieve whatever sharpness of focus we need in order to envisage a practicable action. The end of action is formed as we approach decision; it comes into focus at the end, not the beginning, of deliberation. (The scholastic doctrine that an end is first settled on reflectively, and deliberation undertaken only to find the means to realize it, is one for which there is little to be said.)

Deliberation clarifies a determinate end out of the indeterminate future of anticipation. Let us consider the example of desire. There are, as we have said, other affective states that prompt deliberation, and there are many desires that never reach the point of deliberation. Yet desire and fear are emotions that often tip the balance from a purely speculative anticipation to deliberation towards action, and they illustrate very well the indeterminacy of anticipation as a whole. (What we say about desire can equally be said, *mutatis mutandis*, about fear.) The object of desire is, by definition, superficial—not in the sense that its emotional effect is trivial, for it may be very great, but that it is the *appearance* of the object, not its origin, identity, meaning, or relation to the present conditions, that excites desire. More intense desire clouds our perceptions of its origin, identity, and meaning, since the resplendence of the object throws the context into shadow. We conceive the desired object as a possibility, but we do not simultaneously conceive how the possibility may be realized. The lion lying down with the lamb is a plausible object of desire, though we cannot yet imagine how a lion can be inhibited from eating a lamb. To revert to an example I have used before, one may see a lovely house in a lovely setting, and react to it with a strong erotic feeling of something missing in life which the house seems to offer: a stable home, a social dignity, a conducive environment for life and work. What it would actually mean for one to acquire ownership of the house, borrowing above one's means, sacrificing working time, betraying the expectations of those who counted on one's residing somewhere else, etc., these things are not at all present to the mind. It is only as one tries to frame the acquisition as an end of action that its impracticality becomes clear.

We cannot live without desire; neither can we live by desire alone. Its pangs are indispensable as motivations, stirring us from contemplation to action, but they are by no means adequate for decision. This recognition shapes the practice of *abstinence*, denying ourselves some things we desire (by no means everything, even were that possible) to train ourselves to endure desire unsatisfied. Deliberation has to penetrate below the superficial glow with which the object of desire presents itself, and find out what good, if any, it opens to us—concretely, given existing commitments, other desires, etc. The hallmark of a life that deliberates too little is vacillation, led by desire into undertakings that prove unsustainable. The beautiful house bought one year is sold the next, having proved too remote and too damp.

All of which is not to say that decisions cannot be made speedily or without a full understanding of the implications. Some of our most important decisions are reached in that way. But that is precisely the point: they are *important*, and we make them with so much sense of what hangs on them that we can justify taking a risk. Great risks can be reasonable when great issues are at stake; yet it is only deliberation, carefully weighing the necessities, that can lead us to the conclusion that they actually are reasonable. It is often noticed with some surprise that people make large decisions, such as taking a job, buying a house, or marrying, with less thorough circumspection than they would use in smaller ones. They can be perfectly right to do so. Some people can recognize an imponderable when they see it! A mother puts down a deposit, which she can hardly afford, to secure a place for her child at a school, without having the first idea where the fees are going to come from. She says to herself that it is so supremely important for the child's education, and the child's education so supremely important for her, that she will go to any length to raise the fees, scrimping and saving, borrowing, working overtime. She makes the decision not knowing whether she can carry it through; what she knows is that it is worth the all-out attempt.

An end of action is formed by a process of decision, and it forms the act decided upon. Even at this point it is no more than a possibility, not bound to realize itself; the more complex the end in relation to the operations, the more open to defeat it may be. As we proceed to action, a possibility we foresaw may diminish or disappear. Someone decides to take a hurried journey to offer comfort at the deathbed of a dying friend, and on the way learns that the friend has slipped into a coma or died. The end envisaged for the journey is unattainable, the action has been frustrated. So a new decision is needed, with new deliberation: what to do now? To turn round and go home? Or to go on with the journey to attend the funeral?

A semantic doubt presents itself whenever we speak of "ends" of action. Endings, cessations, terminations break into the stream of life, interrupting its flow and bringing whatever is in hand to a stop. Can these terminations be the object of a practical purpose? Can we go so far as to think of death itself as a goal of life, completing and satisfying the effort of existence—an idea which invites some suspicion of being a refuge for sentimental minds? We may be inclined to refuse the paradoxical concept of an "end" that combines "cessation" and "goal," and to dismiss it as a simple verbal equivocation, using like names for unlike things. But the two senses of "end," distinct as they may be to the mind, cling together persistently in reality.

It would be hard, in the first place, to imagine a "goal" in which nothing was terminated. We think of our goals as "ends" precisely because we need to articulate our active lives into distinct projects; starting and stopping is a condition of deliberation. The end of action is a goal that confers meaning on our act, and to be conceived as such it must be a termination, too, a view of how things will be when the exertion is spent. When we are at the end of our strength, we tell ourselves that we must manage "just one more push"; to envisage a termination of effort is the only way we can envisage the end of our action. When one cooks a dinner, one thinks of getting it "ready," which means one may leave the kitchen and sit down at the table. There are, as we have said, things we do for the sake of doing them, not for any end: to whistle a tune, to kiss the one we love, not to *have* whistled or to *have* kissed. But complex activities depend on completion, and completion demands termination. This is not to say that we don't undertake complex activities in order to enjoy them. It is simply that complex activities involve first aiming and then attaining, and when we enjoy them, what we enjoy is aiming at and attaining those ends. We may say, with Robert Louis Stevenson, "To travel hopefully is a better thing than to arrive," and yet what makes our traveling "hopeful" is that we should have an arrival in view. A carpenter enjoys working with wood; but "working with" wood involves designing and executing pieces of furniture; if one did not enjoy finishing a table, one would not enjoy working with wood. All acquired practices like those of crafts and professions depend on a clear idea of what counts as finishing a task. But there is no finishing without stopping.

It is not hard, on the other hand, to imagine a termination that is not also a goal—a sudden death, for example. With its apparent incomprehensibility it defies our reasonable expectations and goals, and subverts the sense of our practical engagements. Yet even this perception, typical of the first wave of bewildered grief and shock, is not the end of the trouble it gives us. As we meditate on this incomprehensible end, we find the meaninglessness seeping back, as it were, to infect every memory of what was ended. As a picture of a mutilated human body is a picture of a mutilated *person*, not only of mutilated *limbs*, so the pointlessly terminated life appears as a pointless life. Let us suppose that it was a young life. Ambitious plans made in ignorance that they would not be fulfilled, youthful energy poured unstintingly into the tasks of living, gifts carefully cultivated and developed through education but never used in a life's work; these, too, appear stupidly pointless. This vertiginous point of view saps away our practical resolve. A world so arbitrary, we think, cannot be host to any reasonable purposes at all. What we need, if we are to avoid the disaster of despair of life, is to recover our sense of the value of the life that was cut short. We need to learn to view it with tender appreciation, to see even its premature end as investing it with the poignant beauty of short-lived things.

We can find someone's end unworthy without finding the whole life unworthy. Discounting the negative meaning of an end when praising a life with much to boast of is surely something we are entitled to do. The loveliness of an object may outweigh one serious flaw; we need not break the golden bowl because it is cracked. Yet still the end qualifies the terms in which we praise what went before; we cannot treat the two as simply separate worlds. Imagine a writer of solid but not outstanding achievement, whose suicide draws attention to the fact that every moment of accomplishment had to be wrung from a lifelong struggle with depression. Seen through that lens, the work may assume a greater stature than was apparent before. The heroic epic knew that death in battle, though undoubtedly defeat, was a death worthy of the most consistently victorious warrior. One way or the other, all thought about our concrete ends must *combine* the thought of an engagement terminated with that of a goal achieved. The idea of a mere termination is the idea of something purely factual; practical reason will always find some trace of a goal in any ending. We have a barrage of words to express the degrees in which the proportion of the two ideas may vary: "cease," "stop," "terminate," "conclude," "finish," "complete," "fulfill," etc., each tipping the balance to one side or the other, but every one in some measure suggesting both aspects in which we view an end.

Some cessation of effort, then, forms the goal of any exercise of deliberation; there must be a future moment of rest envisaged in any action. Correspondingly, nothing "rests" unless it has striven, labored, or exerted itself. Motionlessness as such is not rest. But since the exertions of life are episodic, not sustained, we can use the term "rest" for intervals of relaxation in between exertions. Rest necessarily appears in two complementary aspects. On the one hand, it is cessation: we rest "from" effort, withdrawing from it, shaking ourselves free of its grip. Rest is the entropy of life, the energy withheld from output and devoted to self-sustaining needs. Animals and vegetables rest in this sense, and in the latter case the appearance is not very different from death. On the other hand, as we take this biological rhythm of exertion and relaxation into our practical reason, rest is a moment of achievement; we rest "in" what we have accomplished. In labor's cessation we find its fulfillment, the goal to which exertions are directed. As it is said that the ambition of every ancient Roman politician was to become an *ex*-consul, so it can be said that every ambition of every human agent is to put some action or other behind him. Rest at the end of labor forms the horizon of deliberation, conferring a reflective self-consciousness upon the end of action we propose to ourselves. Resting-in is not merely "stopping" but "finishing," not clawing back energy for life-sustaining functions, but crowning and embellishing activity by making it the occasion for reflective self-possession. Hegel spoke of the "objectification" of ourselves: by resting *in* what we have put out, we find ourselves given back to ourselves through what we have done. This reflective element marks the difference between "labor" and "work."

Ends of Action

Further and Latter Ends

Whenever we hold a possible future in our mind as an end of action, that future suggests, vaguely discerned in the middle distance as through a window, another possible future, or futures, beyond it. These in turn contain, yet more indistinctly, further futures, and so on into an infinite distance. I cancel a subscription to a paper I rarely read in order to save the expenditure. That aim is self-explanatory, but behind it there lurks some sketchy calculation of what the savings might amount to over a longish period, and what I might possibly do with them in the end. The decision needs no *definite* ideas of this sort; yet if there were no thought of this kind, "saving," which figures as the immediate object, would be an empty notion. But I can go further back behind these vague ideas of how the money might be useful; yet more distant and more indistinct, there are thoughts of a more satisfying life that could be open to me, as a homeowner with a mortgage, a holidaymaker in the Caribbean or (as I may say to myself) "whatever."

This succession of nearer ends leading to further ends may often be referred to as "means," but that term fosters confusion. If we put side by side two expressions of purpose which look very much the same from a formal point of view, we shall see the difference between them: "I am draining the ground in order to build a house"; "I am painting my pictures in order to give my great-grandchildren something to remember me by." The difference is actually very great. Draining ground is something one does *only* in order to do something else—if not to build a house, then to prevent flooding, to reduce the population of mosquitoes, to make a road, to cultivate crops, etc., etc. To any of these undertakings it is indispensable, but without some one of them to justify the trouble it is unintelligible. Painting pictures, on the other hand, needs neither great-grandchildren nor anything else to justify it. A picture well painted is good in itself. We can express the difference by saying that drainage is an "operation," painting a picture a "deed" or a "work." Operations are the typical instances of "means," intelligible only in relation to further ends. Such moral or spiritual significance as they have is borrowed; the good lies not in the operation but in the action it contributes to. "Who sweeps a room as for thy laws. . . ." We may sweep a room for God's laws, we may sweep it because it is our regular task for Tuesday, we may sweep it simply because we want the room cleaned up. The flexibility of operations allows them to serve many ends, including bad ones: we may sweep a room to remove evidence of a crime. But if we sweep the room for no reason at all, we are behaving eccentrically. With a deed it is different; it has an intrinsic end, which *may* tell us all there is to be told, and certainly tells us *something* of what is to be told. Maybe I canceled the subscription to spend more on alcohol—a dubious project, to be sure—yet, after all, one buys a paper to read it; buying a paper one will not read is a waste asking to be saved.

The chain of nearer and further ends we have described is not a chain of means to ends—that much is clear. Each end is intelligible on its own as an end of action, and there is no need to look beyond it. Ends, like actions themselves, form complexes in which nearer units are part of further-reaching ones. Again, we are not talking about anticipated *consequences* (though anticipated consequences may help us formulate broader ends), but about ends of action we intend. They are not atomic units, but clusters, one nesting in another. The preparation of the meal is to celebrate the birthday; the birthday celebration is to get some friends round; getting friends round is a tactic for relaunching life after a depressing period, and so on. Any one of those ends could frame an action without the others; none of them is a mere operation. But taken together, they form a complex we may view as a whole, a single object of a single purpose.

The expansiveness of the practical horizon from nearer to further ends can give rise to a great deal of confusion. To overcome it, we must remember the two defining features of ends. In the first place, ends are *anticipations*, which can be stretched out as far as imagination can trace future possibilities. The future recedes indefinitely with diminishing predictability, until it fades off into the unimaginable. Not only does it have no natural term; it has no natural order of value. More important events are not further in the future than less important ones. Only some of the events we anticipate may occur in our lifetime, and of these the same principle holds, that those that come later are not necessarily of greater importance to us than those that come sooner. If I anticipate writing a book that will make me a great deal of money, that does not mean that I think having money more important than writing a book. In the second place, anticipations are *taken into the formation of purposes*. And here an order of value does prevail. This order *may* correspond to a temporal order in anticipation: I plan a trip to Berlin to improve my German, and that is to help me make better progress with my studies when I return, and that is to get a better degree, and that is to be in line for a better job when I graduate, etc. The sequence of future events is organized to serve a series of ends, of which the last is the most important. But perhaps that happens more rarely than we think. In the example of the birthday party, celebrating the birthday, having friends round, and relaunching life after a depression are organized in ascending order of importance, but are realized synchronously, in one and the same event.

And that offers a clue as to how we may think about the most important of our ends, that our life should be lived worthily. To raise the question of this end can often make us feel uncomfortable. It is difficult to address coherently, and we may fear that it makes a demand on longer-term meaning which reality simply cannot satisfy. Yet to brush it aside can only be an act of self-censorship, based on a *metaphysical* doubt about the possibilities the world contains. Practical reason spontaneously raises it, since practical reason can abandon neither the formation of ends nor their ordering by value, the further ends reinforcing the nearer for as long as it can anticipate life's continuance. The answers we give or fail to give to the widest-reaching questions affect how successfully we answer the nearer questions, and refusal to address the question of what our life is for, takes its toll in an immediate loss of purpose. My longer-term vision for my work organizes how I set about what I have in hand. But when we ask what our successive actions are, in the end, to add up to, the answer by no means lies simply with the most remote anticipation. To have an ambition for our lives as a whole is to look further than the next action, to be sure, and as far as we can imagine being alive; but it is also to look to the present. Such an end can encompass the now and the then, the near and the far, and seek to make a whole of them. That is why it is our most important end, not because it concerns the temporal end, the last day of our lives, but because it concerns the integrity of the agent-subject we are, both on our last day and today. One traditional way of expressing this, attributed by Herodotus to Solon in conversation with King Croesus of Lydia, is to say that the decisive moment is the moment *after* death, when our lives can appear whole.[2] That moment is not accessible to us, however, but only to those who observe us. The last end becomes detached from our practical horizon, and is simply a judgment that will be passed upon us without our knowledge of it.

The ancient philosopher who explored the implications of this most thoroughly was Qoheleth (Ecclesiastes). It troubled him that the whole conception of ends of action on which we depend was unsupported by the natural order of the world, where one could find nothing one could think of as achievement, nothing one could think of as an innovation. Action was a conceptual surd within the observable world.

To describe Qoheleth as a philosopher is, of course, to stretch a point, though it is not a bad point to stretch. "Philosophy" suggests the Greek

---

2. Herodotus, *Histories* 1.32.

endeavor to give a *logos* of phenomena that cause wonder, and we have no ground to situate Qoheleth in relation to that endeavor, resonances of Solonic wisdom notwithstanding. His debts are held by the wisdom writers of the Hebrew Scriptures, and perhaps the Psalmist of Psalm 49. Yet if "philosophy" may be extended to any attempt to wrestle with fundamental antinomies of thought, Qoheleth is undoubtedly a practitioner of it. Nobody would be tempted to call the compilers of the Book of Proverbs philosophers; they are moral teachers with pedagogic aims and distinctive methods; they collect and compile proverbs, and they supplement them with poetry in praise of a wisdom which crowns and coordinates all other human goals. They are unconcerned when their proverbs do not see eye to eye with each other. Some of these things Qoheleth does, too. He includes clusters of proverbs along with his own reflections, and he writes in moderated praise of wisdom. Yet he presents the pursuit of human goals, wisdom included, as generating irresoluble contradictions. The nearest we come to this project in the Hebrew canon is the book of Job, which also explores contradictory perspectives. But Job concludes in a theological resolution, and no such resolution occurs in Qoheleth. His one contemporary commentator, the nameless disciple who issued and perhaps assembled the book we possess, drew attention to the sharpest of the differences between the proverbists and Qoheleth: "The sayings of the wise are like goads, and like nails firmly fixed are the collected sayings of one shepherd" (Eccles. 12:11). The earlier wisdom tradition inducted its readers into the grand tradition of stimulating thought through collected and recollected wisdom, accumulated and passed down from ancestors (the "mother" and the "father," in whose voices much is said), but it could not have assigned such value to a single-author book. As "shepherd" of his disciples Qoheheth leads them through a moral wilderness, offering his own unique experience of wisdom-reflection without the evident certainties to sustain a cultural tradition. In place of educators for a successful life we encounter a dedicated élite, pursuing questions, doubts, and affirmations drawn from a single thinker, wary "of anything beyond these" (12:12). There was, of course, a model for them to follow: the disciples of Israel's prophets.

If we can stretch the category of "philosopher" to encompass this isolated figure in Israel's literary landscape, may we stretch the category of "scepticism" to characterize his unique position?[3] As Hellenistic philosophy

---

3. See Stuart Weeks, *Ecclesiastes and Scepticism* (London and New York: Bloomsbury; T & T Clark, 2012), a source of insight on this as on other questions of interpretation.

understood the term, it explored antinomies and contradictions, putting them to the service of a distinctive *epistemological* strategy, that of always keeping doubt open and avoiding assertoric finality. Contradictions keep the mind turning over, but they do not impede the living of practical life. One may live comfortably, and act responsibly, on the basis of plausible suppositions. Qoheheth is more troubled than they were. He is a moral philosopher, not an epistemologist, and the contradictions he explores go to the root of practice, leaving no room for the comfortable pragmatism of those who are content to live with theoretical foundations up in the air. He wants to know what can possibly justify human action when all apparent justifications turn out to be unfounded.

The primary insight that pursuit-of-an-end is a human projection with no support in the way things are is a paralyzing insight, in the face of which Qoheleth propounds a modest strategy for redrawing the horizon of action with less ambitious scope. These themes shape his three great rhetorical set-pieces: two poems and a passage of counsel to the young. The opening poem is on the aimlessness of nature (Eccles. 1:2–11); the expression *hebel*, commonly translated "vanity," refers to the illusoriness or pointlessness of human aspiration (v. 2), while *yge'im* "weary," refers to the incessantly recurrent character of nature (v. 8). The question, "what does man gain . . . ?" (v. 3) points forward to the declaration that the new never occurs (vv. 9, 10), and is illustrated by images of endless repetition (vv. 4–7) both in time (generations, days) and in natural phenomena (wind, streams). The last words of the composition take the thought onto new ground (v. 11): the illusion that action can be purposeful is possible only because there is no sustained memory. Memory might unify the sequence of generations and so allow for real progress, at least in accumulating human experience; it might also caution us against imagining progress in what is no more than the repetition of the past. The absence of memory leaves us attempting to impose our ends upon a world that is incapable of harboring them; it therefore leaves us frustrated of our ambitions—an experience elaborated in the quasi-autobiographical narrative (which may be in the nature of a thought-experiment), reporting the successive pursuits of wisdom, pleasure, and business, and each time arriving at the conclusion that they have been fruitless (1:12–2:26).

The second poem (3:1–9) introduces the category on which a more sober concept of action will be built: time. This, too, speaks of repetition; the characteristics of any time are characteristics that will turn into their opposite, and then recur: birth and death, planting and reaping, weeping and laughing, etc. But there is a difference now, for these experiences confer a practical form upon the times at which they occur; there is a time "for" doing this and "for" doing that. The wise man, as is stated in the important verse 8:5, knows time and judgment—time being what the moment is good for, judgment the act that can be shaped to fit it. At the end of the poem Qoheleth poses again the question that led the first poem (1:3), "What gain has the worker from his toil?" and in the commentary that he adds to it (3:10–15) he introduces the elements of a view of action ("the business God has given to the sons of men"), which transforms the terms of that question. It is not a question of gain or achievement. It is a question of (i) the moments in which a given beauty is allowed to appear in the world; (ii) our capacity to see the coming and going of such moments in time, even though we cannot see an overall pattern or final outcome (v. 11); (iii) our capacity for enjoyment of passing beauties (vv. 12, 13). Out of the essentially theistic but in no sense covenantal statement of the relation of man and God, contrasting man's immediate temporality with God's eternal sustaining of all that is (vv. 14, 15), it is possible to form the conception of an action worth doing. That conception refers to the enjoyment of beauty and the moment of opportunity, but not to consequences or to longer-term purposes.

Qoheleth's "time" might be compared with the "moment" of Kierkegaard—to whom, of all modern thinkers, he can sometimes seem closest. His idea is passed through a variety of little illustrations, negative and positive. There is a change of government when a young champion arises from the people to displace the old ruler who is set in his ways. No one doubts it is an improvement. But if only they had memory, they would recall that the old ruler was young and reforming once, and they would anticipate the days when the popular young ruler would become a burden to his people (4:13–16). A poor wise man invented a clever device that rescued his city from a siege; no one acknowledged the achievement or rewarded him, nothing *came out of* what he did, yet it proved true that "wisdom overcomes might" (9:16), for the city was actually saved. Though nothing else was to be said about it, *that* could be said about it.

The theological reference comes into play—a bare reference, without any elaboration whatever—as a *limit* of thought, a necessary point of view on action, invoked independently of whatever we ourselves project and whatever others may or may not think of it. "God will bring you into judgment," he says (11:9, echoed by the editor at 12:14). It is not an eschatological warning. It is a reminder of the necessary truth that every act, in its time, has an objective reality that may be described. The wise man may possibly know judgment, and so discern the reality of the act; God certainly does so. And so the third long composition of the book is a counsel addressed to the young, which, with its grimly comic invocation of the failings of old age, serves as a parody of those exhortations to the young that occupy the first nine chapters of Proverbs. There the search for wisdom is a quest for an armory of experience and reflection that will see the young through life, assuring stable and successful maturity. Here the young addressee is told to be glad while he can, responding freely to the goods that present themselves in their time—there is a time for buying smartphones and a time for throwing away smartphones—yet cultivating objective self-awareness by seeking clarity about what he is doing at any point. For there really *is* something he is doing—playing with a toy? diverting his attention from making friends?—and that something, however clear or unclear to him, has a terrible objectivity in the mind of God who makes a "judgment" on it. That is what it means to "remember your creator": each moment is a gift to be appropriated; each moment must be grasped clearly for what it is, free of the seductive illusion that there is something better to which it leads.

Qoheleth imposes a necessary *ne plus ultra* on practical thought, a critique of ambition that halts the headlong rush of anticipation. Yet the alternative he poses is only an *ideal* alternative, as he himself understands; moment-by-moment living-in-the-present can never wholly be realized, but only act as a restraint. The young man addressed at the end has to imagine *something* about the future, and the cartoon-picture of old-age provides a kind of astringent askesis for the futureward gaze. God has put temporal transcendence, the scope of time, "eternity," or however else we translate *'olam*, into our minds (3:10), and the persistence of that horizon is what generates *hebel*, seeming to offer a prospective view that cannot possibly be made good in reality. There is no way, then, that Qoheleth could pronounce the *last* word about ends of action. He could only, by demolishing so many false words, leave us asking what kind of word the last word would have to be. The eschatology of later prophetic Judaism and Christianity grasped the point: the only, and essential, purchase on the future is the word of a true prophet, which is both a warning and a promise. An ultimate end, which can anchor the retreating series of ends that practical thought constructs, must be a divine revelation. What, then, if "judgment" were more than present objective reality, and were to become eschatological finality?

And so to the "end of all things," as Scripture calls it. There is an order of moral importance and an order of historical sequence, the one culminating in a supreme good, the other culminating in a last day, two orders which, in experience, by no means always coincide. By what right can we think of these two culminations brought together as one, promising ourselves their ultimate convergence in a last-and-best-thing, a Kingdom of God? There is nothing self-evident about it. We have no immanent reason to think that a supreme good ("for the sake of which we seek all other things," as it was classically defined) can ever become an actual reality, and we have no inherent reason to think that an end of all things can be good for us, and therefore take its place in the order of *our* ends. Only when Christian eschatology entered philosophical thought did the possibility arise of correlating them. But the condition on which the correlation could occur was that the highest good could not be discerned by natural anticipation. The identification of the highest good with the Kingdom of Heaven, as taken for granted in the ethical writings of the nineteenth century, ends up as no more than an ideal projection, and was, as such, a reversion to paganism, though recast in the light of the Christian valuation of history as an immanent eschatology, cultural "progress." The significance of Augustine's bold reconstruction of the edifice of classical eudaemonism in the nineteenth book of the *City of God* involved major surgery upon this paganism: it denied the possibility of a "highest" organizing good realized within the time of this world, and so within the reach of practical anticipation. The Kingdom of God is promised, not immanent. It shapes our ends, but is not itself a further end we may form within the sequence of ends for the yet-more-perfect realization of our active lives. It lies beyond the horizon of self-realization, but that is precisely why it can come to the rescue of self-realization, for it discloses an end which no practical reason could project for itself, an end to which God alone could determine it.

In what sense can the end-of-all-things become an end of action, too? The idea has intrinsic difficulties. An end of action, even a distant one, is something we anticipate, perhaps with some clarity, and purpose to bring about in due time; a world-ending can hardly be thought about at all, and no one but God could bring it about knowing what he was doing. The "rest" which the ordinary end of action offers is an articulated moment in the rhythm of our activity, closing one engagement and making space for another; a final rest has no further engagement in view. Yet if we are to think of an end of all things, to think of it as a simple *termination* is to think of it as wholly destructive, an invasion of the moral order. Thus the prophet spoke of the day of Yhwh as a "gloom with no dawn . . . darkness, not light . . . as when a man runs from a lion and a bear meets him, or turns into a house and leans his hand on the wall, and a snake bites him" (Amos 5:18–20). Another prophet sees it as a reversal of the *fiat lux* of creation: "I saw the earth, and it was without form and void; the heavens, and their light was gone . . . I saw, and there was no man" (Jer. 4:23–25). Yet such a view of God's final intervention into world-process cannot be the last word for any theology that speaks of a promise, as Jewish and Christian theology necessarily does. The promise speaks of a *Kingdom* of God, an exercise of rule, bringing order to creation confused and disabled by sin. "Heal the sick, raise the dead, cleanse lepers, cast out devils" (Matt. 10:8): in such goal-oriented activities as those we may find an interpretative matrix for the end of all things.

If, of course, we make the mistake of thinking of an end of action as something we ourselves purpose and produce, the contradiction between our end and the world's end becomes absolute. We could never posit the world's end as our own end, except perhaps in the abstract game-theory machinations pursued by nuclear strategists a generation ago, or in the act of suicide. But an end of action, as we have insisted, is not a *projection* of the purposing mind; it is an *anticipation* of a future state that the world we now encounter harbors, though concealed, among its possibilities. It is an anticipation that reflects our purpose back to us, and discloses what it is about by representing what the world shall be in its wake. An analogy of nearer and furthest ends appears more plausible when we take into account the sequence of intermediate, middle-distance ends that have opened up to us in response to the sheer need of practical reason to envisage human life as a whole. Without any tutelage from theology we can form a vague anticipation of an ultimate goal of life; we cannot imagine it with any clarity, but we can still speak of it, and call it "happiness." The desire to be happy generates its own inner tensions and contradictions, which is why an early Christian reader of Cicero, agreeing with him that the task of moral theory was to harmonize "the decent and honest" with "the advantageous," declared that only *eschatology* could provide a framework for that harmonization. "We define advantage in terms of what is decent and honest, but we measure it by the rule of the future, not the present. Advantage is what is conducive to the gift of eternal life, not to present satisfaction."[4] Neither "advantage" nor "honesty," on this account, was capable of interpreting the other. Honesty (conspicuous, but short-term) and advantage (long-term, but obscure) shed no light on each other. If honesty held the whip hand, as the Stoics said, we could not be sure it would be to our ultimate advantage. If we looked to

---

4. Ambrose, *De officiis* 1.9.28: "*Nos autem nihil omnino nisi quod deceat et honestum sit, futurorum magis quam praesentium metimur formula, nihilque utile nisi quod ad vitae illius aeternae prosit gratiam definimus, non quod ad delectationem praesentis.*"

advantage to shape our sense of honesty, we could not be sure where it ultimately lay. Only a Kingdom of Heaven could bring the question into clear focus. Which was why, on Ambrose's account, the paradigm of the "honest" act was the act of worship.

It is the task of moral teaching to teach us how to envisage ends of action. But moral teachings do not find themselves speaking with one voice about what may be hoped for. Their differences are reflected in their debates about the nature of human happiness. "Happiness" is not the goods we pursue; it is not even the goods "for us"; it is the way in which those goods offer themselves, in combination or separately, as possibilities to be realized in our lives. So Augustine, in developing the seed-thought he found in Ambrose into the greatest discussions of the foundations of morality in Christian literature, held that all moral teachings from any provenance could be compared with each other in terms of how they conceived of "happiness," and that the crucial difference of Christian moral teaching lay in the way it understood future happiness as simultaneously eschatological and social.[5]

Theological Ethics in this tradition has claimed that the a final end of action, an anticipation of "happiness" supporting our purposes for life as a whole, can only be a response to what we have been *told* about the fulfillment of God's plans for history. It is for apostolic proclamation, and within the theological disciplines for Dogmatics, to give content to what may be believed about the ultimate future, to bring the indiscernible absolute end within our conception. In speaking of the end of all things as a *promise*, we take up just one of the categories through which they do so. The ultimate future is not a promise by virtue of any immanent necessity of practical reason; rather, it is a threat or a simple uncertainty. It can be thought of as a promise only as there is warrant for that thought in the communications of God to man. Ethics can only hear and learn of that warrant. But Theological Ethics, conducted within and by the community that has heard and learned, can show how the promise resolves stubborn antinomies in practical thought.

Judgment

Together with an end of action, we anticipate a moment of reflection upon action, a moment at which we may appropriate its meaning for ourselves.

---

5. Augustine, *City of God* 19.

Ends of Action

This is not the first moment of reflection in practical thinking. A reflective view of the world and our place in it was presupposed by deliberation in the first place. The difference in the second reflection is that our own acts, too, become an aspect of the world we reflect on. The archer standing with drawn bow takes careful note of the length of the target, the strength of the breeze, the weight of the arrow, and seeks to use this information in judging the aim of his eye and the tautness of his arm; a moment later he will be taking note of the flight of the arrow, and drawing conclusions about how well the eye and arm were judged. In the second reflection we no longer have privileged insight into our own actions. While we deliberated on them, we saw them in our own way; now they are objective facts, and the world knows what we have done, perhaps better than we do. The archery coach may tell us, as a matter of information, that we sent the arrow into the bush; the military inquiry may tell us that the soldier we had shot as a spy was in fact loyal. Embedded in objective history, our acts will become of a piece with other people's; we may even casually forget which were ours and which were not. We may repeat someone else's witty remark believing that it was our own original thought. Yet when we come to reflect on our acts, they will still be ours. We shall see our agency expressed in them, and shall feel responsible for them. When an act is *fait accompli*, to be sure, responsibility takes a different form. If, in deliberation, we experience our responsibility as a sense of competent agency, a freedom to determine what is undetermined, in reflection we experience it as a need to know the truth of how we acted as a truth about ourselves. The question bears on us whether our acts have constituted "good works." Are they accomplished? Can we be satisfied in them? May we offer them to God as a service that will acknowledge his working within us? In this second reflection action is passed through the prism of *judgment*, tested for its coherence in the light of what God has done and is doing.

In a novel by Iris Murdoch a character who is dying declares, with no religious belief to support him, "I would like to be judged." "Do you mean judgment as estimation, a clear account, or as punishment?" he is asked. "Oh both. I think one *craves* for both. To look over the Recording Angel's shoulder. I would want to understand it all. I would want to have it exhibited, explained."[6] This desire for judgment springs directly from the need for "rest." If an end of action marks a "rest" where exertion can cease, it does so because it represents a state of world and self in which the act has been well accomplished. We imagine ourselves, as we prepare

---

6. Iris Murdoch, *Nuns and Soldiers* (London: Chatto & Windus, 1980), p. 67.

to loose the arrow, relaxing the shoulder muscles, lowering the bow and perhaps wiping our forehead, as the arrow quivers in the bullseye. But if we find the arrow ending up in the bush, there may be no comfortable wiping of the forehead, only a stamping of the foot. Failure denies us rest. It is, as we often call it, "unfinished business," interfering with our freedom to attend to the next challenge. If, on discovering some terrible mistake I have made, I say, "I cannot live with myself!" what I am saying is that a certain power of facing the future has been taken from me. If I am to face the future again, I must be able to discern a past horizon in which I can rest. Judgment threatens me with dispossession of my freedom, disempowerment in relation to future action. That is why confession and forgiveness are so important to active life. Yet as we look ahead to our end of action, we demand judgment, for it also offers a hope of well-grounded rest that will add strength to our agency.[7] The question about the nature of our action demands to be resolved with a word, a communication that puts us in possession of the truth of ourselves, an account viewed objectively "over the Recording Angel's shoulder."

From this point of view we may understand the phenomenon sometimes referred to as "the prospective conscience."[8] The term is paradoxical, since the judgment of conscience is primarily retrospective. It is a reflection on past action which has become part of the world's objective history. Yet when we decide upon an end of action, we anticipate, and the anticipation includes the future moment of second reflection, when we shall look back on how our projected act *will have become* part of the objective world. That is how conscience, though in principle retrospective, enters prospectively into deliberation. The prospective conscience is easily misdescribed. It does not, as some theories have maintained, grasp moral laws or principles. It does not, as other theories claim, direct or command us. We do act on moral laws and direct commands; but these are not derived from our self-consciousness but come from without, to be interpreted and understood. What conscience does in its prospective mode is simply to project a future moment of self-awareness: there *will be* a moment at which the now malleable, projectable, arguable, renounceable act on which we deliberate *shall have become* a fixed item in world history, open to public interpretation and critique, and at that moment

---

7. Cf. Georg Christian Lehms's perfectly balanced encomium of rest (the text for Bach's BWV 170): "*Vergnügte Ruh . . . Dich kann man nicht bei Höllensünden, Wohl aber Himmelseintracht finden; Du stärkst allein die schwache Brust.*"

8. I offer a fuller account of the development of the concept of conscience in *The Ways of Judgment* (Grand Rapids: Eerdmans, 2005), pp. 301-8.

we shall know ourselves to be unnegotiably bound to whatever judgment is passed on it.

To the future-perfect tense of prospective reflection, in which we imagine looking back on our future acts as past, we can append the prospect of yet further anticipations of the future. That we *shall* know that we *have* acted in such and such a way, means that we *shall* know that such and such further futures will have become more or less possible. The inner rationality of our acts includes their reach into the future and their likely failure or success in attesting the purposes of God for the world. It is possible to state this receding perspective wrongly. I have criticized elsewhere the thesis that all perception of the good is *ipso facto* a perception of the future.[9] If that were so, there would be no straightforward enjoyment of worldly beauty, only the ambition to make something of it. That misunderstanding apart, however, we may still say that *some* reflections, and supremely those second reflections which take a retrospective view of our own works, open up anticipations of possible futures. These can be either negative or positive; we may as easily be terrified as elated by the thought of what may follow from what we have done.

In reflecting on our past acts, then, and in anticipating such reflections when our acts are done, we may look forward to the prospect of an ultimate future, a world made new, which is not the *given* world of God's goodness, with which we came to terms in our first steps in practical reason, but a *promised and completed* world, supervening on history to judge it and restore it. We may anticipate this either with hope or with fear, for it is this world that will finally determine the fate of our agency. Either our lives will have a place in that world, and we shall rest in them, or they will be made of no account by it. It is, indeed, this prospect of a world completed that allows us to think of our lives as a whole, and ourselves as continuous self-identical agents. "It is appointed for men to die once, and after that comes judgment," says the apostle (Heb. 9:27). The significance of that one death is that it marks *life* as one, the ensemble of our many practical engagements forming a single utterance of the self, a definite word about God's world, to which, in turn, there will be a definite word to be spoken. This word, however much we may fear it, is more fundamentally the object of a hope, an implication of the thought that our lives are something for which we can and may take responsibility. That there should be something to be said about them in the end, that there should be something our scattered efforts might add up to, is

---

9. See *Resurrection and Moral Order* (Grand Rapids: Eerdmans, 1994^2), pp. 58-60.

the lynchpin on which the intelligibility of moral self-direction, with all its piecemeal resolutions, finally rests. Here, at the apex, the Gospel brings to articulation the moral ambitions concealed within human practical agency. The meaningful, judgeable unity of each human life depends on the fulfillment of the world's destiny, and that is offered through the decisive act of Christ's death and resurrection. "So Christ," the apostle continues, "having been once offered, will appear a second time to save. . . ."

The ultimate judgment sets in a purely relative light all interim judgments we may pass on our works, or which may be passed upon them by others. The positive or negative verdict, whether of conscience or society, only anticipates a further verdict, which may overturn it. The coming of the Kingdom of God is proclaimed as a liberating message to those whose knowledge of their responsibility terrifies them, a threatening message to those whose sense of responsibility is their comfort. Not that there is anything automatic about the reversal of judgments, as though a sense of failure were in itself comfortable, or a sense of success in itself threatening. That way lies superstition. The point is simply that our sense of achievement, or lack of it, looks forward to a disclosure to follow; it is not a sufficient ground on which to rest. It encourages us to accept the forgiveness of our sins and to step forward into the next future God is giving us. Unless we become familiar with repentance and renewal, it is never possible to rest, for even the deeds in which we imagine we may rest can very quickly appear in another light. As we grow older, we find ourselves ashamed by the accomplishments that gave us pride when we were young. The best performances are open to doubt and deconstruction. The radical prophetic dictum that all our righteousnesses are as filthy rags (Isa. 64:6 KJV) has a purchase on us here. There is, however, another side to the matter. Once we have grasped that we may see our actions only in the light of promised redemption, that light may fall precisely on what *we ourselves* have been given to do, so that our deeds become an occasion of satisfaction, not for their own sake but as witnesses to what God has done and is doing. They can be echoes of the greater promise of the greater rest. Deeds "done in God," for all their ambiguity, tell us not only of our frailty and incompetence, but also of his strength and will to work his good through and in us.

CHAPTER 3

Communication

Ends and Community

What is the logic that ties together the idea of an end of action and the idea of a community? Intuitively it may seem obvious that a last state worthy to be the last end of striving should be communal, but intuition must be required to produce its accreditations at this point. We shall attempt to do this by tracing the connection in both directions, first from the end of action and then from community.

First, then: an Aristotelian doctrine taken up by the scholastics held that ends of action are selected *sub specie boni*, "because they appear good." That is to say, ends are not simply "chosen"—for no other reason than that they are chosen—but are decided on for a reason, and all the innumerable reasons that might possibly motivate someone to act in a given way fall under the formal condition of practical rationality: the end for which one acts is conceived as a good. The doctrine does not impose the condition that the end should actually *be* good, only that it should *appear* so to the one who acts. Acts that are morally good from the point of view of their intention will be those in which the good end is a true appearance, and yet acts that are far from good may be perfectly rational on their own terms. The bank robber, the terrorist, and the lying politician act *sub specie boni* quite as much the philanthropist, the nurse, and the moral teacher.

When we seek to justify an action, either to others or to ourselves, we claim for it a certain measure of objective moral intelligibility. We assert that the appearance of the good on which we rely is not a fleeting and illusory apparition, but a clear and true intuition. If it were not, the only reason that could be given for the action would be an explanation of how we were deceived; but as long as we offer reasons *for our action*, not merely *for our mistake*, we believe that the end for which we acted was a true and intelligible good, making sense of what we did. But if intelligible, then communicable; what is open to understanding can be grasped by anyone with sufficient understanding. That rule does not exclude acts performed solely for our own benefit—preparing a meal, say, to be eaten alone. Solitary actions, too, conform to patterns that others understand and approve. Reading, writing, watching a video, or listening to music alone, we rest in ideas, experiences, and forms that are a common possession. Preparing meals is a practice of community, learned from others and practiced by others. When tempted to wonder why I should bother to prepare a meal when I could grab a slice of pizza and eat it on my feet, I shall remind myself that formal meals are a link to the well-ordered life as the community understands it. I shall determine not to "let myself go," but to allow the common expectation of orderly life to figure as an end of action in my practical thought. That may not be easy; the sense of lost significance surrounding lonely meals is one reason why people throw pizzas in microwaves. But it is also a reason why people look for housemates and partners, a measure of the powerful socializing force that meals continue to exercise. I may, of course, resolve the tension in neither of these ways, but simply appreciate, in solitude, the aura of social order that the meal invokes. In laying claim to the objective intelligibility of our intention, then, we appeal to a community of understanding to support our moral intuition. It remains to be seen whether that community will prove to be there. But when we maintain the end of our action to be good, we must at least suppose that it is there, waiting in the wings of possibility, so to speak, to step forward and express its support. If it fails to materialize, we may plunge into self-doubt, or, alternatively, persist in thinking it is there in principle, somewhere under the surface of things, silenced, perhaps, by timidity or lack of self-knowledge, but all the time recognizing our projected good as a real good.

An end of action depends on the *idea* of an approving community for its justification, and for its complete vindication it depends on the actual appearing, in concrete objectivity, of an approving community. And so the act of God in restoring moral reason is brought to completion, as the prophet of the Apocalypse sees it, in the disclosure of a community, a city "descending from heaven from God" (Rev. 21:10). Always looked for in every faithful endeavor and endurance, the city cannot appear on the stage of human history until endeavor and endurance are completed. No less paradoxical than the announcement that presents the slain lamb as "the lion of the tribe of Judah," and intended to balance it, the city's appearance is heralded as that of "the bride of the lamb" (Rev. 5:5–6; 21:9). To John's readers who, like ourselves, will have been used to thinking of the church on earth as the bride awaiting the appearance of its Lord from heaven, the inversion of spatial imagery suggests that the reality of the church cannot be seen until its struggle is over and the "marriage" of the lamb is consummated. The lamb has not been secluded in heaven, but active in history, winning victory through his servants' endurance. Only finally can the fellowship to which the lamb has pledged himself appear as it is destined to be, a city, a site of unity and common praise.

Now, let us reverse this line of connection and follow the same passage of thought backwards, filling in some of the intermediate conceptions in more detail.

A community is not simply a set of relations with a common term, but a relation of relations, a reflexive relation among participants in common relations. There are many relations in which one has something in common with others — a name, a country of residence, a diet, a piece of information, etc. As a piece of carrion forms a common source of nourishment to birds of prey and sarcophagus grubs without either of those predators giving the other a second thought, so human beings may have common interests that imply no interest in one another: can anyone say what Conan Doyle's "Red-headed League" would have found to discuss had it ever convened a meeting? The simple fact of commonness means little or nothing to us. But a community is conscious *of itself*; its members are interested in one another as fellow-members. When the sharing of a name ceases to be seen as a curious accident and becomes a bond, we recognize those who bear it as our kinsmen; when the sharing of a place of residence becomes an object of interest, we view those who live beside us as our "neighbors." Community is a cultural good that reflects upon and values itself. It is a form of attention to a double object of interest: the good shared, on the one hand, and the good of its *being* shared, on the other.

In stating so much we have already said that the emergence of a community depends on a certain intentional disposition of its members, a readiness to look sideways at one another as they look forward at their common object of interest. To express this intentional disposition we have at our disposal the verbal noun "communication," a coinage of medieval Latin used to convey the dynamic side of the New Testament's *koinōnia*.[1] It describes the practical

---

1. In the Greek of Saint Paul κοινωνία could be used both actively and concretely, of the act of charitable giving (Rom. 15:26) on the one hand, and of the church itself as the "community of the Holy Spirit" on the other (2 Cor. 13:13).

disposition that constitutes a community, the treating of goods as common and the readiness to discern private interest only insofar as it is compatible with common interest. The logic of communication is summed up in the phrase: "what is 'mine' is 'ours.'" Not "what is 'mine' is 'yours,'" which is the logic of bestowal, nor "this 'mine' is yours, and this 'yours' is mine," which is the logic of exchange; both have a place within the logic of communication, but are subordinate to it. And certainly not "this 'mine' must cease to be mine and become ours," which would be a denial of particular interest that could have no place in the logic of communication and would have no credibility.

For the particular initiative is an essential element in the mutuality of communication. To communicate is to embrace a structure of meaning in which the particular is located within the common—not abandoning its particular fulfillments, but finding them in, and not apart from, the fulfillments of others. Simply because we are living bodies, materially individuated, we have individual interests in our own physical welfare. However pleased I may be for the patient in the next bed when he goes home from hospital, it does nothing to satisfy my interest in getting well. I may suppress the interests of my body in the service of wider interests—going without sleep and food to do something others require of me, for instance. But to pursue the welfare of my body, I must ensure that a certain quantity of food ends up in my own stomach, ignore what other people are doing, and go to sleep. This takes us back to some elementary truths about matter and spirit: material entities are as they are, shared only by division, consumed only through the increase of another body, enlarged only by the displacement of another body, not *related* to anything, since relation is a function of meanings, not of bodies. But communications involve the sharing of meanings together with the sharing of material goods. Their material basis involves divisions and transfers, as when money moves from my own to someone else's account or a sandwich from my picnic basket into someone else's stomach, but the communicative effect of these movements depends on what is meant by them. If we cast our savings at the apostles' feet, or offer a sandwich to a neighbor, or explain something to a student, there is a communication—not just a material event, but an act constituted by common meanings into which we induct one another without diminution or loss. The meaning is not transferred with the sandwich or the sound waves; it is simply held in common.

Material goods taken into the social practices of communication acquire meanings they do not possess when they are merely necessities of life. And when a grasp of the common meaning is lacking, communication cannot occur even when material transfers take place. Lazarus may keep close to the gate of Dives for the benefits of economic "trickle-down," the scraps from his table and the nursing care afforded by his dogs. But since Dives never *meant* the benefits that came to Lazarus from his wealth, there was no community between them. Conversely, communication may fail when the intended meaning meets with no comprehension. A memorable (and anti-theological) story from Edmund Gosse's *Father and Son* tells how the boy Edmund, eager to exercise pastoral care, saved up the princely sum of seven shillings and sixpence in order to relieve the necessities of an extremely poor couple, and then took his gift to present to them. "All John Brooks said was, 'I know'd the Lord would provide,' and after emptying my little bag in to the palm of an enormous hand, he swept the contents into his trousers pocket, and slapped his leg. He said not one single word of thanks or appreciation."[2]

Like an alchemist's cauldron, then, communication transforms our personal interests in the material conditions of life into common moral forms and meanings. Without the material object community would be no more than an idea; it is because the widow will die without food that the deacons' ministry is a spiritual vocation, not only a material service. And because the physical units of human life are individual, communication preserves the dignity of the individual within the social whole. There can be no "we" that does not find points of contact with our various "I"s, no "I" that does not depend upon the context of the "we" for its significance. Communication means a certain self-bestowal of the "I" upon the "we," and a corresponding self-bestowal of the "we" upon the "I," with neither being the poorer for giving away itself. Any suggestion of a language of "property" in this connection will mislead us. If I have a "property" in myself, it is not like any other property I have, and in bestowing it upon community, I do not deprive myself of any part of it. Saint Thomas, in seeking to identify this second movement from the community to its members as "distributive justice," set us on a false trail.[3] "Distribution," as we (and Aristotle) conceive it, is a disappropriation of the common material stock, treating it as a resource for private enlargement. There are, indeed, acts of material distribution, and they demand to be practiced with justice, but this is not the right model on which to understand the relation of the community to the individual. As the early church learned from Jesus, "it is better to give than to receive" (Acts 20:35). The strength of the individual does not depend on getting fair

---

2. Edmund Gosse, *Father and Son: A Study of Two Temperaments* [1907] (Harmondsworth: Penguin, 1970), pp. 145–46.
3. *Summa Theologiae* 2–2.61.

shares from the commons, for it is giving materially *to*, not taking materially *from*, by which one receives oneself back in a "second nature," becoming a "son of encouragement" with social strengths and competences for service, authority, and practical initiative.

At this point we should give some thought *en passant* to the institution of property as a paradigm of communication. Property secures ownership, which is *exclusive* interest in the possession of a given object. But as soon as we say "exclusive," we imply a party to be excluded. Ownership is a social notion; Robinson Crusoe had no need to own anything. Exclusive possession may be asserted by an act of war, when we threaten or harass the other party into leaving our possession alone, or it may be asserted by a claim of property, which appeals to common terms on which exclusive possession can be defended. Property is a pattern of social argument, an intellectual form determining possession as a right commanding public recognition. It frees the possessor from the need to defend his possession by a constant use of force, but it does so by reference to a common interest that enframes and justifies the private. If I appeal to the law of property, I concede that I hold possession on terms that are not mine to lay down. My property is not absolutely my own; however wide the permission to exclude others, it is *permission*, founded in common agreement. I own what I own within, and in some sense on behalf of, the community's understanding of what is right. The community limits and determines private interest, while at the same time it secures and preserves it.

By no means do all communications involve property. The nurse who cares for the sick, the householder who gives a meal to a beggar, do not transfer ownership in anything. Neither, strictly speaking, does the thinker who shares ideas through lecturing or writing; "intellectual property" is one of those mercantile concepts which, like slavery, conceal from us what we are doing. Western attempts to reconstruct practices of education, healthcare, and social welfare according to the economic paradigm of manufacture and exchange, have had bizarre and damaging results. And as the scope of ownership is not universal, so neither is the scope of monetary exchange, which floats on the choppy sea of social conditions that are, in the end, an aspect of human mortality. Prominent in Jesus' teaching is the parable of the rich fool who did not understand the limits that mortality set on the power to exchange and consume.

Yet even transactions that are most amenable to the laws of property, being open to measurement and exchange, acquire their social meaning by being made part of the communication of goods of meaning. Those who deal in market exchange firsthand want more out of the market than buying cheap and selling dear. We like to get our citrus fruit on special, but not *so* special as to close the supermarket down. We have a longer-term interest in the stability of economic communications, the essential component of which, as the economist J. K. Galbraith understood, is not profit but work. Deeper still, we have an interest in the political order underlying social communications, which we call "justice." Every offer on the supermarket shelf represents to us some other, more important good: human goods, such as work, rest, community; divine goods, such as creation and preservation. The "fair trade" movement, which taught us to use the mechanics of retail to lend support to social improvements for producers of basic foodstuffs, was not, as its detractors suggested, introducing alien ideological considerations into the dynamics of pure market exchange. No market exchange is "pure," if that means set apart from the social conditions that support it. Though we frequently cannot see very far behind the market, when we do see some distance, our engagement in the market will be affected by the meanings we see there. Not to see the good behind the goods, not to perceive each commodity as a communication with a distinctive source and content, is simply not to see what makes things happen. And the blindness goes further back: the communicative potential of each social good can be grasped fully only as we receive the greater communication offered us by God with himself and with one another. At the very heart of all failures of communication is the difficulty in seeing social relations truthfully in the context of God's calling.

Community, then, is constituted as the spiritual end to which each particular agent strives in striving for any private or material good. We return to the doctrine of *sub specie boni*, which we may now gloss as *sub specie communicabilis boni*. The communicable good is not all the good there is, for not all good is accessible as an end of action. There is good we can only admire, given for our wonder and enjoyment without further possibility of action. Much good in nature is of this kind: the music of the wind in the trees, the lowering clouds scudding across the sky above the dark luminosity of snow-covered fields. The very difficulty of appreciating these things adequately (unless we happen to be an artist) is that there is nothing to be done with them. We are richer for them, and they are therefore a good "for us," a communication we receive. If we receive it in solitude that is all there is to it; the communication is theirs, not ours. But when we speak of a good that we may initiate, an end of action, we speak of a good that is not only *communicated*, but *communicable*.

The Christian tradition has spoken of an *original act of communication*, an act that overcomes the dichotomy of the "good in itself" and the "good for us." It has dared even to speak of God himself as the supremely self-communicating good. That does not mean that God is exhaustively accounted for by our communications. It is simply that our communications find their origin in God's self-communication, and are therefore open to receive a radically greater communication than they can themselves achieve. The implications of this approach become clearer through the lens of the late medieval theologian John Wyclif, who, building on the legacy of the early friars, advanced a concept of non-proprietary dominion founded on the act of communication.[4] God's lordship over creation, he suggested, was exercised by "communication," by not keeping his own to himself. Nothing was more characteristic of God than to "lend"—not to *give away*, for God cannot alienate his lordship of any created thing, but to bring human beings into communicative fellowship with him in the disposition of what he has made.[5] But our interest in God's communication depended on our responsiveness to it, and so, in his most famously controversial conclusion, "any and every righteous man is lord of the whole sense-perceptible world," and in receiving any thing we receive the whole world with it.[6] Communicating the goods of creation with each other, we discover radical equality with one another in our creaturely relation to God. None of us is a *source* of a communication to others, for we hold what we communicate from Christ.[7]

We come to the point, then, on which the moral questioning of our ends must be focused: *how* is the action we propose communicable and intelligible? Communicable *as* what, and intelligible *in relation to* what? A communication may be successful or unsuccessful, a community formed around it real or suppositious. It is to be evaluated in terms of the meaning it conveys, and we expect this meaning to be grounded in the created ratio-

---

4. Wyclif, *De civili dominio* 1.18.40c, p. 495. To assist access to these hardly known but astonishing texts, I add page references to excerpts included in Joan Lockwood O'Donovan and Oliver O'Donovan, *From Irenaeus to Grotius: A Sourcebook in Christian Political Thought* (Grand Rapids: Eerdmans, 1999).

5. Wyclif, *De divino dominio* 3.4.78a, pp. 487-88.

6. Wyclif, *De civili dominio* 1.7.15d, 16d, p. 488: "God can give nothing to a creature without giving grace . . . and cannot give grace without giving the Holy Spirit. . . . The conclusion is: man cannot be the recipient of that gift [the created good] without thereby having the whole world with it."

7. Wyclif, *De civili dominio* 3.13.93d, p. 491: "All men other than Christ, when they coexist in love, communicate in whatever domain they possess, without one holding this or that domain as a fief *from* the rest, since every member of the church holds that domain immediately from Christ the principal lord."

nality that composes and undergirds the world in which we live and act, and in the purposes of God for the world's fulfillment. The objective content of a communication may be good or evil; we communicate sorrows as well as joys, judgments as well as commendations, bad news as well as good. Good communications may encompass these tensions in their contents (punishing the bearer of bad news was always irrational), yet there may be evil communications, too, for it is not good to pass on malicious gossip or to share a laugh over a common enemy's misfortunes. The bearing of bad news may be done successfully or unsuccessfully. The success of such a communication consists precisely in its ability to present what is evil in the framework of the good, not by concealment or fantastic denial, but by situating it in the working of God, which is the meaning-giving frame for all communications, the criterion by which they must be judged.

God's working reaches its fulfillment, in the vision of the prophet, with the disclosure of the city which shares all history as a common possession for praise in the presence of God and the lamb. All our ends look forward to that end, and take shape as communicable goods that anticipate that final community.

The Common Good

At this point we may begin to speak not only of the good of action as such, not only of the moral good of action well intended to good communication, but of action *for the common good*. This phrase "the common good" refers, self-evidently, to a good distinguishable from other goods. What is added to "good" by the qualifier "common"? It does not mean "what is commonly considered good," nor "what is good for the largest number of people," and yet a "common good" must in some respect be commonplace, available to the enjoyment of many participants. The phrase identifies the good of a sphere of general communications, the flourishing of an identifiable community. The "common good" is not always the good we should be striving for. The philosopher who seeks to elucidate ideas of such complexity and abstraction that not one in a million will understand him, certainly aims at a *communication*—with the few who are capable of thinking his thoughts—but hardly serves what we would generally call the "common" good, a good to be enjoyed by those around him, whether or not they understand. Perhaps philosophy is incapable of serving the common good, or perhaps it serves it indirectly by opening up new trains of thought that prove their general value only after slow dissemination and appreciation (like that mysterious biological research which is promoted as offering undreamed-of cures for unheard-of diseases!). Either way we must defend philosophy (and biology) against the charge of irrelevance. More may be looked for in the Kingdom of Heaven than is current among us now. What is spoken of as the "common good," then, is a limited form of good, a good immediately communicable, conforming to existing spheres of communication, socially comprehensive but imaginatively constrained, in which we can recognize a special claim that may sometimes take priority over other valid claims made by other real goods.

To which, if we emphasize the definite article to speak of "the" common good, we may add a focus on something both concrete and universal, an *ensemble* of communications which form a coherent totality. There are as many common goods as there are communities, as many communities as objects of communication, and any one person may participate in a multitude of them. But the definite article invites us to think of them all as comprised in *one*, "the" common good, a set of varied communities and communications valued not only for themselves but for their mutual compatibility and support. This may be stated intelligibly by saying that the common good is "not a sum, but a new value, formally distinct from individual welfare and from the sum of individual welfares."[8] "The" common good excludes, on the one hand, the idea of an aggregate, a Pareto calculus of interests in which the overall advantage is the advantage of some to the disadvantage of none. On the other hand, it excludes the totalitarian community that asserts itself by degrading the particular interests of its members. Let us be content to say that "the" common good is the good of the community *of* communicating members, consisting in their capacity to realize fulfillment *through* living together.[9]

The common good is a resonant and adjustable concept; large claims are made for its foundational status in political reason that we need neither

---

8. Joseph Höffner, *Christliche Gesellschaftslehre* (Kevelaer: Butzon & Bercker, 1978), p. 47: "*Das Gemeinwohl ist keine Summe, sondern ein artmäßig vom Einzelwohl und von der Summe der Einzelwohle verschiedener neuer Wert.*" More ambiguously, it may be stated by calling it "the sum of those conditions of social life which allow social groups and their individual members relatively thorough and ready access to their own fulfillment," for the *sum of the conditions* of social life is something qualitatively more than the sum of particular interests and fulfillments (Second Vatican Council, *Gaudium et Spes*, 26).

9. Cf. John of Salisbury, *Policraticus* 3.1: "*Est igitur salus publica quae uniuersos fouet et singulos incolumitas uitae.*"

endorse nor reject. We may plead for the common good against secessionist impulses in a region smaller than a nation-state; we may urge the common good in support of international law and justice against the interests of a nation-state; we may bring it to bear in criticism of the unbridled effects of market-competition in a given industry. Three features are present in any appeal to it in moral argument. First, a demand is made on behalf of a *wider horizon* than we would otherwise take note of; it challenges us from the side of a projected universality over against the restriction of our own perspectives. Second, its claim is a *concrete* one, made by some *existing* community, to which the obligations we owe can be specified; it makes no demand on behalf of new or undreamed of spheres of communication. Third, its appeal is made t*o our own social selves* on behalf of some community of which we know ourselves part, with no claim on purely altruistic impulses. It draws concentric circles around our heads, evoking loyalty to wider communities—localities, institutions, nations, continents, or even the world—that, from where *we* stand at present, can be seen to embrace us. But the common good cannot reach so far as to speak for universal humanity against *every* structure. It lacks the ultimate critical purchase, because it speaks in the name of what is finite and limited. It cannot support the claim of every possible good communication, while those that it can support lie within existing spheres, capable of evoking our sense of identity. The common good engages us on behalf of an established order (not only the nation-state, to be sure, but any social order capable of occupying our practical horizon), defending achieved community against the danger of neglect. It demands conformity, recalling us from distracting ambitions, warning against the urge to reinvent communications *de novo*.[10]

We are not still insisting here on the priority of the public and communicable good over the private good. We are dealing with an *established form* of the public good, which makes its claim against speculative adventures and innovations, public as well as private. A poet may interrupt the composition of a poem, an aid worker interrupt the planning of a shipment of aid, to fill out some tedious bureaucratic form in the name of the common good. It is not that bureaucracy is of greater public interest than aid shipments or poetry. But bureaucratic forms stand guard over a common interest in the established order of law, the political sphere. As we reconcile ourselves to the

---

10. Gaston Fessard may have been right in combining his reflections on the common good with reflections on *authority*, and in insisting that authority not only served, but "mediated," the common good. See *Autorité et Bien Commun* [1945] (Paris: Ad Solem, 2014^2).

necessity of bureaucratic forms that interrupt real services to the public, we renew our commitment to the political community of interest. Conservative, but not blindly conservative, the common good may refuse support to proceedings that no longer serve communications of any kind; it may be a rallying cry to support slashing excess bureaucracy or reforming structures that fail to defend freedoms. But it cannot be a rallying cry for ignoring established orders of communication altogether.

Clearly, then, the claim of the common good depends on the capacity of the political sphere to occupy the horizon of our practical imagination so as to appear, for all practical purposes, universal. Only for as long as the political succeeds in sustaining this appearance can the common good present its concrete claim as paramount, and that can never be for very long, because the moral field is constructed not only of *actual* but of *possible* ends, and possibility is always in a position to hold established arrangements to ransom. In the light of what may emerge as a possible future we come to see that duties of loyalty imposed upon us as "the" common good are in fact no more than "a" good. The concrete common good shines with the reflected light of the universal, but as their paths move in relation to each other, the light shifts and falls elsewhere. By its appeal to universality, the claim of the common good dooms its own concrete manifestations to be transitory. There is, then, as well as an innate conservatism in the concrete demand of the common good, also a reference to the universal that will transcend and relativize the concrete.[11]

There are two misunderstandings we have to be especially on guard against in deploying this elusive and self-transcending language. One is what we may perhaps be permitted to call (with a historical reference) "the Prussian doctrine of the State": a political organization supposedly comprehensive of all actual and possible communications, itself a concrete universal, at once the achievement and interpretation of all the purposes of God, commanding us as a categorical imperative. The universal good may be represented, by the state or some other established order, in a form we can conceive as universal for the practical purposes of the moment. If our nation is engaged in just war, for example, we may intelligibly think that meeting its claims is a condition for meeting any other claims whatever. But this is a contingency of the moment; it does not anticipate all possible moral demands. Events may outrun every concrete embodiment of moral claim; we may be called upon to do what at present we cannot imagine doing. And

---

11. Cf. *Gaudium et Spes*, 74, "*ad commune bonum semper melius procurandum.*"

so experience of concrete obligation can always be reduced from the status of categorical to hypothetical imperative. If we are no longer tempted by the Prussian doctrine of the *State* these days, we must recognize that the same misunderstanding can easily colonize larger-scale bureaucratic organizations of a multinational or international character. One false universal the Scriptures can acquaint us with is that of empire. The thrust of the common good towards the universal is not simply towards territorial totality or organizational comprehensiveness, but is always qualitative, enriched by newly discovered relationships, requiring depth of personal "communion," as Fessard names it.[12]

The other misunderstanding concerns the relation of the universal common good to history. Language about action in history cannot be assimilated to language about *making* things. The universal common good is not an artefact, to be constructed, replicated, copied, and so on, with time as a kind of material element out of which it is wrought. The question of the universal is inevitably a question about eschatology, the "fulfillment of the times." As this is not at the disposal of human imagination, so it is not at the disposal of human construction. What is realized historically can only be watched and hoped for, refracted indirectly through the prism of anticipation. In biblical eschatology we encounter a warning that the future is infinitely more than an echo or projection of the present. Its availability to us is represented in the image of the "sealed scroll" of prophecy, which offers itself to faith and hope, but not to sight. The future must be waited upon, known in the interim through prophecy and promise, in which human freedom has the space it needs to bear its responsibility for the present. Of the many powers possessed by the state and other established institutions prophecy is not one, and insofar as the state pretends to that function, it will be a false prophet, projecting the reproduction and expansion of its present dispositions of power. The opening of new communications is not something at the state's disposal; it can only respond to the opening horizons of the community. (If that sounds strange, it is only because the use of the word "communication" has shrunk from the event in which one shares with another to the techniques or facilities that may serve the event.) But a real breakthrough of communications occurs on the small scale commensurate with the imaginations spiritually

---

12. Which is a reason for preferring the Latin text of *Gaudium et Spes*, 74, or the French translation, "*en vue d'une réalisation toujours plus parfaite du bien commun*" to the rough paraphrase offered by the English version, "toward an ever broader realization of the common good," which introduces the disturbing idea of spatial expansion.

primed to receive it. One of the various things that has been meant by "liberalism" in the past has been the preservation of a space for prophets and disciples of prophets in a little circle of non–state-governed communications.

Let us consider Saint Luke's famous description of the "communism" of the earliest church: "No one said that any of the things that belonged to him was his own" (Acts 4:32). There is, here, an assumption of the good of property as an institution, but also a transcendence of it, entering a sphere of communications that do not depend on it. It exemplifies the moment of breaking through, in which a prevailing common good is dismissed and reconstructed. Luke does not imply that property was an unhelpful social fiction that the young community ceased to believe in (which was the line the church took with slavery). In throwing what they *owned* at the apostles' feet, and so *disowning* it, they declared the radical devaluing of this symbolic form of the common good. The idea of outright gift is paradoxical, as many philosophers have insisted; the alienation of a good can never lift us above the realm of social interaction and reciprocity. Yet gift does imply a new initiative in social reciprocity, a point of discontinuity where a fresh input can be made, where what we introduce into the circle of communications is no longer simply a return for what we have already drawn out. In this way it can radically revalue the *forms* of reciprocity that prevail in a community, reorienting its communications to their God-given goals. We know that those who cast their possessions at the apostles' feet did not "solve" the problem posed by property; indeed, by shaping the church as a property-owning corporation, they merely helped property evolve, and the friars who later confronted the problem in this new form with their ideal of non-proprietorial community, merely helped it evolve further from real estate to liquidity, encouraging the economy of salaries, investments, etc. with which the modern world is familiar. But that objection misses the moral point: the setting aside of property, that paradigm of orderly social communication, is the prophetic sign of an overcoming of communication by communication, a breakthrough to a higher level of relationship.

The language of the common good, like the language of property that exemplifies it, is Janus-faced. Looking back, it points to a concrete givenness of community, a present and existing form within which we have been given to communicate with others, and which we cannot ignore without great blame. Looking forward, it can invite us to think of a City of God, a sphere of universal community, and encourage us to seek intimations of it from the future. But only so far can it take us. It cannot ease us through the portals of the City of God up the steps of a ladder of dialectical reconciliations. To the extent that it can open the imagination to be receptive to a further future, it can serve us. But what will take possession of our open imaginations? A word of promise from the self-revealing God of the future? Or seven devils worse than those that have been cast out? Nothing in the idea of the common good can answer that question for us. Nothing can spare us the task of discerning the prophets.

Two Cities

This brings into sharper focus the meaning of "private" spheres of communication. The philology of "private" points us to a *privatio*, which is, on the one hand, an "exclusion," and on the other, a "diminution" or "restriction." Enthroned as a ruling principle, exclusion can only diminish communications; it takes us to the heart of sin in the public realm. Put to the service of social communications, on the other hand, exclusion may provide a definition that is essential to agency. Such is the case with property right. There can be no material gift if there is no competent agent of the gift, and no one is competent to give material goods who lacks a proprietary title to the goods that are given.

Our real experience of community, then, combines two contrasting experiences: one is of giving and receiving a word of truth, an experience that opens horizons that will stretch as far as the truth itself demands; the other is of finding our communications intercepted and cut short by the need to settle on a position that allows of action. In *both* experiences we remain the communicative human beings God made us and calls us to be. The negative experience of interception only has meaning in relation to a communicative destiny. In both experiences, moreover, we are under the rule and direction of God, who calls and makes us ready for the communication of his perfect rest. Interception cannot defeat God's purposes for communication, and it may actually serve them. It is a truth we cannot escape, and for which we may learn to be grateful, that God preserves communication in the face of the limitations that restrict it. This truth can make conformity to restriction something better than resignation, introducing a note of cooperation which makes it milder to experience and more communicatively enriching. It is what we are taught to pray for in our relation to political institutions.

So we may take a nuanced view of the dialectically conflicting demands for "inclusion," on the one hand, and "clarity," on the other. It is not the case that whenever we find ourselves caught up in the excitement of communication and the joy of mutual understanding, we are always in touch with the truth God has to communicate to us. The excitement that heralds new avenues of communication and puts us in vital contact with people and concerns we never knew, is a hint, but no more than a hint, of the unending communication God wills to share with mankind. Neither is it the case that whenever we find our communications "cabin'd, cribb'd, confin'd," limited to the approved, the safe, and the official, God may not use that restriction as his instrument for resisting sin and bringing us nearer to true communion. In every practical sphere of communication there is some limiting and foreshortening. Even voluntary associations have to have their constitutions and rules, diverting time and effort from their primary concerns and giving rise to endless frustrations. In the classical eschatological vision of Jesus of Nazareth the universal rule of God is heralded by judgment, and in the vision of the Apocalypse the heavenly city has perpetually open gates only because there is that which, simply by its nature, cannot enter it (Rev. 21:25-27).

Two communities, or two "cities," as Augustine famously designated them, *civitas terrena* and *civitas Dei*. Not "state" and "church," as that polarity was traditionally understood (or misunderstood) as parallel organs in a single society, but two societies, overlapping but distinct in their membership, moral character, and history, representatively embodied in political community, on the one hand, and in worshiping community, on the other. On the one hand a community that exists by "judging," i.e., by accepting and rejecting, allowing and forbidding, and on the other a community that "judges not." If we recognize this polarity as a perennial tension of social life between the "already" and the "not yet" of God's saving purpose, political and ecclesial communications will frame all the possibilities of communication that we recognize. If we fail to recognize the meaning of the polarity, putting it down to temperaments, or to left-wing and right-wing views, we shall make the mistake of conflating different levels of possibility, substituting material practicalities for moral vocations, investing restrictions and limitations with a priestly aura of high moral rhetoric.

The puzzle at the heart of Augustine's theory concerns the earthly city: how it is supposed to represent at once the administrative entities that govern political life and a community of corrupted moral sentiment; how it provides for the organization of worldly affairs, while being destined for ultimate repudiation. The puzzle arises precisely from the mystery of human destiny: the furthest horizon of the earthly city, which is peaceful economic coexistence, is *not* the far horizon that God has given to mankind to live towards. The earthly city is a reduction, abstracting from the fullness of the human vocation. Every pursuit of nearer ends of action must be in view of the ultimate promise, but the earthly city is structured precisely to make the nearer ends its furthest ends. Augustine has therefore something important to say, unfashionable to our ears, about what we call *secularity*. It is not a neutral ordering of things, to be put to good or bad uses as may happen to be, for no such neutral ordering can exist. Secular organization offers itself to us as a universal, and as such proposes an alternative destiny to that which God has set before us. Those who accept its ends at face value perish with them. Not only does it not extend its scope to encompass the depth of mankind's calling, but it tends by its operations for the common good to conceal that calling. Only those who know themselves to be members of the heavenly city "pass through" the limited ends of the earthly city, intellectually and temporally, to inherit the promises God has given mankind.[13]

The two cities are alternative destinies represented in coexisting social forms. Neither representation can be a wholly pure presentation of its organizing principle. To look for a state that confines itself to formal acts of judgment, or for a church that has no interest apart from evangelical proclamation, is to look for an abstraction, for each reaches out to impose its form upon the varied structures of life that surround it. An element of competition between the two is therefore to be expected. And though each in principle concedes that it is not the other, each, in seeking to colonize the social ground, can transmute itself into the shape of the other. The church, bearing its communicative treasure of the word of God in earthen vessels, will sometimes seem to shrink into its earthen appearance and become an ungainly and stultifying form of social organization. John Donne's prayer, "Show me dear Christ, thy spouse so bright and clear" is not simply the cry of a man in doubt as to which confession to belong to; it is the prayer of anyone who has sought with any seriousness to be faithful to the church.[14] The church is not simply there to be seen; it must be shown us, since its true

---

13. To supplement too gnomic a presentation of a large theme, I may refer to my previous attempts to give it more detailed substance, chiefly to *The Desire of the Nations* (Cambridge: Cambridge University Press, 1996) and *The Ways of Judgment* (Grand Rapids: Eerdmans, 2005). On the two cities doctrine in Augustine I have written in "The Political Thought of *City of God* XIX," as revised in Joan Lockwood O'Donovan and Oliver O'Donovan, *Bonds of Imperfection* (Grand Rapids: Eerdmans, 2004), pp. 48-72. On the treatment of church and state in Christendom the relevant sections of *On the Thirty Nine Articles* (London: SCM, 2011²) have something to add.

14. Donne, *The Divine Poems*, ed. Helen Gardner (Oxford: Oxford University Press, 1952, 2001), p. 15.

appearance depends on the light that is diffused through its form. The "visibility" of the church, as theologians call it, which ought to mediate the "invisible" reality to our sight, may instead make it all the more invisible. And when the "invisible church" is so wholly invisible that it has disappeared, the visibility that remains is not that of the church, but of a set of organizational conventions serving no noticeably useful function.

The political community, correspondingly, can appear bathed in a luminous glow of reflected truth, too easily mistaken for its own, as when the sunset falls on castle walls, turning an instrument of brutal warfare into a fairyland. So it is with the optical illusions of nationalism, which can prompt men and women to die, kill, betray their nearest neighbors, and believe their cruel acts to be ennobled by the service of their people. The illusion is not confined to the idea of the nation; it may attach to any political idea, to democracy, communism, equality—even "justice," if we impose a single intuition of it undialectically and never pursue the questions justice poses to us. "Show me, o God, the state!" may be a prayer every bit as necessary to us—a prayer for the *true* state to be shown us, the political structure which, in attending to resolutions of conflict and affronts to right on the ground, imposes just that measure (and no more) of social conformity and consistency to facilitate growth in community. Both types of disappearance, the church into institutions, the state into big ideas, are evident enough in their catastrophic forms, but the tensions that give rise to them exist in any collective agency.

The church is a sign of contradiction. True communication contradicts partial and false communication, and the church points forward to a communication that will judge history. It proclaims God's judgment without itself judging; so Marsilius of Padua (whatever misgivings one may have over other parts of his account) saw with brilliant clarity.[15] The immediate judgments we make, the judgments we expect to see enforced around us, are suspended (not denied) in favor of God's ultimate judgment, which it is the church's task to uphold before mankind to the fullest extent that the public realm can accommodate it, the judgment by which God acts to redeem the world and banish the evil that would destroy it. The church's contradiction cannot come down to founding an equal and opposite political community, a city that appears as a city with alternative laws, judgments and officials, for that heavenly Jerusalem has yet to descend to earth. It stands as a surrogate for that future city, declaring the "whole counsel of

---

15. Marsilius, *Defensor Pacis* 1.6.

God," forming the eschatological community around itself as it delivers its message. Without judging, but not without struggle and contention. As it is a paradox that one who came to bring peace could say, "I have come not to bring peace but a sword" (Matt. 10:34), so it is that the community that lives by not-judging embodies the contradiction of human judgment rather than a perpetual agreement.

The political community, on the other hand, is a sign of compromise. Not that it can live without the communication of truth, for if it could, it would be neither human nor divine. But it cannot live wholly on the basis of it, either. The truth with which it has to make do is the incomplete perspicuousness of the good and its own limited capacity to enact it. Called into being to uphold God's judgment on untruth, it must live with the fact that its competences are not God's, that the truth it can actually vindicate is deficient. Even disciplined by a political theory that acknowledges its imperfectibility, it must enact judgment. To do so, it must terminate inquiries into truth which for human beings are in principle interminable; it must settle self-consciously for what is evident and on the surface of things. For the truth it cannot express it must shrug off responsibility, with whatever degree of melancholy self-awareness.

Between the two paradigms of church and political community we find a multitude of associations and social forms, for work, for life, for art, and for wisdom: banks, families, media, universities, industries (and perhaps, though I know nothing of them, blogs), which stand in some degree of proximity to one or the other of these two poles, always at risk of being sucked into the train of one and losing touch with the other, so that their distinctive characters are put in danger. We have seen civilization-shaping quarrels over whether education, on the one hand, marriage on the other, are the preserves of the church or the state, when in fact they belong to neither, though they participate in both. They are created goods, for the free pursuit of which both church and state must answer, from different angles and within different horizons.

There are various ways of thematizing the limited possibilities of cooperation and coexistence between the two. The most prominent way in Christian political thought was through the concept of "natural law," not badly described by Pope Benedict XVI as a "blunt instrument"—blunt, since the attempt to observe a created order other than from within a historical situation is an abstraction, always threatening to shift its view as the ground shifts beneath our feet and our own perspectives shift. Creation is like a mountain with different profiles; it does not actually change shape, but it seems to do so as we move round it and change our angle of vision. To describe the mountain as it *really* is, not seen from north, south, east, or west, nor flattened out as seen from the air, is to describe what no human eye can see. To describe a natural law apart from creation's history is to settle oneself in a front row seat among the morning stars as they sang together when all the sons of God shouted for joy, and to overlook the question put to every human being about that moment: "Where were you?" (Job 38:4–7).

Yet a mountain of created goodness and truth there is, just one mountain, from however many angles we may view it. Discourse about it is possible and necessary among different people who stand in different relations to it. Out of that discourse there may come agreements, as one learns from another or as two views converge. Beyond agreement, there may come a measure of compromise, a "public doctrine," to which no wise participant will be more than provisionally committed. How that doctrine is composed must depend on what the parties see in common, which varies from moment to moment. To mistake public doctrine for an abiding truth is to take the first step towards ideological politics; to insist on being consistent to it in the face of reality is to take the second. Public doctrines are compromises—not *guilty* compromises, but *shameful*, all the same, since they remind us of our incapacity to bring more than a fraction of the good we know into public view. They must be recommended, sustained, and endured precisely *as* compromises, and as necessarily transient. They cannot sustain public endeavor in isolation; the tensions in their construction must be consciously felt if they are to serve their public uses. Each party, knowing what it knows, must not be persuaded *not* to know it simply because other parties do not know it. To sink oneself wholly in a compromise is to lose the power to criticize it and to incur blindness. What gives human value to the embrace of partial common knowledge is the hope, cherished by each participant, that God may grant a fuller common knowledge to increase it. The space left for stable public doctrine, a natural law on uncontested ground, "moral values and ethical principles that undergird any decent society," is not much wider than that point of a pin on which the angelic beings were once rumored to dance. Yet just wide enough, perhaps, for a modest work of cooperative order to stand on without dancing.

Augustine understood this when he warned that the "cooperation between the two cities in mortal affairs," the "consensus of human wills in respect of the resources for man's mortal existence" was always liable to be disturbed by demands to worship "a multitude of gods to be enlisted in support of human enterprises," demands resisted by the heavenly city's determination to "use" the earthly peace in its pilgrimage, subordinating its claims to those of "the only peace worthy the name."[16] For if we cease to be interested in seeing the neighbor enjoy the freedom God intends for him, we cannot address the neighbor's needs in any way that takes his status as a spiritual being seriously. Public doctrines, when accorded an improper standing, foster consumerist materialism. There is no way they could do otherwise, since the immediate demand for a "consensus of wills" arises "in respect of the resources for mortal existence." A style of welfare-rhetoric terminating in the power of material consumption has been our age's typical way of erasing the neighbor as spirit. "Community" has been about consumables—food, medicine, shelter, broadband, and so on—worthy objects within their proper horizons, for without some material support no one can live freely. "Give us this day our daily bread," we are taught to pray, since without bread we cannot go further; but we are taught to continue that prayer to temptation and deliverance, to moral decision and action. And if our prayer should lead us there, it should lead our neighbor there, too, created like ourselves to be not a consumer but a spiritual agent.

The Sin against Community

We ask, then, about the sin against our end, which is the refusal of God's sanctification and the refusal of a testimony of thanksgiving. As a sin against the ultimate arbitrament of love, it is directed against community in its twin forms of consensus and compromise. Ultimately it takes up arms against the City of God. Traditionally described as the *sin of pride*, it is often placed at the head of a hamartiology, as sin's origin and source. We present it as the eschatological sin, but without departing very far from the insight that saw it as pre-historic and angelic. Ethics, to be sure, cannot share whatever knowledge of the motivation of angels speculative doctrine may lay claim to, but is forced to begin its tale of sin later on, where Adam and Eve began theirs, with doubt and folly and anxiety. But because practical reason is intent on the future, and searches for a promise of final rest, Ethics can discern the tendency of doubting, foolish, and anxious agency to erect itself into a self-built fortress of solitary isolation. Armed with this discernment, it may then be ready to learn that this end of sin is also its beginning. Of action that could not be said; but it can be said of the failure of action, since disobedience is as circular as obedience is forward-looking and linear.

---

16. Augustine, *City of God* 19.17.

What do we mean by "beginning"? Of the two narratives of sin's origin which have caught the imagination of the tradition, the narrative of the temptation in the garden recounted in Genesis (3:1–15) and the narrative, alluded to in the Babylon oracle of the Book of Isaiah (14:12–15), of the fall of the angelic daystar that tried to place himself upon God's throne, neither intends to describe a "beginning" in a causal sense—i.e., how sin came about when there was no sin before. To approach them with that expectation is to find them question-begging. Their interest is in *what befalls* when the creature turns in rebellion against the creator. The one, concerned with what befalls *mankind*, rehearses the elements of human psychology that come together in sin: doubt, deception, alienation from law, ambition, enthrallment with beauty, collusion in concealment, all of them present in the Genesis story. The intention of the other in taking sin back to a pre-mundane level is to abstract from anthropological and psychological phenomena, and to reflect on what befalls *the cosmos* when the creature rebels. Here we have a picture of absolute separation between the false will to be God and God himself. So when later Wisdom writers, referring to these narratives, speak of a "beginning," which for Ben Sirach was "overweeningness" (*hyperēphania*, Sir. 10:12–13) and for the author of Wisdom "idolatrous imagination" (*epinoia eidōlōn*, Wisd. of Sol. 14:12), their interest is to achieve an interpretative focus, pointing to what sin essentially is for the universe on the one hand and for mankind on the other.

If we can think of these two protological interpretations of sin as mutually complementary, they remain, nevertheless, distinct. Each has its own point of reference, that of human self-awareness, on the one hand, that of the uncompromisable holiness of God, on the other. The one is a familiar datum of human experience, the other an absolute object of belief. And when the New Testament gives sin a place within eschatological expectation, it overcomes the difference between these two perspectives. God's absolute opposition to sin is anticipated through the prism of our historical experience. If the goal of world history is a climactic moment of the disclosure of God's purposes, sin, too, must be disclosed. When all that is hidden will be made plain, sin, too, will be made plain. We are to expect an "abomination of desolation," the appearance of a "man of lawlessness," an Antichrist gathering forces to war against God in the wake of the triumph of Christ's resurrection (Mark 13:14; 2 Thess. 2:3; Rev. 13). In sin's eschatological appearing the unity of the two perspectives on sin is discovered, sin emerging from its concealment among the ambiguities of our moral experience to take form as the angelic sin of pride.

Among the half-dozen or so lists of vices in the New Testament one stands out by virtue of its eschatological interest: "Understand this, that in the last days there will come times of difficulty" (2 Timothy 3:1).[17] In the list that follows there are nineteen items, eighteen vices and one negated virtue. The two first and the two last, beginning with the prefix *phil-*, form a framework for the list: Men will be "self-lovers, money-lovers"; they will be "pleasure-lovers rather than God-lovers" (vv. 2, 4). There is a chiastic structure: self (at the beginning) corresponds to God (at the end), money (in the second place) corresponds to pleasure (in the penultimate place). From self-love to the refusal of God, from love of money to the love of pleasure, there is a progression. The intervening fifteen items describe its course: two pairs of personality-defects in third, fourth, sixteenth, and seventeenth places, separated by eleven varieties of relational failure. The defects in third and fourth place are aspects of pride: "pretentious, overweening." The two that balance them in sixteenth and seventeenth place suggest loss of rational control: "reckless, carried away." Here, then, is pride's progress, with attitudes of pretentious superiority acquiring a dynamic energy through the eleven relational failures, resulting in ever more extravagant behavior.

There is no overt protology in this list, and the eschatological allusion is only sketchy. It is, nevertheless, an *unfolding* of sin from an immanent to an explicit form, and so makes indirect allusion both to first and to last things. The occasion of the list is what will emerge in "the last days." Through the changing face of sin we become aware not only of the multiplicity of moral error, but of the pressing pace of history, leading to more and more concrete expressions of disobedience. The beginnings of the list are not absolute pre-history, but neither are they chance beginnings, as though love of self and love of money were merely two possible points of entry. They are sins pregnant with possibility, and so reminiscent of the absolute beginning of sin in pride; they are forms of sin which forewarn of the absolute end in prideful warfare upon God. So the first and immediate presentation of the sin that the list describes is "self-love," which, set in opposition to the love of God, reminds us of the apostle's contemporary, Philo of Alexandria, for whom *philautia* is the "stubborn passion" giving rise to every other evil conduct.[18]

---

17. On the vice lists in the New Testament, which have an exploratory character, each different from the others and each led by its own thematic preoccupation, see my article, "Pride's Progress," *Studies in Christian Ethics* 28.1 (2015): 59–69.

18. Self-love and the love of God are two opposed "resolutions" (δόξαι) represented by Abel and Cain (*De Sacrificiis Abelis et Caini* 1.2–3, *De Fuga et Inventione* 15.81). Self-love is "generative of" other sins (14.58). It is "the greatest evil" (*De Congressu Eruditionis*

That is to say, pride begins in *self-immanence*, preoccupation with one's own life and tasks, withdrawing the precious self from the harsh light that encounter with others might shed, declining to find peace in community. Pride takes initial form as an individuality whose only peace is to do its own thing undisturbed. Pride is narcissistic, or in John Donne's phrase, "selfe-tickling."[19] That the presence of others could offer a broader and better peace, lies beyond its comprehension. It is a state typified in drama by Shakespeare's Coriolanus. Though intensely interested in honor, Coriolanus cannot bear to hear his achievements publicly praised, ostensibly for the modest reason that what he has done is merely what any loyal Roman should do. But his self-effacement hardly conceals his conviction that no achievement could be of use to Rome that was not a replica of his own. Picturing himself as the paradigm Roman, he finds other Romans an embarrassment, and that he should need to canvass their good opinions to achieve the honor he believes his due, is humiliating. Coriolanus is a social being; he needs human approbation, as we all do. But he is not prepared to pay the price of sociality, which is mutual communication.

Turning away from other people is a psychologically destabilizing move, and the aloof, "selfe-tickling proud" looks for ground on which to stand. So it is that at the other end of its progress pride has taken the world of other people substantially into itself. Not in the way that it was *positively* available, through the communication of social gifts, but in a self-referential form which constructs engagement with the world around personal experience, "love of pleasure." We might have anticipated that the sequence would end in oppressiveness, the proud imposing their terms of coexistence upon other people. That situation is recognized, but in the middle of the list, through the eleven socially disruptive traits: "abusive, disobedient to parents, ungrateful, irreverent, unaffectionate, implacable, libelous, uncontrolled, unfeeling, ungenerous, and treacherous." The catalogue does not end with these, but returns to the focus on the subject from which it began: self-abstraction now converted into dependence on the world for satisfactory experiences. Disdain must make terms with the world, and it ends up by being taken hostage

---

Gratia 23.130). It is a "stubborn passion" (*De Iosepho* 21.118). That said, the tally of occurrences of φιλαυτία/ος/έω in Philo's extant works is 39, as compared to 31 occurrences of φιλήδονία/-ος and 48 of φιλόθεος; but φιλάρετος, not used in the New Testament, counts 64, and φιλανθρωπία/-ος, with one passing New Testament use, 91. The great service of P. Borgen, K. Fuglseth, and R. Skarsten's *The Philo Index* (Grand Rapids: Eerdmans, 2000) has been to temper some of our New Testament parallels, though without making them less interesting.

19. Donne, *The Divine Poems*, p. 14.

by it. Pleasures, offering a premature rest and shaping our unreflective sense of what to expect of life, "encamp," as Saint James says (4:1), in our bodily members, asserting the world's control over our instinctual reactions.

It remains to notice one further striking feature of the vice list of 2 Timothy 3, which is the early position, immediately after self-love, immediately before arrogance and overweeningness, assigned to the love of money. If self-love, love of pleasure, and love of God are all familiar presences in the Philonic moral theology, love of money is less so.[20] Yet it mattered to the earliest Christians: the saying that "the love of money is the root of all evils" (1 Tim. 6:10), a Greek proverb already five centuries old when Christians first quoted it, continued to echo through early Christian writers.[21] The vice list of 2 Timothy 3 looks like a conscious undertaking to situate the love of money within the Philonian understanding of self-immanent pride. It is thus interpreted as a spiritual failure accompanying the immanence of self-love, and its relation to more worldly and social manifestations of sin is seen as one of root to fruit.

In warning us against the love of money, the New Testament has in view precisely the power of wealth to offer us a dignified but deceptive self-image. Wealth is the burghers' version of Coriolanus's military self-consequence. Not all dealings with money are love-of-money, not even all wrong dealings; sins in relation to money can be of many kinds. But there is an always-beckoning possibility for pride, as seductive to those who do not have money as to those who do. Ancient legends saw gold as a reflecting mirror. It pretends to give us ourselves, ourselves in a form we can value, cherish, and defend. In Jesus' parable of the rich fool there is a striking rhetorical effect at the point where the protagonist, having deliberated on what he will do, resolves to speak to himself: "I shall say unto my soul, 'Soul . . .'" (Luke 12:19). We feel the elemental narcissism at work. It is the indeterminacy of money that allows it to reflect a projection of our own false self-image: we come to "hope in the indeterminacy of wealth" (1 Tim. 6:17).[22] As the most purely instrumental of goods, wealth represents *indeterminately* our power to act *determinately*. It confers the power to do "something," without specifying what that something is. In clinging to the indeterminate, we become indeterminate in our purposes, hoping merely to be sufficient for *anything*. Such

---

20. There are 10 occurrences of φιλαργυρία/-ος noted in *The Philo Index*.

21. See Polycarp 4:1 for a direct quotation, but there is constant allusion to φιλαργυρία in the apostolic fathers.

22. ἐπὶ πλούτου ἀδηλότητι.

a hope is sick, either of an inability to value real things or of an indecision as to which things one is called to pursue. Love of money begins when the notice we pay it exceeds the serious uses we have for it, and it terminates in "acquisitiveness," amassing resources only to withhold them from communication, either as currency or as conspicuous possessions.[23] Whether we have it or whether we don't, the thing we should really appreciate about money is that it comes and goes. To cling to it is to lose the power it might have conferred to do something worth doing. The object for which money was useful recedes in the imagination, and we become unable to conceive a determinate desire and plan a determinate course of action. The moral question the New Testament poses to wealth, then, is precisely the question of its use (1 Tim. 6:18): how may resources be put to the service of a well-formed moral reason.

Pride, as military self-consequence, as wealth, or in any other form, is the sin that arises *after* the experience of self, world, and time in action. Pride is a sin of rest. It is the doubtful privilege of angelic beings to refuse good immediately and absolutely; human agents are protected against the immediacy of the "No!" that they might otherwise pronounce to God's purposes for their good. In rejecting the good which God calls them to at the last, they must identify another, less fitting point of rest. Concretely they do so in treating ends of action, which ought to be transparent to further ends, as termini rather than staging posts. Ends can be both innocent and vicious, and so can our "pride" be spoken of in innocent and vicious senses. We are innocently proud of concrete accomplishments, our own or other people's, that simply cause us joy; we are proud of our grandfather's knighthood or our daughter's Olympic medal. We "boast" of them to others, we objectify them and take satisfaction in them as happy gifts, draw courage from them for the tasks ahead. We take "pride in x," we are "proud of y," etc. But when we are simply "proud," we have not kept our satisfaction focused on the concrete object, just one accomplishment among many possible accomplishments, but have taken it into our own moral self-consciousness. The achievement drops out of sight; what remains is the standing that it leaves us with. This halts in its tracks the dynamic progress of practical reason from one provisional end to the next, from faith to love to hope and back to love again, keeping faith and hope in play until the final end is reached. Pride thus makes absolute the sins against self, world, and time. Agency is re-founded on what we have made of ourselves, instead of being received afresh in faith as God's gift. The

---

23. πλεονεξία in the Greek of the New Testament, translated into Latin as *arrogantia*.

social world becomes our prey, raw material for our self-valuation. Time is seized and overmastered, since it cannot be endured. The proud individual, people, or civilization no longer learns or does, for it is always having to maintain its position, scanning the world of appearances for proof of its power, technique, or wealth. At the root of its impotence is a moral vacuum, an intolerable doubt as to the point of existence, an inability to live without a surrogate for the meaning it has lost sight of.

CHAPTER 4

Sanctification

A Dogmatic Preamble

"Sanctification" speaks of God's saving work in Christ, but speaks of it from one particular angle. The renewal of creation, the disclosure of the second Adam, the perfect sacrifice, the overcoming of death and the vanquishing of the Devil are not included in the term. It is focused, rather, upon the transformation of our experience as agents. Its primary concern, then, is pursued in common with Ethics, the recovery of human agency from the death of sin. But its approach is very different, and the two discourses are pursued in relative independence. A doctrine of sanctification begins from the holiness of God, manifest through the life, individual and corporate, of God's people. Ethics approaches from the point of view of human moral reason. It is not for moral reason to comprehend the acts of God, nor for Ethics to comment on them; they can be spoken of only as we step back from living our lives, and see the signs of God's hand stretched out to bless us. What God does must be thought and spoken of in ways that recognize him as the sole subject of his action and revelation. There is an irresistible logic, then, in the conventional distribution of responsibility between a Dogmatics that speaks of God's sanctifying work and an Ethics that speaks of a human work corresponding to it.

Yet that offers no more than an introductory orientation to a borderland difficult to map. Dogmatics speaks of God's work both narratively and theoretically. It speaks of his active presence among us in the Holy Spirit, and speaks predictively, on the basis of promise, of our fulfillment. These topics form tributary streams in the discourse of sanctification, but to bring them together in a fuller account also means speaking of God's "cooperation" with man's work, understanding that as it should be understood, not as a partnership of equals but as the giving and receiving of gift. Following the discourse of sanctification downstream towards an account of moral experience, then, we might think it natural to elaborate some kind of "special anthropology," an account of human nature as it functions in its revival under the sway of divine grace. This could take the form of a psychology (as with Edwards's "religious affections") or of a normative map of spiritual progress (as with John Wesley's "regeneration, entire sanctification, perfection"). The eighteenth-century theologians of revival were not the first to follow this path; they had plentiful antecedents in the spiritual writers of the patristic and medieval eras. But the path proved liable to erosion, since the general experience to support the special anthropology was not to hand. Sanctification is a happening, and a happening in which we are presently caught up, not yet (as is the death and resurrection of Christ) complete and entire. The experience that bears witness to it unfolds from day to day, following life's unanticipated directions. Evidence for sanctification is not absent, but it is not coherent, gathered, and systematic. A heavenly Dogmatics can have a doctrine of renewed human nature, disclosed like a bride ready for the bridegroom, but in the meantime it is for prophets to point towards it.

The revival theologians were led by an urgent need to renew the discourse of Ethics, and it was a measure of their attentiveness to the age of Enlightenment in which they lived that they conceived this as a systematic descriptive theory of psychological powers and processes. The correct way to connect sanctification with experience, I shall argue, is not descriptive, but narrative and confessional. We live and act as members of a redeemed mankind, in whom, generically, the powers that God gave, and were lost, are restored; we live and act particularly, as individuals and as members of our own communities, each given a life to live and to thank God for, like others, but never simply conformed to the life of others. Charles Wesley was surely right that it would take a thousand tongues (or should it be a hundred and forty-four thousand?) to tell the great Redeemer's praise: every particular narrative application of the truth of sanctification, every autobiography and community history, which Dogmatics has excluded from its view. Dogmatics tells one narrative, the sacred narrative of Israel and the Christ, and beyond that it speaks generically. It knows and declares that God is made known in the holiness of the saints, but *which* saints—Saint Teresa? John Wesley? Savonorola?—is not for Dogmatics to say. That involves a particular moral discernment. Only moral reflection engages directly with the distinctiveness of particular acts, particular lives, particular histories. Yet if our talk of sanctification leaves the particular out, it remains airy and aspirational. To moral reason it must fall, then, to recognize God's sanctification of the saints, and of our own lives and communities. To Ethics as a discipline it falls to ask what is involved in that act of recognition.

The verb "to sanctify" and its corresponding adjective and noun, "holy" and "holiness," translate a range of New Testament words that draw on priestly imagery to speak of the church and its members as dedicated to God.[1] The verb may have God as its subject, but also human worshipers (1 Pet. 1:22; 1 John 3:3). Holiness may be attributed to church membership (as at Acts 20:32; 26:18; 1 Cor. 1:2); to baptism (1 Cor. 6:11; Eph. 5:26); to the effect of Christ's work (repeatedly in Hebrews; also 1 Cor. 1:30); to the presence of the Holy Spirit (Rom. 15:16; 1 Cor. 3:16; 2 Thess. 2:13; 1 Pet. 1:2); to the reception of God's word (John 17:17); and, distinctively, to the eschatological perfection of the church as Christ's bride (Eph. 5:27). The specific application of the term to the moral character of the life of faith is based on a selection of New Testament uses which speak of sanctification as progress towards completion. In 1 Thessalonians 5:23 Paul prays, "May God sanctify you wholly; may your spirit, soul, and body be kept whole to be found blameless at the appearing of our Lord Jesus Christ," adding "faithful is the one who calls you; he will do it." Completion, as attained through purgation and correction, is a term echoed in 2 Corinthians 7:1 and Hebrews 12:10. The adjective "holy" may appear in a list of virtues (Titus 1:8), or in parallel with "righteous" and "blameless" (1 Thess. 2:10), or with "blameless and irreproachable" (Col. 1:22; blamelessness accompanies holiness again at 1 Thess. 3:13, while at 1 Tim. 2:15 it accompanies faith and love and is tied to discretion). Sanctification is the moral goal of believers at 1 Peter 1:15–16 and Hebrews 12:14 (associated with the church's peaceful relation to society). The only specific moral topic in which the term is deployed is sexual, referring (1 Thess. 4 repeatedly) to restraint and consideration for others in contracting marriage. In 1 Corinthians 7:34, however, it refers not to morally approvable marriage, but to the special dedication of virginity, reminding us that "holy" never loses the overtone of the numinous, forbidding us to translate it simply as "virtuous." This quick overview would be lacking if we failed to add that the New Testament speaks of progress and completion corporately as much as individually.

The terminological pairing of justification and sanctification as a sequence, derived from Romans 6:19, 22, is a distinctive idiom of Protestant

---

1. ἅγιος, ἁγνός, ἁγιάζω, ἁγνίζω, ἁγιωσύνη, ἁγιότης, ἁγιασμός.

Dogmatics. It served to focus the term "justification" more sharply upon the acceptance of mankind in Christ, in whom the Father is well pleased. "Sanctification" was focused more sharply, too, upon the work of bringing worshipers to maturity.[2] That sometimes prompted the thought of sanctification as a *second work of God* in salvation, either a repetitive shadow of the first (so that in some contemporary theology we read even of a "sanctification by faith"), or on lines so different as to undermine the principle that faith is the root of action.[3] The safe rule of the scholastic theologians, that what God's word declares it effects, and the safe rule of Saint Augustine, that the persons of the Trinity are undivided in their external works, can both be lost sight of in catechetical presentations which suggest that God, having declared our acceptance in Christ, must then do something *else* to give his gracious word real effect. Justifying and sanctifying is one saving work of God, connecting the past death and resurrection of Jesus, on the one hand, with the present active life of his disciples on the other. We may speak of two "moments," but without any suggestion of separation or independence. The distinction is aspectual, between what God has done *in Christ for us*, and what God has done *in us through Christ*. Whatever God does for our salvation is done in Christ; whatever he does in Christ takes effect in us. There is not one work of God and then a second, but two points of purchase of one work, representative and incorporated aspects of our solidarity with the Redeemer through the Holy Spirit.

The problem is compounded when it is also suggested that to these two works of God there correspond two *biographical experiences*, an experience of "regeneration" first, and subsequently an experience of "sanctification." In this normative biography individual experience seems to have floated free of its communal context and acquired a shape which does not belong to the life of the church. That is what imposes upon the doctrine of sanctification the burden, which it can never bear, of accounting for Christian

---

2. To get away from the "perpetual see-saw of argument about definitions" Hugo Grotius proposed (*Annotata ad Consultationem Cassandri*, ad 4) doing without the terms "justification" and "sanctification" entirely, replacing the first with "forgiveness of sins" (*remissio peccatorum*) and the second with "cleansing from faults" (*emundatio e vitiis*). But these alternatives unfortunately narrowed the scope of the original terms, focusing on the specific effects of divine work, rather than on God's working itself. So Saint Paul's observation that Christ was "delivered for our sins and raised for our justification" (Rom. 4:24) would lie very awkwardly with the proposed substitutions.

3. Cf. Henri Blocher, "Sanctification by Faith?" in *Sanctification*, ed. Kelly M. Kapic (Downers Grove, IL: IVP, 2014), pp. 57–78.

"perfection." Properly, talk of perfection belongs to eschatology; but when it has a secondary place on the penultimate horizon of moral reason, it is bound up with the life of the community. Cut off from the radical change of moral orientation, which corresponds to incorporation in the community by baptism, sanctification is left looking solely to a horizon of individual experience. Speaking only of continuing, and not also and at the same time of beginning, it is sucked towards a discourse of further post-conversion experiences demanding special description, with eschatological and perfectionist overtones. (It was a path that quietism had beaten a century or two before the experiential theologians of the eighteenth century, reopening an old highway once traveled by Origen of Alexandria and his admirers.)

No effective criticism can be made of this false turn without first accepting one proposition from which it arose: theology must be able to speak of the sanctifying work of God so as to prepare the ground for a confident and hopeful unfolding of faith into moral thought—on the part of the individual believer and on the part of the believing community. It has proved possible to mount an all-too-defensive orthodox reaction, which, sheltering behind the Lutheran *simul justus et peccator* formula, takes only its second half seriously. Sanctification was mentioned only to be bound and gagged, reduced to a disillusioned consciousness of moral possibilities unrealized, speculation on a gracious work of God that was never to be performed. The barrenness of the outcome can be seen in the withering away of vital moral categories, leaving only the reference to "good works," which (like wild animals, or enemies one cannot talk to) must be ignored if they ever thrust themselves on the attention. This was the high-road to deism, indeed, premised upon a God who worked only through man's inactivity, leaving "sanctification" as a doctrine entrenched in the curriculum with precisely nothing to talk about. Small wonder that Protestant Ethics, for lack of a sound doctrinal point of departure, so often reverted to echoing secular platitudes, the whole exercise of moral reason having become unsanctified and unsanctifiable!

Five dogmatic principles, then, must be established at the outset of a discussion of sanctification: (i) The restoration of human agency in Christ is wholly God's work, and it is *one* work, performed in Christ and consequently in us. (ii) To talk of this one work in these two aspects is to talk *evangelically*, of the possibility of joy in life and action under the empowering Spirit. (iii) God's activity and human activity are each realized in the realization of the other, not excluding or restricting each other, human action following in faithful correspondence and obedience to God's action. (iv) Human action that reveals God's sanctifying work lives in constant and conscious sequence

Sanctification

upon the one holy sacrifice of Christ, the atonement that assures the forgiveness of sins. (v) The demonstration of God's activity in man's activity occurs primarily within the community called forth for this very purpose, and consequently, but no less determinatively, in the shaping of individual believers' lives within that community.

And with these principles in view we may begin to ask about the contribution Ethics may bring to the topic, introducing first, as a word too long delayed, a category that ought to stand at the head of any discussion of sanctification, but rarely does. That category is "love," which follows upon faith as its only possible expression in act. Faith is "operative through" love, as Saint Paul puts it (Gal. 5:6). Saint James, to be sure, retains the expression "works" to make his polemical point, speaking of "faith operative with works and brought to completion by works," but the essential coherence of the believing life, for James as for Paul, is still, in the expression he especially favored, "friendship" with God (2:22–23). The real point of the distinction of justification and sanctification is to reflect in whatever we say about God's work the lived experience of faith taking active form as love. That, as we have said, is not a biographical sequence; it is an ongoing dynamism accompanying and governing the restoration of the moral life at every stage. But it is too important to allow a return to the pre-modern use of "justification" as an all-embracing term, or, indeed, the substitution of "sanctification" in that function. Rahner once proposed speaking of "justification by love," perfectly mirroring the Reformed proposal of "sanctification by faith," and the reason for hesitating over one of these proposals is the reason for hesitating over the other, namely, that they lose sight of the dynamic of faith pressing forward to enactment in love. Together with that they lose sight of the trinitarian dynamic by which the Son, "exalted at the right hand of God" on the completion of his work, "poured forth" the promised Spirit that we now see and hear (Acts 2:33). One work of God performed in two moments, historically in the passion and resurrection of Jesus of Nazareth, contemporarily through the Spirit in the church: it is not a *single* moment of renewed moral experience, whether we call that moment "faith" or "love." Believing in the historical accomplishment of justification in Jesus, we are opened to love in the present. We may speak, of course, of "works done in faith," provided that we remember that these same works are, in their own character, works of love, of which faith is the root. There are various things we can say to tie the work of sanctification to its source and origin, while preserving the dynamic of its unfolding: sanctification as "not withdrawing from the sphere of faith," sanctification as "a corollary of faith . . . never severed from its relation to the mercy of God." There are more adequate ways to express a unity-in-duality that must not be allowed to fall in on itself.[4]

Since it is the dynamic expression of faith in love that is at issue, we may be attracted by Barth's proposal to extend the parallel with the three theological virtues by adding a third term to the justification-sanctification sequence: "vocation" is the work of God that Barth associates with the virtue of hope.[5] This focuses the discussion of sanctification on the new *moral orientation*, preventing us from rushing precipitately upon "works" and encouraging attention to themes of importance to the Enlightenment-era revival theologians who reflected most constructively on the topic, with their consideration of "religious affections" and the "gracious temper wrought in the heart." There are, however, difficulties. Separating sanctification/love/temper off from vocation/hope/works risks conjuring up some well-known romantic paradoxes about lovely souls performing ugly deeds. "Vocation," in its turn, points especially to the particular and the innovatory. By using the term to organize the whole sphere of action, we risk devaluing that routine and law-governed activity central to any practical expression of love-of-neighbor, a devaluation of which Barth, with his somewhat bourgeois horror of the bourgeois, was often guilty.[6]

So it is better to treat faith and love as two poles, which need not impair the faith-love-hope triad if we recall that love, in its second reflection, returns as the concluding moment in Christian moral thought. It is *from the beginning to the end* of the active life that the phrase "faith operative through love" builds an arch. If conscious agency arises with the hearing of God's summons to faith, agency is crowned in the loving thanksgiving offered for what he has done in and through a life and action of love and hope. The theme of sanctification is properly located at this concluding retrospective moment. Not all thanksgiving is retrospective; we may be thankful for cre-

---

4. These phrases are those of G. C. Berkouwer in *Faith and Sanctification*, trans. J. Vriend (Grand Rapids: Eerdmans, 1952), pp. 20, 26-27, a presentation of the issue from a couple of generations back which, for all its Reformed orientation and now wholly dated polemic against Catholic theology, displays an admirable sense of the question and a fine judgment.

5. I embraced this proposal, on which I now have second thoughts, in "Sanctification and Ethics," in *Sanctification* (ed. Kapic), pp. 150-66. On the wider scheme behind the proposal in *Church Dogmatics* IV/1 §58 I comment more extensively in *Self, World, and Time*, pp. 100-102. The appropriateness of exploring the category of vocation under the general heading of hope I have sought to demonstrate in *Finding and Seeking*, pp. 214-37.

6. Karl Barth, *Kirchliche Dogmatik* IV.1 §58.2 (Zürich: Theologischer Verlag, 1986), p. 118. The standard English translation renders "bürgerlich" by "middle-class" (*Church Dogmatics* IV/1 [Edinburgh: T & T Clark, 1956], p. 109).

ated goods that the world offers us here and now, and by anticipation for goods promised in the future. But a thanksgiving that concerns itself with a work of God in our lives and communities is bound to be retrospective, for there is no other angle from which we may speak concretely about God's working within our own work. The sanctification of the saints is a strand in the history of the world; our particular sanctification is a strand in our own particular history. We can speak of it only as we can draw on the experience of having lived and acted.

Let us propose, then, as a provisional definition to guide our thoughts, that God's work of sanctification is to reveal his working in the members and communities of the church, through experiences of living and acting in the faith of Christ, as a matter for thanksgiving and a ground for hope. There is a self-reflective character in the work of God: he is at work within the Christian experience of acting, and he is at work within our recognition that he is at work. Recognition and attestation are therefore the first distinct task which the work of sanctification lays upon us. The church is given to live by the "communion of the Holy Spirit," the shared experience of God's working in its differentiated life. This requires the testimony of each individual and community. And here we must speak of the second task which this work lays upon us, that of "sanctifying ourselves" (1 John 3:3) in reflective correspondence to the holiness of God revealed to experience. For the way in which any member or any community within the church is given to bear the testimony of thanksgiving is materially distinct, and presupposes moral discernments made by particular agents, whether individuals or communities of believers. As a reflective discipline, Ethics cannot supply them. But Ethics can indicate the parameters within which these discernments may be made, and here we shall make some observations, first, about the positive content of sanctification as thanksgiving, and second, about the way in which the concept of "perfection" may and may not shape past and future horizons of our agency.

Thanksgiving

To speak of sanctification is to speak in thanksgiving for God's work in our experience, and therefore to speak *retrospectively*. Though we may speak in anticipation of sanctification yet to come, we do so secondarily and by way of corollary, following the inferential logic of Philippians 1:6, that "he who began a good work in you will bring it to completion at the day of

Christ." To speak of our experience in thanksgiving is also to speak *interpretatively*, since the sanctifying meaning of our experiences may not lie on the surface of our recollections, but may need to be drawn out by the discipline of thanksgiving. If memory can be a labor, needing to be sought out, weighed, puzzled over, and given attention, so may thanksgiving; if memory can cause us pain, thanksgiving may be tempted to evade the hard edges of the pain. To bring all to thanksgiving is not quickly accomplished, nor, in this life, completely. The souls of the slain beneath the altar in the vision of John have not yet been shown the meaning of their unjust deaths, so that they may thank God for them, but are bidden to wait "a little while" till the higher and greater justice of suffering time has reached completion (Rev. 6:9–11). To speak of sanctification, third, is to speak *continuously*, since the work of sanctification for which we are thankful and the work of thanksgiving for sanctification are one ongoing work. It is not simply that God works in our experience while we give thanks. The very way in which he sanctifies us is by leading us to thankful reflection and recognition of his work, so that thanksgiving itself becomes a continuation of his sanctifying work.

That answered petition should always be followed by thanksgiving is a major theme in the Hebrew Scriptures: "Praise is due to thee, o God, in Zion, and to thee shall vows be performed, O thou who hearest prayer! To thee shall all flesh come" (Ps. 65:1–2). The "coming" to make petitions and pay vows is recurrent; it belongs to the celebration of the annual feast. This cyclical asking and answering has its proper logic in the worship of a God who, year after year, acts in the lives of his people. But in the ministry of Jesus this rhythm is suspended; the crisis of the ages leaves only expectation and petition for the once-for-all gift, "Thy kingdom come!" Jesus himself does not instruct his disciples to give thanks, as Paul will later; yet at one very climactic and decisive moment in his ministry he *himself* gives thanks: "I thank you, Father, Lord of heaven and earth, for hiding these things from the learned and wise, and revealing them to the simple. . . . Everything is entrusted to me by my Father" (REB). Luke places this moment at the triumphant return of the seventy (10:21–22), Matthew at the conclusion of his exposition of the ministry of John the Baptist (11:25–27); it is dawning of the Kingdom in proclamation and belief that excites this special word of thanks from Jesus, not only for the *fact*, but also for the *manner* in which the "babes," the attentive and unprejudiced, lead the way. Matthew follows it at once with the invitation to the humble to "take my yoke . . . and learn from me." In our thanksgiving we are invited to take up the yoke of Jesus' thanksgiving, and to learn for what, and how, our thanks are due.

In *Finding and Seeking* we followed the petitions of the Lord's Prayer to characterize the three moments of faith, love, and hope in moral thought—a purely *expository* arrangement, let it be understood, for which no exegetical ground is claimed—and are left now with no further petition to follow "Deliver us from evil." There is, however, the common ascription, "For thine is the kingdom, the power, and the glory for ever" at Matthew 6:13, the earliest appearance of which dates from the fifth century. Jesus did not teach his disciples to pray in these words, yet we may find in them some reassurance that the Holy Spirit did not abandon the patristic church, for any form of words that could be appropriate to append to Jesus' prayer would surely have to have been a reflective ascription of praise. The ascription builds on a petition Jesus did teach, for the final disclosure of world history, "Thy kingdom come!" The appendix thus serves to reflect on the new situation of the church in the light of the coming of the Kingdom in the resurrection and ascension of Jesus and the renewal of human action by the sending of the Holy Spirit. Taking these words as a suggestive example, may we not propose as the prayer of love's second reflection Jesus' own words, "I thank you, Father"?

The crowning virtue of the new humanity in Colossians 3 is love, "the perfecting bond" (v. 14), perfecting *because* it is a bond that unites the new humanity in one community. To this love all the practices of restraint that have just been itemized (vv. 12, 13) contribute. The concluding phrase "over all these" (NIV) does not simply indicate an addition, but a culmination, love bringing coherence and final purpose to restraints which left by themselves require further explanation. Four practical requirements follow: First, Christian peace is to be an arbitrating consideration in the individual's doubtful decisions on how to act—the "hearts" in which peace is to exercise its sway are the sites of moral deliberation, not merely registers of emotional satisfaction (v. 15). Second, we are to "be thankful" (v. 15), finding in this bond of love the supreme demonstration of God's work in our midst. Third, there is to be constant communication of the Gospel in teaching, counseling, and worship (v. 16). Fourth, in what we are given to *do* in this respect, we are to find a further matter of prayer ("in the name of the Lord Jesus") and, yet again, thanksgiving (v. 17). The command that authorizes talk of the perfecting bond of mankind is the command, "And be thankful!"

How, then, are the themes of love and thanksgiving bound together? Thanksgiving, we may say, gives love its historical form. Inverting the order of immediacy in which we proceeded in the case of the first reflection of love from love of the world to love of God, we now place love of God first of all, because in the events of history he is the first agent.[7] The controverted term "theodicy" refers essentially to this service of love in praise, an eschatological anticipation given on the basis of reflected experience, the praise of God's sanctification of his name in deeds of reconciliation and salvation: "Great and wonderful are your deeds, O Lord God the Almighty! Just and true are your ways, O King of the nations! Who will not fear, O Lord, and glorify your name? For you alone are holy. All nations will come and worship you, for your righteous acts have been revealed" (Rev. 15:3-4). But in thanksgiving, too, we express love "of the brotherhood," the church—which is to say, the neighbor seen from the point of view of his ultimate calling, to be a child of God. In framing the thanksgiving due to God we enrich the tradition of praise we have received, offering further resources for faith out of our own experience. And in the third place we love *ourselves within the church*—for as in the three steps of faith, love, and hope there is a discovery of and acceptance of the self, so there is in the second reflection of love. It is only as we gladly recognize that we have been a part of God's work within his community that we can finally and fully come to terms with ourselves—accepting what we have been given to be, not pining to have been something else. Self-acceptance is a highly valued state of mind in the age we inhabit, but any ground that we may think we can find for accepting ourselves will seem shabby and complacent unless we can learn to say of ourselves that somehow God has touched us and owned us.

 Let us reflect briefly on the latter two points. The church is the site of the prayer of thanksgiving, the agent of it, and the ground for it. The life of the church is seen in it, and by thanksgiving we prove our works as done in and for the church. In the upper room on the evening of the day of resurrection, we are told that Jesus breathed on his disciples and spoke the words, "Receive the Holy Spirit. Whoever's sins you remit, they are remitted for them, whoever's sins you bind, they are bound" (John 20:22-23), an authorization for them to act together in community, to define themselves as a common agency and to expect the blessing of heaven on their decisions. If Jesus' ascension into heaven was, in one aspect, the last word in the drama of Christ, it was also a first word for those who were given to follow him, the beginning of an answer to prayer which drew them into his triumph and enabled them to do what they could not possibly do otherwise, to recapitulate and build on his life of witness and service. Precisely this authorization formed a new kind

---

7. See *Finding and Seeking*, pp. 70-81.

Sanctification

of prayer for a new kind of action. And so the first prayer of the church of which we read after the Ascension is an exercise of this collective authority, claiming the insight of God, "the searcher of all hearts," to reveal "which one of these two you have chosen to receive the place of ministry and apostleship from which Judas fell away" (Acts 1:24–25). This prayer, so different from the forms of prayer taught hitherto, did not look forward to its answer but back to it, acknowledging a favorable answer already given, a decision made by God that needed only to be disclosed through the church's decision.

A prayer for the church is at one and the same time a petition, a proclamation of God's work, and an action. It is a prayer that extends from its center, the bestowal of the Holy Spirit, out to the ends of the earth, not only within the bounds of the church as it exists, but to "all nations" destined to gather before the throne of Christ. And what is prayed *for* the church in this triumphant way is at the same time prayed *in and by* the church. Jesus taught disciples to pray "*Our* Father." Not that the prayer, "My Father," is forbidden. Jesus speaks of God as "my father," and though we do not find that phrase in his prayer, we find expressions that amount to it.[8] Jesus speaks of God to his disciples as "your Father," not only using the plural possessive but the singular, too.[9] To each of us God is Father, and to all of us acting as a whole. But to accompany this extension of the community of the church to each individual, there is a contrary movement, the weaving of the experience of each, the particular experience *this* life has been entrusted with, back into the thanksgiving of the whole, resuming the expression "our" with a strengthened sense of the body. The thanks that each gives for his or her own experience, the church takes into its collective thanks for the coming of God's Kingdom in history. Each person, each community, brings a thread to the weave. As the thread is woven in, the individual who contributes it is confirmed as a member of that whole, redeemed from the shadow of regret or resignation.

That is why it is not the smallest part of our work of thanksgiving to praise God for his working *particularly*, in our individual lives and the lives of our communities. The contribution of our own experience to the eternal praises of the Father must be articulated. To live as those redeemed is to bear a testimony that is in each case unique, not to be replicated by any other. Nature sings God's praises generically, history particularly. The "hundred and

---

8. Consider, for example, John 17:21. Not to be overlooked in this connection is Mark 15:34.

9. Matt. 6:4, 6, 18, in close proximity to the Lord's Prayer in the Sermon on the Mount.

forty-four thousand" whose songs are to be added to the very satisfactory songs of created order which open the visions of the Apocalypse, sing the songs of history, redemption accomplished in the ways their own lives have been stamped with the manifestation of God's holiness. And we, too, are called to be part of the praise we articulate: not only "His blood can make the foulest clean," but also "His blood avail'd for me."[10] Not a thousand tongues, but a hundred and forty-four thousand distinct tongues, each speaking of a work "for me" out of its own experience.

Sanctification is the work God has done for and in us. We praise God for his being and his works; we thank him for how his works have constituted our good, "for our creation, preservation, and all the blessings of this life."[11] But in thanking him for *this* blessing, the blessing of our moral experience, we speak *in* thanksgiving *about* thanksgiving. The holy life for which we give thanks is itself already an act of thanksgiving, made "not only with our lips but in our lives," for God's "inestimable love in the redemption of the world by our Lord Jesus Christ." Thanksgiving for sanctification, then, is always a second moment of thanksgiving, a moment at which we become gratefully implicated in what God has done in restoring our agency in Christ. To speak of sanctification is to speak of living thankfully. But to speak thankfully of that thankful life extends it, draws it out into a further act of thankful reflection.[12] It *sanctifies sanctification*, takes what we see of the cooperation of God with our own endeavors as a moment to "sanctify ourselves," opening ourselves to his further working by recognizing and rejoicing in the work we have seen.

What, then, becomes of the moral ambiguities of our experience? All experience is uneven, not only in its emotional content but in its moral tone. In giving thanks for sanctifying grace we do not adopt a point of view from which past sin is invisible. The whole burden of thanksgiving is that sin, which blasphemes God and resists his working, has not been given the last

---

10. Charles Wesley, "For the Anniversary Day of One's Conversion," in *Charles Wesley: A Reader*, ed. John R. Tyson (Oxford: Oxford University Press, 1989), p. 109. Cf. Berkouwer, *Faith and Sanctification*, p. 125, commenting on Ps. 26:1-3: "The expression of joy over the mercy of God and distinguishing self from others are naturally related; they find their point of convergence on the altar of reconciliation."

11. The "General Thanksgiving" of the 1662 *Book of Common Prayer*, the work of John Cosin.

12. A point expressed with crystalline clarity by John Webster, *Holiness* (Grand Rapids: Eerdmans, 2003), pp. 9-10: "A Christian theology of holiness is an exercise of holy reason . . . ; it is a work in which holiness is perfected in the fear of God." Again: "The act of acknowledging or, perhaps better, confessing the holy God . . . is the fundamental act of the holy Church" (p. 66).

Sanctification

word in the shaping of our lives. God has drawn our inconsistency under the control of his own consistency. "If we are faithless, yet he is faithful, for he cannot deny himself" (2 Tim. 2:13). *Simul justus et peccator* does not mean "partly sanctified, partly not," but subject, in all our vacillation and inconsistency, to the sovereign grace of his holiness, which imprints its presence upon our lives in correction and judgment as in strength and accomplishment. We cannot pretend that there is nothing in our past deserving regretful moral assessment, but we can find in regret a moment to recognize God's patience in giving new proofs of his love: "Whom the Lord loves, he chastens . . . that we may share his holiness" (Heb. 12:6, cf. Rev. 3:19). "Sanctification" is the dynamic operation by which God takes hold of us with all our moral imperfection, and by correction, chastening, teaching, and strengthening brings us to safety. Such is the work of judgment which is to begin, Saint Peter declares, with the household of God (1 Pet. 4:17).

The New Testament speaks of a "good conscience" (Acts 23:1; 1 Tim. 1:5, 19; Heb. 13:18; 1 Pet. 3:16, 21), and hardly at all of a "bad conscience" (possibly Heb. 10:22). Yet it does speak of a conscience that is clearly *not* good, a conscience "seared with a red-hot iron" (1 Tim. 4:2) or "kept at bay" (1 Tim. 1:19), which is to say, insensible and non-functional. A conscience may be "good," not by being comfortably "unaware of anything against me," which proves nothing at all (1 Cor. 4:4), not simply by not being "bad" (as an unhelpful line of modern commentary maintains), but by being reflectively attentive, quick to grasp the significance of our works, including those in which we have unquestionably failed, within the context of God's works. In seeing and naming failures the conscience opens them to the redemptive work of God who forgives sin and brings good out of the evil we have done. That is the sense in which the active conscience is "pure" (1 Tim. 3:9; Heb. 9:14) and "free of offence" (Acts 24:16)—not by the simple absence of anything to notice, but by taking notice of the cleansing and purification God has accomplished.[13] Sins and moral offences, drawn into God's purposes, give offence no longer.

Perfection

The little parable of 2 Timothy 2:20–21 calls us back from such reflections with the reminder that some vessels in God's house are for honorable, some

---

13. Contemporary English translators who like to render καθαρά and even καλή and ἀγαθή as "clear," have apparently succumbed to the attractions of the negative view, unwisely.

for dishonorable use. On reflecting thankfully we may find that as individuals or communities we have served God in either capacity, and quite probably in both. We have been humbled, made an example of, perhaps; perhaps, also, we have been used to bless and strengthen others directly. Looking back, what does it matter, if either way we can praise God for what he has done with us? But looking forward, the distinction between honorable and dishonorable does matter. And look forward we must, for the pause to reflect and give thanks is only a pause, not the final rest. "If anyone cleanses himself . . . he will be a vessel for honorable use." Thanksgiving must be a *cleansing* pause, a preparation that will make us *more fit* for the service that remains.

Here we have to look more closely at the difficult term "perfection." John Hare comments on two aspects of the requirement of perfection: on the one hand it is "indeterminate," on the other it is an "ideal."[14] It is indeterminate in that while it applies to *anything* we do, it does not instruct us on *what* we are to do. It is simply wrapped up in the notion of "doing" that *certain conditions must be fulfilled*. "If a thing is worth doing, it is worth doing well," we say, which is simply a truism about what it means to consider something worth doing. It is a truism, however, only about the *particular* deed, not of the *kind* of deed. If I sit down to play a piece of Brahms on the piano, I must try to get it right, hitting the right notes with the right fingers, sustaining the right tempo, shaping the phrases as they are intended, etc. It does not mean I should never attempt a piece I cannot play well. When Chesterton wittily inverted the saying, "If a thing is worth doing, it is worth doing badly," he hit on another truth, which is that there are some kinds of things that are important to do, whether or not one can fulfill all the conditions of doing them. It is worth stumbling through a piece of Brahms if one is capable of playing it somehow, but not well. What is *not* worth doing is playing it worse than one is capable of.

This is relevant, too, to the living of our lives as a whole. I cannot set out to live the life of a Bonhoeffer or a Mother Teresa, but I can, and must, intend to live the best life given me to lead. But there is something else to be said about perfection, which is expressed in the term "ideal." Not any life whatever could count as the best life given to me to lead. My being perfect is, in some sense, "a perfection of the common nature 'humanity.'" Being human is the supreme example of something too important not to attempt merely because we cannot do it perfectly, and yet there are conditions for living humanly in the pattern of Christ, and they are conditions we are bound to intend to meet, whether or not we think we can meet them—in which

---

14. John E. Hare, *God's Command* (Oxford: Oxford University Press, 2015), pp. 45–46.

the knowledge that grace will be given will encourage us, but not make us certain of never failing. That is why the early Methodists, wishing to lay fresh emphasis on our responsibility for living life as a whole, had some necessary business to transact with the term "perfection." The practical horizon we face invites and allows no compromise, but makes the demand, "Be perfect." Yet it was a mistake, a result of the eighteenth century's anthropological turn, to treat perfection as a stage of achievement in the general description of a redeemed life.

Whether in John Wesley's version as an inner purification of the affections, or in Charles Wesley's version as a perfection to be attained on the deathbed, this introduced a new threshold between the sinner's conversion and the final entry into God's glory. That could only have the effect of reducing the decisiveness of conversion itself as a turning from death to life, since the words "Repent and believe the Gospel" no longer conveyed the totality of the encounter with a justifying and holy God. It also introduced within the company of disciples a notional élite, not set apart by calling to a special service but simply by their level of attainment. The pastoral convenience of this conception for those who had to wrestle with difficult tasks of organizing communities and counseling individuals at every level of moral seriousness and confusion, is easy enough to see. But pastoral priorities afford only a restricted view of moral realities, God having reserved the judgment of all souls to himself. In the more general context of their teaching about the Christian life the doctrine of perfection could foster one of two misrepresentations: an additional threshold intruded *behind*, an additional threshold intruded *ahead*. In any given life, of course, there may be any number of moral thresholds, but that is because there is in reality one threshold, enacted and reenacted hour by hour and day by day in decisions made about great matters and small. There can be *no one* additional threshold, unless we view death itself (not the deathbed!) as such. Within life there is one crisis and no second, however it may be distributed across the mixed experiences of our days and years, the crisis of confrontation with the perfect humanity and perfect sacrifice of God's Son. The encounter of sinful man with the holy God turns him round in his tracks once and for all, or else it is a fabrication.

(*a*) Suppose we imagine an additional threshold intruded behind us: it posits a plateau of accomplishment (if only in the realm of motive, leaving much to do in the concrete tasks of life), on which we may look back with satisfaction. In the anxious pages of the dogmaticians this raises the specter of complacency. That specter had better be exorcised, since an anxiety that prevents our telling the praises of God's deeds in sanctification is a dangerous anxiety indeed. But exorcised it can be, if our talk of sanctification is wholly thanksgiving, wholly governed by its true object, the gracious working of God, wholly oriented to its true goal, the faithful service of God.

The bare declaration of thanks is no insurance against complacency. In Jesus' parable of the Pharisee and the Publican (Luke 18:9-14), the very hearthstone of justification by faith, the prayer of the Pharisee could not be faulted for want of thankfulness, nor for failing to draw its topics from personal moral experience. Yet the experience he recalls is so closed off against the working of God that we can hardly avoid thinking of the thanks themselves as hollow. It is instructive to compare his prayer with that of someone else who thought he could be thankful for his own moral integrity, the poet of Psalm 66: "Come and hear, all of you who fear God, and I will tell what he has done for my soul. I cried to him with my mouth, and high praise was on my tongue. If I had cherished iniquity in my heart, the Lord would not have listened. But truly God has listened; he has attended to the voice of my prayer" (vv. 16-19 ESV). We feel at once the drama of dependence, the pressing peril of losing touch with God, the decisiveness of God's intervention. In the Pharisee's prayer, on the other hand, there has been no peril, no cry for rescue, nothing much, indeed, for God to have done. The subject of every verb is "I," but worse, the verbs speak only secondarily of what the "I" has *done*, and primarily of what the "I" *is*, or, yet worse still, is *not*. Defining himself against someone else, of whose inner life he knows nothing, the Pharisee gives thanks simply for the static separateness of his own being.

The meaning of sanctification cannot be that a certain moral status has been attained. In thanksgiving for sanctification the principle holds, "Let any one who thinks that he stands take heed lest he fall" (1 Cor. 10:12). Only "thinks" he stands, because "standing" is not what progress in the Christian life can ever be about. "Resting," yes, for there are opportunities for thanksgiving, when we pause, reflect and look back, but the resting is always a preparation for the challenges ahead. Holiness is to be "pursued" (Heb. 12:14, where it is linked suggestively with "peace with all," the goal of universal communication). The signs of God's working may be recognized and enjoyed, but they must also be made the ground for tackling the next frontier of decision and action. With further signs come further demands, never free of risk, for "To whom much is given, of him will much be required" (Luke 12:48). And so we may find the Pharisee's prayer inadequate on the prospective front. Augustine, who saw him as the archetypal Pelagian, commented that he gave thanks but failed to ask, "as though there was nothing

Sanctification

he would wish to be added."[15] A retrospection so fixed on attainment could not be open to future demands and dangers. To which there corresponds his unawareness that what is given is meant to be passed on for others' benefit. There is no echo of the Psalmist's "Come and hear" on the lips of one who, in Luke's suggestive phrase, prays "apart" and "with himself."

Yet we may speak properly of what has been given. "I know your works," says the Lord of the church to the seven churches of the Aegean littoral. In subsequent church history there are many works worthy to be known, and spoken of. Along with good works done, there are good habits formed, practices engrained, both in individuals and communities. A habit, as Aristotle first described it, is a disposition, a bearing, in relation to action, which allows decision to draw on a certain legacy of acquired experience and instinct. Nobody could go through life without acquiring dispositions except someone utterly devoid of the powers of memory. Typical habits are piano-playing, courteous and self-controlled reply to rudeness, love of the impressionist painters, single-minded attention to making money, etc. Habit is the realization of a power of memory, working convictions and practices deep into the self-recalling structures of continuity in the mind, to guide and reinforce our convictions and purposes. Habits include those "capacities for perception" of which the Epistle to the Hebrews says that they must be "trained." They include the wisdom which Saint Paul says is "for the mature." Yet it would be a strange life in which all habits acquired were perfectly good or perfectly bad. What Aristotle's theory of the habit did not know how to say was that we can change bad habits for good, and the capacity for change where necessary, for strengthening habits where necessary, is God's own self-communication to us, a work of the Holy Spirit witnessing to the righteousness of Christ.

Good habits relate to specific activities: doing certain things, or doing certain things well. Being patient may be a habit, or being cheerful; but we could never speak of a habit of being holy, or even of being good. Being holy and being good are not the kind of thing one *could* make a habit of; they are not specific patterns of behavior to be replicated and learned. They are the verdict of God's reality upon our lives and works as a whole. Sanctity is simply the fact that God has touched us, and has worked his work through us. It takes form in habits, as it takes form in acts and emotions. But habits are not spiritual relationships, not souls, not new natures. They are formations of the soul that remain under God's judgment. So if habits are spoken

---

15. Augustine, *Sermones* 36.11, 115.2.

of in classical antiquity as a "second nature," we should not mistake that for a theological claim about a *restored and redeemed* nature. Anxiety over excessive claims for habits has led some theologians to refuse the use of a perfectly serviceable anthropological concept. But forming habits is not, as such, putting on a new nature, for we form bad habits as well as good, and neither is changing bad habits for good, as Augustine knew when he commented approvingly on the "good habits" of ancient Roman civilization, yet judged them without "virtue." If neither works nor emotions nor habits comprise the renewal of our nature promised in God's sanctification, they are surely *implied* in it. We need not be afraid to see works, emotions, and habits as signs of the Spirit, who is called the *arrabōn*, or "pledge" of what is yet to be given (2 Cor. 1:22; 5:5; Eph. 1:14).

(*b*) What of an additional threshold intruded ahead of us? Is there an ideal, a point of self-possession, to which we may approximate in this life? This is, perhaps, the most difficult aspect of the theme on which to speak judiciously. Sanctification relates to our experience of God's working in us within the living of our earthly lives. The question arises over how these experiences license expectations of further such experiences, and whether that projection is simply indefinite, or whether it tends towards a fulfillment that can be accommodated in our earthly lives. There is a great deal said in the New Testament about "growth." Much of it is about the collective growth of the church rather than the growth of the individual, and yet growth "in grace and knowledge of our Lord Jesus Christ" (2 Pet. 3:18) can hardly not *include* individual growth. The example of growth that comes first to hand is the progress from childhood to maturity, in which a major component is the formation of habits:

> When in the slipp'ry paths of youth
> With heedless steps I ran,
> Thy hand unseen conveyed me safe,
> And led me up to man.[16]

Sanctification can hardly be confined to teenagers. How can an analogy between natural growth and moral progress be developed? And is there an analogous state to that of having been "led up to man"? C. S. Lewis plays with the idea, wittily but not scornfully, in describing his life as a walk that should now be coming to its "supreme stage ... reserved for the late afternoon,"

---

16. Joseph Addison, *The Spectator* 453 (August 9, 1712).

Sanctification

when he would meet "majestic rivers" of charity, "forests of contemplation," "silvery temperance," and "mists of chastity," and then adds:

> I can see nothing like all this. Was the map wrong?
> Maps can be wrong. But the experienced walker knows
> That the other explanation is more often true.[17]

We can say correctly, but too quickly, that the map was wrong in confusing the work of God, who sanctifies old age as he sanctifies youth and maturity, with some of the more attractive features of accumulated experience nature bestows upon advancing years. Nature bestows unattractive features on advancing years, too. Quite apart from the moral side effects of diminished powers (deafness breeds a defensive tetchiness, memory loss encourages paranoia), there is fixity of mind, and sometimes paroxysmic revolt against fixity of mind (another form of rigor), all of which may cut us off from hearing the calling of God.

But we should not leave the matter with that correct, but too quick answer. God's holiness may sometimes dawn upon us as a theophany at a particular never-to-be-repeated moment, but since his holiness is seen in his consistent pursuit of his purposes, it must make its imprint also upon our passage through time. If we may speak of sanctifying grace within the conduct of life over time, we must be able to speak of it within all our typical experiences of time, and these are passive as well as active: not only as we bend our deliberation upon the future horizon to discern our next act, but also as we discover our powers have been secretly enhanced or eroded by time's passage. Life in time is an experience of change, improvement and regression, growth and loss, accumulation of responsibilities and responsibilities discarded. All may be sanctified—not only learning when we are young, but memory loss when we are old. And what may be said of an individual life in this connection may be said *mutatis mutandis* of communities embodying the church on pilgrimage, who may see God's hand at work not only in establishment but also in exhaustion.

Yet we should go further than this. The future and the past are not alike to us, and our passage through time is future-facing. The past is closed off from change, open to knowledge; the future is closed off from knowledge, open to change. The future presents us with our next task, together with

---

17. C. S. Lewis, "Pilgrim's Problem," in *Poems*, ed. W. H. Lewis (London: Bles, 1964), pp. 119-20.

which it presents us with the one task that embraces all tasks, the task of life itself. When we speak of "experience" we speak of a continuity given to our life as a whole, which may draw on its past to address its future. Though in facing the future we are vulnerable to disruption and loss of what we have attained, we face it with experience behind us, and that experience, if we take the trouble to draw it down, is at each stage a somewhat ampler resource than before. For those who are capable of learning, the next future is approached with new experiences added to old, and in that respect, at least, better equipped. In that sense, if in no other, men and women may gain wisdom with time, acquiring a greater purchase on themselves as they grow older. In this respect, too, we may look to see the potential of nature taken up in the working of God. Not that faith or hope necessarily grows stronger, for Christian hope may be exercised with the greatest courage from the first moments of faith and may sometimes weaken with the weakening of natural energies, but our *reflection* becomes more deeply habituated, and therefore a richer resource to strengthen faith and hope with love. We may speak in some sense of "progress" in life—a natural progress, to be sure, but since progress is not alien to human living, God's gracious working can and will work through our natural progressions, too.

The "new heart" of the prophet's vision is a new moral center, a new orientation arising from the encounter of faith with God's appeal to mankind in Jesus Christ. The "nature" to which the "new heart" belongs is always and wholly a human nature; it is new in the sense that it is renewed from the death of sin. Called to be "sharers in the divine nature," as it is expressed in 2 Peter 1:4, human beings are not called to be other than human, but to attain the fulfillment that God set before his human creation from the beginning, to be in fellowship with him, freely directed by him to share his work and enjoy his glory. We may not and must not intrude an imagined self-possession short of this fulfillment into an account of mankind's redemption. Since fulfillment lies beyond the limit of our earthly lives, we must accept the judgment of philosophers who deny that the "I" can ever wholly possess itself within time. Yet in the very constitution of humanity there is an opening to a "second nature," which is the capacity of the first nature to unfold, to cultivate the experiences it has been given and assume a more perfect self-possession with the formation of social habits and practices. If these relative horizons of attainment to which our created nature is open are given back to us by God, renewed and restored as a sign of his ultimate purposes for us, they become prisms through which the light of final rest is diffracted through immediate practices and actions, no more than provisional, of course, yet,

Sanctification

if God sanctifies them, no less than glimpses anticipating fulfillment. And at this point we must surely concede Charles Wesley his moment of insight. Are not the glimpses *most* powerful and *most* telling when the condition of our nature can tell us only of our collapse and dissolution?

Social Transformation

In speaking of sanctification we have to ask about the working of God beyond the limits of the individual believer and the believing community within the wider affairs of society as a whole. That God is at work there is hardly a thesis to be questioned; it would not be the work of an omnipotent God to allow society simply to go its own way—if we can even imagine what that might mean. The question arises whether we are to think of this work simply in terms of omnipotent providence, or whether it shares in the character of his work in our sanctification, making himself known in Christ. The proclamation of the Gospel which occurs, according to John of Patmos, not in heaven but in the "mid-heaven" (i.e., in the sky above the earth, for all the world to see and hear), speaks of an impact of the disclosure of the Incarnation upon the political realm: "Fallen, fallen is Babylon the great!" (Rev. 14:6-8). All talk of politics and society that is open to us—the categories of "state," "law," "secular," and the compromises that each of these imply—lie downstream of that great fall, the overcoming of the purely bestial in collective life. In *The Desire of the Nations* I proposed that the triumph of Christ could be seen in what I called the "reauthorization" of the fallen and humbled powers, and, in what struck some critics as a provocative "defense of Christendom," that such a missionary impact could, and did, occur in medieval and early modern Europe.

Christendom itself had various ways of speaking of the relation of church and political rule after the fall of paganism. Broadly speaking, it conceived them as two poles, realizing that to think in unified terms of a single city/bride was to think of eschatology. It spoke of cooperation between the poles, realizing that a stable world-order turned on the acknowledgment by each of the other's place in the purposes of God. At its most reflective, it spoke of the two as in tension, each recognizing that the terms on which the other functioned were in polar opposition to its own. Neither could will the other's absence; neither could will to *be* the other, and to function as the other did. Since the very existence of the church was a provisional sign of God's purpose for the Kingdom of Christ, so, in general, was the existence of the cooperation-in-tension between the two. Christendom itself was a sign of God's sanctifying of the world order to the service of the Gospel. But that general answer demands to be given more specificity. In what particular ways did the Holy Spirit's work in the church extend to sanctify the relation between the two and mark it in distinctively evangelical ways?

That question may be approached from two angles: whether the proximity of secular order was a means by which God sanctified his church, and whether the proximity of the church was a means by which God sanctified the secular sphere. If the first angle of exploration is the more implausible from our modern point of view, at certain periods in the life of the church—notably after the conversion of the Roman Empire in the fourth century, and after the Reformation in the sixteenth—it appeared to be very plausible indeed. We are speaking here of what was referred to, in a broad sense, as the "establishment" of the church. That term, which in the modern world has become confined to the selective privileging of one or another branch of the church, originally meant simply that the church could take recognized form in society as a licit and organized human institution, a structure with legal personality that can interact with other structures. In a society where the corporate life of Christianity can find a legal presence, the churches are "established" in this wide sense, even if the legal personality attributed to them is no more than that of a public corporation. When we allow the distinction in ecclesiology between "visible" and "invisible" church, or (more precisely, in the terms perfected by the Reformed Confessions) between "particular" churches and the "church catholic" (for the church on earth can be *visible*, without being *organized*), we speak of how the secular order gives shape to the sacred. Synods, tithes, buildings, canons: all belong to the secularity of the church. That the church should be endowed with these secular functions was certainly seen, at a time when their legitimacy and possibility were constantly contested, as a great work of God to strengthen the church. If we have any capacity for sympathy with historical agents at all, our sympathy should surely extend to the newly legitimized bishops at the Nicene Council who, we are told, thought that the Kingdom of Heaven had come. The attitude of some of the Reformers to their "godly princes" was not very far removed from this.

If such an assessment was doomed to suffer a reaction, it was surely because the necessary strains and tensions involved in the legal personality of the church were never long in emerging. We do not need to speak of the *corruption* of the church to appreciate this. Institutional forms of the church can obey the logic of mission. They can afford openings to effective witness.

Sanctification

It is foolish to think that they could be dispensed with, or to yearn for the catacombs as though there were no temptations down there! Churches that like to parade "disestablished" status, while sheltering behind secular gospels of state neutrality and universal human rights, are often the ones that become imaginatively trussed up in their legal forms. Yet while thanking God for giving us institutional forms in the service of his mission, we must not fail to view them with a certain irony and distance. They are a necessary concession to life in the world, an embodiment of the lack of transparency of practical endeavor to spiritual meanings. To claim to see the Spirit's sanctifying work in a particular church polity, whether "independent" or "established," suggests a serious loss of focus. The present age cannot be overcome by idealizing our institutional self-representations. Their tensions are in evidence wherever Christians, meeting together in twos or threes as their Lord commanded, find it necessary to appoint a chair and agree on standing orders.

Let us turn, then, to the other aspect of the question which in the end must be judged the more fruitful. May we observe the effects of the Spirit's mission in transforming the conduct and norms of worldly organizations—not bringing the heavenly city to earth from heaven, but simply imprinting a character on them that speaks of sanctification, making their compromises more humane, their practices more appreciative of the virtues the Incarnation calls forth on earth, their ideological constructions less impermeable by the truth of man's call to fellowship with God and fellow-man? Is such an effect identifiable? Is it accumulative and progressive, when it is? And what are the criteria by which it might be recognized?

In my earlier attempt to take the legacy of Christendom seriously as an element of Christian tradition I recognized various contributions to European political culture as gifts of God: the emphasis on the rule of law; the definition of the polity by territorial limits rather than by tribal membership; the consultative disciplines of policy-making and of parliamentary representation. They were legacies of political actors who sought to be obedient to the rule of Christ—not only the few great political actors, but the very many small ones. I also took the view (unobserved by many critics) that Christendom was now a past era, and that the influence of their legacy had in some important respects been reversed. Those who took issue with me divided on either side of this position: to the left those who insisted on the perennial opposition of the spiritual and secular communities, so that any Christian service in the world must be alien, revolutionary, against the cultural grain; to the right those who refused to doubt the permanent gains of Christian civilization, and championed features of modern life such as democracy, human rights, and the place of women (but not usually economic globalization!) as living strands in the Christian tradition.

I see both responses as affirming different aspects of a complex truth. Certainly, to live in the world as a Christian is to be forced to make painful and difficult discernments between the work of the Spirit and of the Antichrist. If we have not learned what it is to live "against the grain" of civilization, we have not learned to take up our cross. Yet the very need to discern the shape of the conflict around us must alert us to the cultural deposits of the Spirit's work, still potent in the minds of our fellow men, still active as leaven in the lump and offering a continued purchase for the communication of the Gospel. It is not unreasonable to find such features in the contemporary world: if commonsense alone and a minimal sense of history should dissuade us from the view that democracy is the only acceptable polity, that does not make democracy entirely dumb about the virtues that Christians have practiced and valued in public life, nor entirely bankrupt in offering opportunities for those virtues to be practiced and valued in our times.

Yet we must be clear what is, and is not, being said at this point. This is no general truth about modern civilization as a whole, but a reflection on one concrete development, one point at which God has sanctified a cultural form to make himself known. All cultural events are under the direction of providence; that is something simply to *believe*. Providence governs the evil as well as the good, the routinely good as well as the exceptionally good. People die of cholera, people love and care for their children, both under the direction of providence. But if we speak of God's "sanctifying" the development of Western medicine or international law, or any other development we believe we are given specially to value, we claim to find traces of the Spirit's working quite specially there, and not everywhere, and quite specially in testifying to God's ultimate purposes, though not within the church where the Gospel is faithfully preached and the sacraments rightly administered, though some historical links will associate the church with such a development.

By this *a posteriori* route, then, there is no access to a universal doctrine of cultural progress. That is simply a speculative version of the doctrine of providence, and if we understand the role of providence in the world's affairs, we shall understand that universal progress is a rather inadequate way of expressing it, incapable of shedding light on a great deal that occurs of a more tragic character. It is a matter of faith, not of sight, that the whole of history leads patiently towards the end that crowns it, God working everything together for good, and to discern that shape in history is to hold to a promise, not to look through the historical records. Yet faith insists on scrutinizing the historical records, too. Though we belong to an age of struggle, even in such a time we may find concrete deposits of wisdom and experience to aid us. The tradition of the Gospel has spread its tentacles wide, and to treat the whole world as incapable of preserving a recollection of what it has heard is no less extravagant a speculation than universal progress. The operative question, then—perhaps the only question that does not fall under the charge of improper speculative ambition, and certainly the only one that Ethics can handle—is how we may recognize the legacy of works that God has sanctified. And the law of practical reason prevails. We discern reflectively only in the course of a deliberative search for the way we are called to walk in Christ's footsteps. God's presence in the culture will be known by those who have learned to long for it, and to give thanks for it when they find it, those for whom the presence of God in what their predecessors have left them is a practical guide and deliverance.

That leaves us with one further question, which is whether we shall find that legacy only within *social* practices—let us say, in aid organizations, welfare provisions, hospitals and so on—or whether we shall find it also in the *political* practices current among us. Building on what I have written, Eric Gregory has pressed the suggestion that we should be willing to see the works of God in the political realm, concluding with non-committal suggestiveness: "Some theologians have written about the American civil rights movement as a Christian event for both church and society."[18] Without prejudicing whatever may be said for or against that suggestion, let me propose the simple thesis that a political legacy, even if real, may be difficult to recognize. Thomas de Quincey, writing at the high noon of nineteenth-century triumphalist cultural Christianity, wrote: "Shyer than gravitation, less to be counted than the fluxions of sun-dials, stealthier than the growth of a forest, are the footsteps of Christianity amongst the political workings of man. Nothing, that the heart of man values, is so secret; nothing is so potent."[19] What is the meaning of this paradoxical secret potency in public affairs?

Let us define the sphere of the political as widely as possible, not confining it to the direct service of state organizations. Any service of community may be political, to the extent that it seeks to establish a just compromise in social communications. That may be undertaken in the fullest consciousness

---

18. Eric Gregory, "The Boldness of Analogy: Civic Virtues and Augustinian Eudaemonism," in *The Authority of the Gospel*, ed. Robert Song and Brent Waters (Grand Rapids: Eerdmans, 2015), pp. 72–85.

19. Thomas de Quincey, "On Christianity as an Organ of Political Movement," in *Essays on Christianity, Paganism and Superstition* (New York: Hurd & Houghton, 1877), p. 1.

of serving God and the church in love. Even a hangman, Luther famously insisted, may do that much, and the shock that this illustration continues to deliver may alert us usefully, perhaps, to certain modern instances that are hardly less paradoxical: a lawyer who assists a client in presenting a case in court; an accountant who assists a business in the prudent reporting of its financial transactions; a politician who composes an election manifesto for his party; a journalist who attempts to elicit a story from a reluctant source. All these may be dismissed by a skeptical and half-considered judgment as permitted forms of deception. A more considered judgment might allow that an optimal state of public truth needs dedicated advocates of partial truths. In that such advocacy is an accepted and necessary role in the wider public service, it may be undertaken with love for the common good and desire for public truth, and may be discharged conscientiously in fitting compromises between total candor and misrepresentation.

If, however, we are looking for a "Christian event" in politics, we are looking for something more hopeful than these conscientious, if paradoxical, services. More hopeful even than conscientious services of a less paradoxical kind, such as organizing health-care provision or working to meet carbon-emissions targets—"good works," without doubt, which witness to the truth by their conscientious search for the best courses of action available. What is wanted is a service that introduces something *new*, adjusting the terms of the compromises generally available to society, making it more hospitable to virtue than it was before. Such an event could only be recognized retrospectively, discerning the work of God in changes that have come upon us in the course of our political experience. They could not be hailed for their Christian significance at the moment of their accomplishment, if only because longer-term outcomes are essential to any judgment on whether, and to what extent, God has made himself known in them. De Quincey's own catalogue of the developments that Christianized politics—the disapproval of slavery, the generation of voluntary charitable societies, the regulation of war—all reflected long-term civilizational tendencies. Their "secrecy" was, in fact, the invisibility of something too large and too slow to be noticed as occurring at one moment. To his list we could add several more: the understanding of political authority as a responsibility, exercised by consultation and governed under law; the tendency to restrict, and finally to eliminate, routine use of the death penalty. These are political changes which, growing in the soil of moral and emotional attitudes taught by Christian teaching and worship, took generations to mature and are visible only when looked at in the long historical perspective.

Sanctification

It was important for de Quincey that changes attributed to Christianity should actually be derived from its beliefs, especially belief in the sovereignty of God and his relation to mankind. The capacity of Christianity to formulate its practices doctrinally and philosophically was, he thought, decisive for making certain patterns of action intelligible. The determination of Christian individuals would not have been enough to accomplish that. A combination of the energy of Boniface and the military power of Charles Martel could get the northern Germans baptized, but not morally converted. Routine habits of thought were needed to permeate society and its ways of judgment. Behind the big changes lay the undramatic reflections of citizens and obscure officials, expressing more immediately the qualities of lawfulness and freedom that God willed for mankind.

Yet why not also particular events, which, in retrospect, may seem to crystallize long-term and deep-seated transforming tendencies? It would be implausible to deny some heightened significance to William Wilberforce's success in persuading the British Parliament to abolish the slave trade in 1807, even if that was by no means the first or the last important Christian repudiation of the notion of the human chattel. (European Christians had eliminated slavery once before, by untraceable degrees in the course of the Middle Ages, an accomplishment overthrown by the dawning of the colonial age.) It would be ungrateful not to acknowledge the virtue of King James VI/I's bravely innovative practice of explaining government actions and policies at length through public speeches and letters—even though the principle that the sovereign should consult was current a thousand years before his time. The importance of those moments was proved by their outcome. It was not automatically implied by Wilberforce's parliamentary victory that slavery would disappear; it did not follow automatically from James's practice that later governments would feel obliged to explain their policies. But God blessed those deeds with happy outcomes.

"Christian events," then, need to be nourished in the wider soil of Christian practice and belief, and to resonate with it as they establish themselves. Which is why not every political act that could reasonably afford Christians satisfaction could be included in that category. A political event is a sign of God's good purposes only to the extent that it evokes the possibility of a coherent Christian life. Christian life is lived as a whole, a seamless robe, not a program of piecemeal policies. Celebrations of Christian influence in developments that actually contributed to undermining large tracts of Christian social life are, to say the least, tendentious. When the coherence of the whole is lost sight of, particular advances or improvements, however welcome, speak with a confused sound, not as a clear signal sent by God.

Suppose, for example, that someone were to lay claim to the allies' combatancy in the Second World War as a "Christian event." Bonhoeffer prayed for an allied victory, and the victory occurred in answer to the martyr's prayer. Yet who can doubt that such an attribution of meaning is compromised, to say the least, by the indiscriminate bombings of Dresden and Hiroshima? Can we separate the victory in our minds from the subsequent direction of the victorious allies, and from the Cold War, especially? Might we not even doubt that we could speak of God's hand in *any* war in quite this way, given the inescapable paradoxes at the heart of the just war? None of which puts in question the judgment that the war against Hitler was indeed a justified undertaking, nor that the allied victory deserved grateful thanks for God's preservation from a great evil. But the quest for a "Christian event" is asking for something more than a preservation; it is looking for a disclosure of the God who redeems and sanctifies the human race even through its cultural traditions. Let us take a more controversial instance: the claim that a great "Christian event" occurred in the changes in the social role of women over the past fifty years. Contemplate for a moment the desperate ambiguities, beginning with the popularization of abortion, and we are surely going to want to find a more measured way of approving of these changes. The social upheaval involved demands a more complex response than the joyful cry that God is at hand. While we must not fail to see the good in them, there are other things that we may not allow ourselves *not* to see.

Not seeing is the risk of too precipitate a claim for revelations in political events. Not to see injustices when they are done in a good cause, not to see commodification of women's bodies or disposal of unborn children when we are celebrating some increase of liberty, not to see an accumulation of weapons sufficient to destroy mankind when we rejoice at the stability of peace in the West, and not to see that these are not *accidents* that have merely chanced to spoil Western liberal society like surface mud picked up on its boots, but are also expressions of its ambitions and values. Not-seeing is the blindness of mortal sin. Which is why we should be specially careful about pressing such claims in relation to events in which we have a strong personal stake, events that shaped circumstances we should wish to be able to take for granted, for it is in those events that we are most likely not to see important compromises. God may have revealed himself in the events that constitute our context, but it is better that we learn this from those whose context they have not constituted. Of one thing, at any rate, we should be quite clear: God will not grant us the privilege of being in the right of any political question *without our having to make a fully political discernment*. We have to weigh and understand the compromises we make. The expectation of being in the right by prescription lies at the heart of the "holy war" mindset, which is a failure of obedience because it refuses the service of painstaking moral reason. The danger of placing a halo round political events and actors, however much they may deserve our approval, is that it tempts us into deep spiritual laziness.

In conclusion, something must be said about the role of conflict. Balanced between the two eschatological alternatives, the destruction and the realization of freedom, community is perpetually imperiled. Whatever progress may be discerned retrospectively, at the point of action we have no security. The good that society has learned may be forgotten in a moment. Those who wished to persuade Christendom in the eighteenth century to accept the commercial necessity of slavery as part of "the great colonial system" were unpicking a millennium of Christian moral teaching, though they thought of themselves as having an understanding of the economic basis of international power that put them ahead of their times. Successful for a while, they could very well have been successful permanently. In 1800 there was no good reason to predict the disappearance of colonial slavery. In our lifetimes we have seen similar readiness to accommodate the Christian conscience to the conditions of late modernity. Christians must participate actively in their communities, but they must do so with their eyes open to the kind of community that is emerging. Witness is not simply a matter of being good team players; it means questioning the compromises society wants to make, incurring the disapproval of socially active people. The prophet complained of those who said "'Peace, peace,' when there is no peace" (Jer. 6:14). To be messengers of peace in a world of strife, we must sometimes be messengers of strife in a world of false peace.

CHAPTER 5

The Communication of Work

Body, Soul, and Spirit

When we speak of God's sanctification of our communications, how we organize the field of communication assumes great importance. Over and beyond the exposition of God's will to sanctify (which is the work of Christian Dogmatics), how shall Ethics identify the specific communications that God wills to sanctify?

Opening a standard textbook of Christian Ethics, we are liable to encounter a series of general subject headings: Responsibility for Life, Responsibility for Truth, Responsibility for the Goods of Creation, Responsibility for Peace and Justice, etc., etc. The special explorations pursued under these headings, if well conducted, may afford students some of their most rewarding moments, yet they provoke understandable heart-searching among those who write thoughtfully on Ethics. On the one hand there is the impression that each of these "spheres" of responsibility can be spun off from the others, and treated on its own. "Bioethics" cut away from Ethics almost as soon as the name was coined. "Political theology," "ecological ethics" and "business ethics," meanwhile, have all made their bids for independence. So Hans Ulrich has complained of Ethics so organized that "it is merely a matter of pulling together a number of different discussion topics and discourses within one overview, not speaking of spheres of *life*, with their specific 'ethos', where men and women live and act, acquire experience of life, and transmit it."[1] But

---

1. "Wie Geschöpfe Leben: Zur narrativen Exploration im geschöpflichen Leben," in *Ethik und Erzählung*, ed. M. Hofheinz, F. Mathvig, and M. Zeindler (Zürich: TVZ, 2013), p. 307.

practical reason *as such* cannot specialize; it is the thought of a living human being, of community, that participates simultaneously in many spheres. If I hurtle along the winding lanes at ninety miles an hour, burdened with a conscientious concern to arrive in time to clinch a business deal, I cannot plead my specialism in business ethics when I kill a cyclist. This caution prompted the late Duncan Forrester to urge on us a "fragmentary" method of pursuing Ethics, by which he meant to resist an undue ambition to systematize, and an openness to trains of thought that crossed traditional schematic boundaries.[2] Moral challenges arise for practical reason not as single values, but as knots in which strands are tied together in contingent ways. It is the task of Ethics to help moral reason find its bearings on *all* the conspicuous landmarks from the point at which it finds itself, and so take an interest in the *occasional* character of every situation that invites serious thought. If this apparently asks for *less* unity than the spheres offer, where Ulrich asks for *more*, the two objections in fact converge on the same point: Ethics must be related to the life-experience of human beings and communities *as they encounter* questions raised by distinct spheres of activity. There is inevitably something occasional about the way Ethics takes up, and puts down, specialized questions of professional interest, for the mandate of practical reason comes not from the spheres but from the common reasoning life of human beings and communities. So together with the occasional, there must be something unifying the way each question is approached, some underlying conception of what is involved in living as human beings in community.

Which is a modest defense of architecture and organization. These serve a number of different functions. One is the "overview," which, however inadequate in itself, may be a necessary starting point, especially for educational purposes. Another, more profound, is achieving consistency. Leading motifs ensure that we do not think about one sphere of life quite inconsistently with how we think about others. So the principle of covenant was invoked by Paul Ramsey as a guiding principle over a range of rather different special inquiries: medical practice, biotechnology and marriage, and war. We may need a different kind of architecture to define the lines of a particular train of thought to keep it to the point and prevent it wandering off to become a discussion of everything at once. If someone asks whether artificial human fertilization is necessarily complicit in contempt for nascent human life, we must be able to determine the parameters of the question, without trying to

---

2. Duncan B. Forrester, *Forrester on Christian Ethics and Pastoral Theology* (Farnham: Ashgate, 2010), pp. 434-36.

answer it with a discussion of the goods of marriage. An architecture may also serve to link ethical discussions to the doctrines of theology or philosophy, as is instanced by Paul Ramsey, again, in his recurrent appeals to the principle of body-soul unity.

Distinct trains of thought evoked by distinct historical developments (there was no bioethics before the twentieth century) continue to draw upon older and more universally applicable trains of thought, and Ethics must be able to show us how. No full account of artificial fertilization could do without *some* attention to the goods of marriage. Moral reflections, like mountains, cast their shadows over many territories, and in exploring a new question we can anticipate seeing familiar principles from new angles and in new relationships. If there is a danger in the occasional approach, it is a tendency to drift with the stream, reflecting *post hoc* from wherever we may happen to have been washed up, never achieving a sense of where we have come or where we might go. That shortness of memory with which intellectuals are so fortunately blessed has obliterated the fashion of the 1990s for propounding a "theology of risk" directed especially to the work of bankers and investors. Those who promoted such an enterprise sought, among other things, a discipline to govern risks some people took with other people's money. But in launching their project grandiosely as a new departure (a "theology," indeed, of "a risk-taking God"!), when they might have approached it humbly through traditional reflections on profit and trust-keeping, they made a rhetorical virtue of cutting loose from the principles that had governed financial morality. Bacon's apothegm, "Time is the greatest innovator," is a doctrine that makes many giddy. A sense of adventure was aroused by practices that would shortly lead to the worst economic collapse of a century—the unsurprising result of embarking on a voyage of exploration without taking the best available chart of known waters.

The imaginative architecture we need if we are to hold the variety-in-unity of the moral landscape secure, avoiding the undifferentiated haze where the same answer is good for every question, as well as the glare in which everything dazzles so distinctly that we cannot see relations between one thing and another, must be constructed on categories of theological interpretation. Not always, and for every purpose, on the *same* important categories. In reply to those who have in the past criticized me for my "architectonics," I may simply plead that to think freshly, and at the same time preserve order in thought, one must be able to think one thing in relation to another according to some pattern of which an account can be given. Thinking stiffly in traditional categories, thinking randomly in whatever sequence leaps to mind, are not exclusive alternatives. To construct a building of thought serves the heuristic purpose, at least, of imagining relations that traditional categories do not reveal, while still accepting responsibility for treating things in their due place—everything as what it is and not some other thing. To be a slave to one's own organization is, of course, to end up talking only to oneself, a somber fate to contemplate, as Barth, that great intellectual architect, was fully aware, treating his own elaborate groundplans more cavalierly than most of his expositors have dared to. But to be a slave to whatever one happens to have on one's mind at the moment is to end up talking *not even* to oneself. No organization of thought is exclusive of alternative organizations; the value of this in comparison with that will be shown by what it can teach us. But it can only teach us anything, if it is followed with some discipline—for the time being!

For the purposes we have before us now it will be sufficient to trace a very simple organizational formula that is capable of opening up to allow more complex ones: "May God himself, the God of peace, sanctify you completely, securing spirit, soul and body integrated, beyond criticism at the coming of the Lord Jesus Christ" (1 Thess. 5:23). Paul's formula, while proposing only the most economical system-building, takes us beyond the purely "fragmentary." Organizational principles can be as simple or as complex as the occasion requires them to be, and Paul's tripartite anthropology is not meant to be the only or the last word. Augustine's division of the duties of love into material and spiritual objects worked on the basis of a bipartite anthropology; the two analyses coexisted in ancient thought, and can coexist in our thought, too.[3] The strength of the tripartite formula is that it disengages the power of emotion from the power of understanding, not that it is inappropriate to think of emotion and understanding as unified in the act of knowing, but simply because there are distinct things to be said about emotion on its own terms. The formula, then, is exploratory rather than conclusive, and the same can be said about the order in which it places its three elements. Following the spatial imagery which locates spirit as "above" soul and soul "above" body, as God is "above" his creation, this is a descending sequence. The outward movement of divine action reaches from where man

3. Augustine, *De doctrina Christiana* 1.22.20: "*In his igitur omnibus rebus illae tantum sunt quibus fruendum est, quas aeternas atque incommutabiles commemoravimus; ceteris autem utendum est ut ad illarum perfructionem pervenire possimus. Nos itaque qui fruimur et utimur aliis rebus, res aliquae sumus. Magna enim quaedam res est homo, factus ad imaginem et similitudinem dei, non in quantum mortali corpore includitur, sed in quantum bestias rationalis animae honore praecedit.*"

is summoned to answer God, spirit to Spirit, out to where man is most obviously other than God and creaturely, his bodily constitution. Answering the descending movement of God, however, there is an ascending movement on the part of the agent, as the work of the body is drawn into an act of worship constituted by emotion and understanding. The divine act encompassing "spirit, soul, and body" commands the human act of "body, soul, and spirit."

Framed by the ordering and peace-giving of God before, the fulfillment of history in Christ behind, the work of sanctification is directed towards wholeness—wholeness of human existence and the whole accomplishment of God's purposes. The repeated *holo-* compounds in the Pauline text combine to reinforce this emphasis, and do not require to be sharply distinguished; when taken together with the elements of human nature, spirit, soul, and body, they carry a sense of *integration* as well as *completion*—wholeness of form as well as wholeness of accomplished destiny. The sanctified person is sanctified as a whole person, in the interrelation of constitutive aspects, which is the special significance of being "beyond criticism," one in the balance of whose communications there is no dissension or incongruity, a completed work of the God of peace. But why does the apostle trouble to make this point about the harmony of human powers when he has in view the fulfillment *of community*, addressed with the plural pronoun? It is to stress that the integration of the individual is accomplished only within a communicative whole. It is there that the perfected service of embodiment, feeling, and thinking is to be found. Sanctification refers to every aspect of what we as human agents are, and of what the world that constitutes our human world is. We are bodies in a material world, centers of emotion and relation in a social world; centers of intelligence and purpose in a world of meanings. God's sanctifying work does not imply a sacrifice of any one of these aspects to the others, but promises a wholeness of existence in which each is present in a perfect balance.

All levels of human existence are brought into play in all human communications. Whatever can be intended is intended in three dimensions, material, social, and hermeneutic. Yet while each communication functions within this triangulation, not all relate to each of the three points with equal immediacy. Dictating thoughts onto a recording in a silent studio, sitting and watching quietly by the bedside of a sleeping patient, digging out a pile of manure and spreading it over the ground: these three acts have differently focused leading functions: articulation of meaning, human presence, disposal of materials. Yet each can be interrogated for its other functions, too: by whom are the recorded thoughts to be heard, and who contributed

The Communication of Work

technical labor to assist the recording? how is the patient to feel the visitor's presence when he wakes, and what are the physical demands of long watching? what plants will grow more effectively, and how will the manure affect the neighbors?, etc. While stressing the wholeness and integration of the three functions, then, we can also use them to differentiate types of communication by their leading functions. In this chapter and the next two, we shall speak distinctly of communications of work, communications of friendship, and communications of meaning, beginning in each case from the created human existence that gives rise to them, and then proceeding, by way of the wrongs to which they expose us, to the work of God in sanctifying them, for service, assembly, and witness.

Work and Existence

"Existence" stresses the point from which reflection on work should begin. Behind the mid-twentieth-century interest in a "theology of work" there lay a strong insistence that it should begin from somewhere else. It became a platitude that theological reflection on work had to take its starting point from the labors of industrial society, not from a notion of creation order, which, whatever light it may have shed upon an earlier, pastoral society, was hardly likely to illuminate the dark Satanic mills.[4] At the same time some theologians wished to distinguish their project from the *ethics* of work and its organization as the Popes especially had promoted it, and address a question at a more fundamental level, which was essentially that of theodicy: what, after all, is the point of work? The answer given to that question was an eschatological one, drawn from the legacy of Hegel as mediated through Marx and the still-unpublished but influential evolutionary spirituality of Pierre Teilhard de Chardin.[5] These theologians of work can seem, after a rhetorical prelude about *l'homme écrasé par la machine*, to give the realities of work rather limited attention. Yet their question, "what is the point of work?"

---

4. M.-D. Chenu, *Pour une Théologie du Travail* (Paris: du Seuil, 1955). Chenu popularized the phrase "theology of work," though it was current, he claims, for about five or six years previously. From a somewhat more naturalist point of view, cf. Yves Simon, *Trois Leçons sur le Travail* (Paris: Téqui, 1936), p. 18: "*Les paysans et les ouvriers sont les travailleurs par excellence*."

5. Hannah Arendt, who rarely noticed any theological discussion among her contemporaries, dismissed contemptuously the "idealization" of "liberal or left-wing Catholic thought in France," which failed to notice the essential difference between motivated work and modern labor. See *The Human Condition* (Chicago: University of Chicago Press, 1958), p. 141.

is one that cannot be escaped by any serious theology of humanity. To be tackled adequately from a theological point of view, however, this question must be approached from an understanding of man's creation and fall, which means that the link between theology and ethics at this point, which should never have been severed, must be reestablished. If it is true that our work is to bring us in the end to the Pleroma (and there is something, at least, to be said along those lines), it must involve us in the meantime with some rather closer scrutiny of the office, the farm, and the factory.

If the platitude about industrial society no longer appears quite so flat as it did, that is because historical situations evolve. Not that the problems of mass mechanized labor have been resolved, though it would be ungrateful not to see that they have been addressed and in some measure alleviated. But they have also been exported, to reappear in the factories of Bangladesh and elsewhere. In the West, however, we have a new set of problems. Now and for the foreseeable future we face a famine of work. Looking around me where I live, in what was once one of Britain's great industrial areas, the former mills are now chic residences, the former mines beautifully landscaped parks; and listening to the taxi drivers' nostalgic reminiscences about their former lives in the mills and the mines, I cannot help wondering what my neighbors actually find to work at. Led by a false antithesis that conceived work merely as the price to be paid for the satisfactions of leisure, we continue to plan, by research in artificial intelligence and in other ways, for a world in which as few people as possible will have any work to do. And since every adult now, not only one in two as a generation ago, looks for paid employment, the sense of scarcity is all the greater. Christian discourse on work, meanwhile, has effectively fallen silent since John Paul II's *Laborem Exercens*, thirty-five years old and predating the communications revolution. Our theological talk about work, following what Arendt saw as the inevitable modern trend, has been swallowed up in the discourse of economics, which is only incidentally about work and is primarily about the generation and distribution of resources for life.

When in the ancient narrative of creation it is said that the Lord God "took the man and put him in the garden of Eden to till it and keep it" (Gen. 2:15), something decisive is said about the place of work among the conditions of human existence. We are in and of the material world, summoned to exploit its potential by acting upon it. In work we make a difference to the world, not merely the kind of difference that any event must make—a herd of elephants trampling vegetation and denying other species their habitat, for instance—but a purposeful difference. In work we not only *affect* things;

The Communication of Work

we *effect* things. We sometimes call our best work "creative," though the analogy with God's creation is only a remote one. If God grants being and sense to a world that would be nothing without him, human creativity is an exercise of sympathetic intelligence, exploring and revealing goods latent in the order of nature. The first example of Adam's work the ancient narrator gives us is not digging or sowing, but naming the forms of non-human animal life, a linguistic and scientific work of recognition and classification, unlocking the order that undergirds the variety of the animal kingdom (Gen. 2:19). To work well is to bring intelligence and love to bear upon the grain of our worldly material, whether that is inert stuff, living beings or abstract relations of things.

We are likely to reap a bitter harvest, then, from investing our energies in putting people out of work. The wise man said, "There is nothing better than that a man should rejoice in his work" (Eccles. 3:22). Because our work shapes our world, it gives us room for satisfaction in our accomplishment, which is to say that we achieve not only a state of the world but also a state of ourselves. The converse is also true: the unhappiness that attends lack of work or its failure strikes very deep at our self-assessment. "I cannot work!" is a cry of existential distress. This, of course, speaking of adults. The meaning of work and the feelings appropriate to it have to be learned by children as they grow up. But learning to work is not like learning practical things, such as weaving, playing the piano, or performing calculations. It is a reflective learning of what is involved in existing as humans. We learn to love, to forgive, to endure suffering, and to hope, and learning to work is like these. As we learn skills and performances and the gamut of practices that make up our acquired habits, we learn also to differentiate them into practices of work and practices of rest. Just how we make that division is determined by cultural context and personal vocation. The practices that constitute work differ, from one culture to another and from one person to another, as do the practices that constitute rest. Earlier generations would have been bewildered by the thought of "working" in sport or politics, and the philosophers would have reinforced their bewilderment by insisting that these activities were not, following the Ciceronian distinction, "useful," but "honest."[6] But work does not need to be "useful"; it has only to be communicable. And what societies are prepared to communicate in changes with fashion, variations of knowledge, patterns of cultural exploration, etc., and the parameters of what counts as work change with it. Yet it remains basic to the structure of

---

6. On the *utile-honestum* distinction, see chapter 2 above.

our active human life that some practices acquire the habits and feelings appropriate to work, others those appropriate to rest.

Work is famously difficult to define in relation to action; sometimes the term is stretched to embrace all free conscious activity, which is too wide, sometimes confined as closely as the making of a living, which is not wide enough. Not all our life's activities can be, or should be, work; our practical calling is to respond to the meaning of the world and the presence of the neighbor, and that will take us far beyond the boundaries of anything we call work, into the life we share with family and friends, into one-off acts of care shown to other people, into acts of reflection, meditation, and worship. These, too, are our calling, and when they seem to demand too much, we may seek to escape from them into our work. On the other hand, work is not limited to what earns us a living; there is work that brings no financial reward, done by those who derive a living from other sources, and this may be just as hard and just as valuable. By "work" we identify a core set of material engagements with the world that determine our presence in society over the longer term. Domestic labor, too, devoted to sustaining the life of ourselves and our families, can also be an opening to an interaction with the wider world where we make our presence felt—buying in the supermarket, equipping the children for school, fostering contacts with neighbors, and so on—and so become the working core of our activities. "Labor" is what we do to sustain our own lives; "work" is what we do to contribute something to the world. That famous distinction, given currency by Hannah Arendt, is best understood as aspectual, referring not to different things we do, but to different ways in which we think and feel about different things we do.[7] Neither the meaning of our life nor our social presence is originally dependent on our work, for meaning is given us in worship, and we have a social presence in childhood; these are gifts of grace that precede the first day of work that we ever do. But public commitments form a nexus of outward-facing practical habits that give continuity to our lives and coherence to the variety of other activities we undertake. If our activities are to be coherent, channels are needed for our practical energies to flow outwards and shape a

---

7. Arendt, *The Human Condition*, pp. 79–93. Arendt's exposition of the labor-work antithesis never seems to achieve total clarity as to what these two terms, and the third of her trio, "action," refer *to*. Are they distinct activities in home, or workshop, or agora? Are they distinct types of life? Or social classes? Perhaps we are not meant to be sure, since her noble protest against absorbing all human activity within the categories of life-sustaining economics, was driven by the conviction that intellectual concepts shaped without remainder what human society would become.

The Communication of Work

social presence. That is what is meant when it is said, paradoxically, that in work we become "more a human being."[8]

Labor, Society, and Self-Realization

Let us explore the concept further from three points of reference on which we have already touched, work as material labor, work as social contribution, and work as personal self-realization.

(i) Material, social, and hermeneutic aspects of communication are all present in work, and yet when we speak of work, we throw the weight of emphasis first upon the communications that involve material labor. We re-order the material world by acting upon it. When young people are advised to do some "real work," the thought is usually that they should do something physical: pushing and pulling, fetching and carrying, "getting their hands dirty" in direct contact with mass and resistance. Of course, there is nothing more "real" in constructing a house than in constructing a graph, but the manual-labor paradigm forces us to recognize that whatever work we do, our physical resources are expended on it. Work exacts toil; it wears us out. If heavy lifting may damage the back and a blowtorch hurt the eyes, so may constant sitting at a desk and gazing at a screen. The nervous strain of meeting deadlines and negotiating agreements, confinement to an enclosed space when the sun is shining, headaches and ulcers, loss of sleep, all these are toils of "real" work, whatever its type.

It is the dignity of work that it elevates our physical interactions with matter, our constant struggles to snatch shelter and subsistence out of nature's grasp. In itself these are no more than moments in the cyclical back and forth of natural motion, but through work they become meaningful contributions to social existence and means of serving the divine purpose for the world. George Herbert's famous poem speaks of how all activity can be directed to God—"what I do in everything, to do it as for thee"—an exercise that makes the world appear "bright and clean," as though we had polished up a dish or a piece of furniture. That metaphor paves the way for the topic

---

8. John Paul II, *Laborem Exercens*, 9: "Work is a good thing for man—a good thing for his humanity—because through work man *not only transforms nature*, adapting it to his own needs, but he also *achieves fulfillment* as a human being and indeed, in a sense, becomes 'more a human being.'" "*Magis homo evadit*," quoted from an unidentified source, could be rendered, perhaps, "more the human being he is."

of work itself, in one of its most unglamorous forms, complete with its toils and responsibilities:[9]

> A servant with this clause
> Makes drudgery divine;
> Who sweeps a room as for thy laws,
> Makes that and th' action fine.

"That and th' action," for work, like all our activity, has an objective and a subjective side to it, an objective effect in the world and a subjective aspiration that produces it. Neither for its objective effects nor for its subjective aspirations alone would we value it as we do, but for the objectification of the subjective. The objective product commands interest because it embodies someone's practical intelligence and exertion. We often resent the "drudgery," the irreversible expenditure of time and physical effort on transitory effects. But it is no hardship that work can be hard; it is the price exacted for the satisfaction we find in acting on the material world, a measure of its significance for us. Most people would rather work too hard than too little.

It was the belief of Teilhard that the value of work lay in its direct contribution to an ultimate state of the cosmos that was to be identified with the *parousia* of Christ. "With each one of our works we labour," he wrote, "in individual separation but no less really, to build the Pleroma; that is to say, we bring to Christ a little fulfilment."[10] It is not an idea to be rejected out of hand that work has something significant to tell us about the end of all things, but we must resist the temptation to pin that significance down too quickly. Instead of passing through the life of the agent in the world, through death, judgment, and resurrection, work is apparently supposed to add a brick or two to the New Jerusalem right here and now. In explaining the pastoral aims of his reflection on work, Teilhard addressed them as reassurance to those who had been told to think of their work as "an exercise, a blank sheet" for the making of their own mind and heart. Instead, he propounded what he regarded as "a psychological truth: that no one lifts his finger to do the slightest task unless moved, however obscurely, by the conviction that he is contributing infinitesimally (at least indirectly) to the building of

---

9. "The Elixir," *The Works of George Herbert*, ed. F. E. Hutchinson (Oxford: Clarendon Press, 1941), pp. 184–85.

10. Pierre Teilhard de Chardin, *Le Milieu Divin*, trans. Bernard Wall (London: Collins, 1960), p. 62.

something definitive."[11] With conceptions of redemption and Christology that were wholly cosmological, Teilhard always had difficulty in focusing on *historical action*, which disappears either inward, into "mind and heart," or outward into cosmic development. Value lay only in an accumulative process which, despite appearances, never came to an end, but grew, piece by piece, materially and formally, into the fulfillment of Christ. From which we might be tempted to conclude that our work would be effective in proportion to the durability of its products. Making the terracotta army would be better than making gingerbread men for the children's party, planting a tree better than cleaning a room, manufacturing the plastic bags that hang around for ever caught in the branches of trees better than making biodegradable ones.

Miroslav Volf, in what was perhaps the last echo of the mid-century tradition, put the same challenge more bluntly. Only "cumulative work," he insisted, could "have intrinsic value and gain ultimate significance." Objecting to Jesus' saying that "Heaven and earth shall pass away, but my words shall not pass away," he continues:

> The expectation of the eschatological destruction of the world is not consonant with the belief in the goodness of creation. What God will annihilate must either be so bad that it is not possible to be redeemed or so insignificant that it is not worth being redeemed. It is hard to believe in the intrinsic value and goodness of something that God will completely annihilate.[12]

But that is precisely what Christians have always believed in: a world *that God made good* brought to nothing by sin and death; a world *brought to nothing* redeemed and restored by God's renewing love. What need, one might wonder, would an indestructibly good world have of a "redemption," a term that speaks of a historical event overcoming a natural fate? The worry that motivates this argument concerns the association of *time* and *evil*, and has a traditionally Platonist character. Rightly defending "the intrinsic value and goodness of creation," Volf does not see how that can be done while attributing impermanence to it. Not that there can be no passing away, of course; a wholly permanent world could be a permanent order of impermanent things. But that would be an order of eternal recurrence, an incessant to and fro of matter and life such as caused Qoheleth to shake his head over human

---

11. Teilhard, *Le Milieu Divin*, pp. 54, 56.
12. Miroslav Volf, *Work in the Spirit* (Eugene, OR: Wipf & Stock, 2001²), pp. 90-91.

ends. To do justice to Volf's hope of a "cumulative" work, something would have to remain behind of each product, a trace of material artefact on which the next material thing can be built.

We should hesitate before reaching such a conclusion, not only from a scruple about ephemeral work, but because we know the deeds we have valued most have often been those whose future effects the actor could know nothing about—such as the hours spent wrestling with a piece of writing that no publisher may ever touch. The effects of our work are not, as a matter of fact, and should not be, forever. When we celebrate the value of world time as "history," we celebrate the value God has set upon what is impermanent. It is through events that God makes himself present to the world, events that constitute time as history and invite the thought of a completion of history. So we must not allow ourselves to be forked on the suppositious alternative of a work that is precious because permanent, and a work that is worthless because its effects are impermanent. Work is *made* precious *as* impermanent, since God has taken time and its works to himself, restoring them through and from their passing away, not "cumulatively" as a process, but by an act that bears testimony to himself as creator and redeemer, which is resurrection.

(ii) The significance of our work lies not only in its impact upon the material world; it has an impact upon the social world around us, building us into society and defining our responsibilities and privileges in relation to our neighboring human beings. Work is not distinguished from leisure in the way one type of activity is distinguished from another, swimming from walking, or reading from singing, for the activity that comprises one person's work may comprise another person's leisure. What distinguishes the two is that work is the point at which our exertions are depended on by others, and so determines the duties we consistently owe to others. The amateur and the professional chef may each earn a *cordon bleu*; the amateur may organize a dinner party when it suits her; the professional must turn up at the restaurant, rain or shine, to meet the expectations of the waiters and clients. In work we spin a thread tough enough for others to weave with. And it is one reason that we desire to work, that it confers a certain social dignity upon us; it makes us an element in other people's worlds, a "something" that they count on.

They may count on us simply for the resources they need to live—as the clients in the restaurant count on the chef to send them away full. But they may count on us more strategically for the opportunity to work themselves—as the waiters count on the chef to provide them with something to serve.

And one of the measures by which good work can be judged is its capacity to give work, or resources for work. God, who calls us to an active life, is the giver of all work, the first and universal employer, as Jesus teaches in the parable of the laborers; there is no middle way between being employed by him and being idle. He has work to give to all who will have it, and rewards work equally with the blessing of effective agency. Downstream from his gift, we, too, are given to "employ" one another—using the verb in its widest sense of what we do whenever we make it possible for another to work. Work is not a possession, but a communication to be received and handed on. To give work generously, together with the satisfactions and freedoms that properly belong to it, to give it continuously and expansively, responding to another's developing capacities for work, is a form of giving someone life. Not to have work to give, not to be able to alleviate the idleness that blights our fellow humans' lives, is one of the great tragedies of any age. Unemployment is the form in which our common impotence to be an effective society is constantly brought home to us.

Beyond the limits of the formal employment contract, work continues to be given in all kinds of informal ways, and one optimistic reading of recent trends might be that informal work is experiencing a comeback. Work may be given reciprocally in a relation of complete equilibrium, when two partners offer their work to one another by collaborating on an undertaking in which each employs the other—the happy relation of an author to a publisher being a model of this. Yet the typical case of giving work is non-reciprocal, in which one gives and the other receives. Inequality is a factor in all gift relations, which are accommodated within the framework of the real equality of human beings simply by being events-in-time, and so only beginnings. God's gifts are beginning-and-end, for God is not our equal; our gifts to one another are beginnings only, and while time persists, beginnings have the advantage of setting the terms for their continuation, but not of dictating what becomes of them in the end. A child depends upon the parents through whom it receives the gift of life, a pupil on the teachers through whom it receives the gift of knowledge. But today's child may be tomorrow's parent and today's pupil tomorrow's teacher. If we are not to step out of the stream of time entirely, we must be content with the equality afforded by the succession of generations, which allows each age to criticize its parents and teachers, and then try to do better for its children.

Administering the gift of work is the focus of that special kind of work we call "management." Management is the way a corporate working body cares for the planning and disposition of its work—among other things, employing the workforce. The weight of authority that rests with management in any complex business is not, as such, an imbalance of power, since the authority is precisely that of the corporate whole to direct its own affairs. Yet when that authority is used badly, there may well arise an imbalance of power, in which one sector of the working community is able to dictate terms to the others. To understand the situation adequately is to understand it as a *malfunction* of the corporate enterprise, not a regrettable necessity of the management-workforce relation. When the corporation works well, its employees work freely and securely. When management becomes oppressive, the corporation fails to achieve its purpose, which is to facilitate collaborative work. There are other possible forms of dysfunction, to be sure, but this one has a strong hold on the common imagination, because it speaks of an archetypal anxiety we all have about our institutional Leviathans, which we both need and fear.

That the work of management is itself hard and demanding is something Christians learned long ago in the ancient world within the microcosmic enterprise of the household business: "The master has more need of patience in ruling the household than the servant in being ruled," as Augustine wrote.[13] The difficulties are, however, enhanced in the context of modern manager-workforce relations, where the scale of enterprises tends to increase beyond the reach of interpersonal relationships. As the business enterprise takes root, it absorbs more entropic energy in securing its position in its social context. Strategic planning, publicity, accounting, appointment and management of personnel, all demand specialized attention with specialized skills, and a business does not have to be very large before it recruits dedicated administrative staff, establishing a department of administrative workers with different working practices, different qualifications, different immediate objectives from the rest of the workforce, and as administrative skills tend to be transferable, may have much more in common with their peers in other enterprises than with those with whom they work directly. We often refer to "administration" *as distinct from* "workforce"—not that administrators do not work, but the immediate object of their work is not the primary object that that business serves (manufacture, retail, teaching, performance, whatever it may be); it is a secondary object, namely, the smooth administration of its internal and external functions. This makes effective collaboration more difficult; it takes sympathetic imagination on either side to grasp the practical problems and aspirations of the other side in the ser-

---

13. Augustine, *City of God* 19.16.

vice of the common business. And the difficulty becomes greater when a third party is taken into account, the provider of capital. It can easily seem that there is a natural alliance between capital and management since, in an age when private enterprises must grow and more capitalization is constantly called for, it falls to management to secure it. Publicly funded work has its own equivalent, which is the need to compete for government favor. There is not one "bottom line" in modern industry, but two parallel bottom lines, economic profit and political profit, both of which can assume an importance so large as to dwarf the work which is purportedly at the center of it.

But, of course, neither of these is what matters most. A business needs to be profitable, but only to such a degree, and public-sector work needs to satisfy government, but only in those aspirations that are genuinely relevant to the work in hand. The real bottom line is the primary objective, the effective performance of the work in hand and an opening to further work which will follow on from it. That is what was meant, I take it, by the insistence of Pope John Paul II in *Laborem Exercens* on "the priority of labor over capital."[14] This should not be read as a demand that the sectional interests of the primary workforce should always trump other sectional interests in a complex enterprise, but that the primary concern of the enterprise, to sustain and make possible a certain kind of human work, has to *remain* primary in the thinking of all the participants, whether they are workers, administrators or investors. It requires a breadth of thinking difficult to legislate for, difficult to inculcate where it is missing, but it is not impracticable, and we can recognize it when it occurs, in well-run enterprises that pay their bills and reward their investors sufficiently (but not excessively), while primarily providing for their own future by recruiting, training, and supporting a well-practiced workforce, renewing the plant, exploring new markets and new techniques, and so on. Good management turns on a capacity to focus the variety of practices involved in any enterprise towards a common ambition, and to elicit from a possibly ill-assorted set of co-workers the necessary breadth of imagination to work together. And together with equilibrium on that front good management will establish some equity in the sharing of the risk, whatever that may be, that the business runs. A specially "imperiled" sector of the workforce, liable to be laid off before anybody else is laid off, will be a sector that cannot acquire and contribute skill, a helot class useful not for its work but only for its labor. And that is a failure in the socialization of work.

(iii) Work is a form of *personal vocation*, a calling to realize oneself.

---

14. John Paul II, *Laborem Exercens*, 12, 13.

Behind the purely trivial German use of the word *Beruf* for a "profession" there lies a real theological insight. The concept of work as the West now knows it—something every adult, whether formally employed or not, does in one form or another until he or she gets too old to go on doing it—is a later fruit of Christian reflection. In earlier periods of history, including Christian history, work was seen as something only certain social classes did. The social presence of the landed classes depended on authority exercised by their families. It was not, of course, that they actually did nothing, nor that what they did was unimportant, but simply that it was not conceived as "work" in the sense that a carpenter or a household servant had work. Yet the idea that everyone has work to do was never wholly absent from Christianity. The parables of Jesus represented the living of life itself under the guise of forms of work—fishing, farming, housekeeping, harvesting, etc.—and the relation of men to God as that of employees to employer. Two parables especially, those of the laborers in the vineyard and of the talents, connect work with the realization of oneself. The one-talent servant in the parable who treats the investment task assigned him by an ambitious master merely as a dangerous liability, does not realize that what he wrapped up in a napkin and hid, rather than developing it and offering it back with interest, was himself.

The traditional contrast between workers and non-workers distinguished those whose activity was governed by "necessity" (i.e., economic need) from those whose activity was "free" (i.e., independent of need). Behind this social distinction lay a wider contrast of types of activity, the "servile arts" and the "liberal arts," those that served economic necessities directly and those with no utilitarian function, pursued "for their own sake." The overcoming of the first distinction (between workers and non-workers) implied the overcoming of the second (between servile and liberal arts)—"overcoming," in the sense that it is seen to have merely provisional status, not to represent the ultimate significance of different activities. But the thought that in the last resort there is no more distinction to be made between liberal and servile arts has filled some thinkers, especially of an Aristotelian stamp, with alarm. Does this not reduce all human activity to the servile? Such was the worry of Josef Pieper, who saw in philosophy the paradigm of the liberal art, destined for "blessing" rather than for "use," to be defended against the purely servile concept of "intellectual work."[15]

We should not deny that there is a danger. Dedicated utilitarians may

---

15. Josef Pieper, *Leisure, the Basis of Culture* [1948], trans. Gerald Malsbary (South Bend, IN: St. Augustine's Press, 1998).

hear the assurance that there is, after all, no such thing as a "useless" liberal art as a welcome confirmation of their prejudices. And the danger may be enhanced in the context of an overarching social doctrine, such as the Prussian doctrine of the State, which assumes that all activity is subsumed in the service of a political whole, making every actor, helot or intellectual, indifferently subservient to ultimate political ends. But this is a corruption that springs precisely from a failure to take the theological content of the universalization of work seriously. Place us before the immediate demands of the household, and there is the greatest difference in the world between sweeping the room and writing a poem. Place us before the summons of God himself, however, and what remains of the difference? George Herbert's line is enough to answer the question: God's summons affords the widest and most ennobling horizon for the meanest and most servile task. Correspondingly, God's summons invests even the most discretionary undertaking with a non-negotiable urgency. To sweep the room is to do something as intrinsically worthwhile as to write a poem; to write the poem is to do something as urgent as to sweep a room. In work, as elsewhere, the law that commands us is the "law written on the heart," which is the law of freedom (cf. 2 Cor. 3:3).

As all deliberation is seeking, so the deliberation that we focus on discerning, taking up and defining our work, involves search.[16] Finding our work is not the only self-finding we have to do in life, nor the most important; we leave our working selves behind when we engage with aspects of life that are, in the last analysis, of higher importance. Yet the experience of finding ourselves in work has often been the starting point for whatever other self-finding we may have had to do. Some people have to look for work from the beginning, seeking an opening, a job offer, a business opportunity, or whatever, and it can be a hard and dispiriting discipline. Others find job offers thrust at them, opportunities falling into their lap. Yet these different experiences disclose a similar spiritual task, which we engage far beyond the limits of job hunting. What we have to find is what we have been given to do, answering not only the question of *what* work will be given us, but also the question of *how* that work is to be our own work, overcoming the alienations of work and discovering our calling in it. It is always possible that we may fill the position and discharge its responsibilities while cheating the world, and ourselves, of a lived engagement with the world through the work we do. Only as we find ourselves in our work, in a convergence of what is required with what we are equipped to give, can we mold it creatively and

---

16. Cf. *Finding and Seeking*, pp. 179–88.

return it to the world as a cultural contribution. Forms of work—farming, teaching, homemaking, etc.—are plastic, and can change as the conditions in which they are practiced change. Within the course of a generation the experience they offer those who practice them may be greatly enriched or greatly impoverished. There are many factors that condition these changes, and the question of which are enriching, which impoverishing, is one that those engaged in the work will discuss indefinitely. But the final answer will have to be proved in experience. Without farmers, teachers, homemakers, or whatever, who are prepared to grasp the opportunities on offer, bring the resources of their gifts and personalities to bear on them, and find themselves within the parameters of the work, the way will be closed to enrichment. It is when work becomes *our* work that it unfolds more expansively for others, opening up new possibilities of personal engagement and disciplines of practice.

And here we must introduce the correlative of work, which is rest. Work depends on rest, and rest on work; work is what we rest *from*, rest what we work *towards*. This truth is easy to misunderstand; it is not simply that we need relief from the expenditure of effort, though we do. A good deal of effort is poured into non-working activities, too—not only leisure activities that we choose to suit our fancy, but the half-working tasks of sustaining life, which are sometimes our work, sometimes our rest: shopping, preparing food, household chores, etc. Rest involves reflection upon work. For if in our work we find a proximate meaning for existence, we can lose sight of what it is all for when the labors are too unremitting or the design of work too imperspicuous. It is only as we rest that we see our work as an achievement to take satisfaction in. It puts us in a position to love our work: to love the world that exhausts us, the fellow worker with whom we have to struggle to communicate, the God who so effectively works even when we are ineffective. This is what it means to rest not only "from" our work, but "in" our work. We let go of our work in order to take a reflective view of it as something to be glad of.

The importance of rest is embodied for Jews and Christians in the institution of the weekly day of worship. Articulated into weekly units of exertion rounded off by a day of rest and worship, work is interpreted as a path to lead us into the purposes of our creator. The sabbath celebration calls us to see our own work and rest within the narrative of God's work and rest. As God "saw everything that he had made" and found it "very good" (Gen. 1:31), so we are taught to see God's creative purposes, which make our human work good, too. It is not simply that we take encouragement from our own achievements and experience; that would make us creatures of our past, no longer open for new work. But as we join in creation's praise of God's work, we hear God's call to us to work once again. It is the hearing of that summons to move forward that makes the difference between rejoicing in our work and "works righteousness." The church fathers said that the sabbath was the one command of the Decalogue that was not "moral" but "ceremonial," i.e., an eschatological sign. The Reformers of the sixteenth century, on the other hand, insisted on its being a "moral" command. Both were, in different ways, right. Rest is the condition for defining work, and the command to rest is as much a matter of natural law as work itself. But man's nature is man's transcendence, as is rightly, if loosely, said. Here is the anticipation of something further, a completeness not limited to a single piece of work, which marks humankind out as the covenanted partner of God.

The Wrongs of Work

The wrongs of work are as old as slavery itself, which the primeval history of Genesis takes back to the sons of Noah. When we look at them we see something primeval, and we see at the same time something contemporary, and it is important to keep these two perspectives aligned. For ancient wrongs remain alive and well, assuming a character distinctive to our time. For an age which has trouble believing in God must inevitably have trouble believing in its own work. The absence of God entails a loss of confidence in the hope that the self may find realization in its work. We forget how to see our work as "for" anything that might support the meaning of our personal existence. Work is therefore bitten by the frost of alienation. Instead of the word "sin" at this point we use the more objective word "wrong," because we are no longer concerned here only with ways in which *actions* may fail, but with ways in which their failure entails failures of communication which leave a structural deficit in community: I fail to work well because you do not work well, you do not work well because I do not work well, and together we make it impossible for others to work well.

As a first glance it is convenient to divide the wrongs of work into those that allow too little exertion in work and those that exact too much. Borrowing terms used by others we may call them "idleness" (from the Beveridge Report)[17] and "drudgery" (from Herbert's poem). "Idleness," as Beveridge

---

17. *Social Insurance and Allied Services* (London: HMSO, 1942).

understood it, was not merely a disposition of some workers who did not want to work. He appreciated very well that it was a feature of any society that failed to conceive and plan the work that was done in it wisely. Where there is lack of effective activity, there is idleness. The wrong of idleness, then, can be traced to whatever restricts and inhibits effective work, not only in formal unemployment. Many an informally employed person is anything but idle, while many activities that count as employment are little more than regulated idleness. Drudgery, for its part, is not limited to forced or unconsenting work. The freest forms of work can turn to drudgery when the social setting is unable to support them adequately, or when there has been a misjudgment of what can be accomplished, or destructive compromises in the standards of work have become institutionalized, and so on.

But this distinction takes us only so far, for drudgery and idleness are symptoms of the wrongs of work, and we need to go a little deeper into the structural causes. The three aspects of work we have identified will allow us a sharper view of how work may degenerate.

(i) Work may fail to set us in a creative relation to the material world. Labor, cut off from the social and hermeneutic functions of work, can never attain to achievement. A gap then opens up between the worker's interests as a human agent and the physical labor he has to expend on work, so that the latter is never justified by the former. The Marxian critique of the worker's "alienation" is the ancestor of all such analyses of this wrong: on the one hand, human consciousness nursing its thoughts, loves and ambitions; on the other, working patterns in which the worker takes no personal interest. It may seem strange that a post-industrial age in which a great deal of white-collar work is done suffers acutely from the problem diagnosed by Marx among the industrial "helots" of the nineteenth century. Yet office work, too, may lack social connection and overall meaning; much of it is, in fact, trivial and inconsequential. Even at a more rarified level than the average office communication, no one who deals primarily in words could fail to worry that so much exhaustion can be incurred for so insubstantial a product, always liable to vanish into the ether; neither, I imagine, is the case very different for those who deal in numbers.

We are alienated from our work when we are not in a position to appreciate the goods it serves and derive our practical orientations from them. What is needed, if we are to renew the contact between work and world, is participation in the social processes of deliberation that shape the work. And here we must notice the very great importance of working practices. These are the primary *intellectual* resource which any business inherits and transmits, the maturing repository of wisdom about the work and its performance. A practice is an ensemble of activities, skilled operations and principles governing them, which can be learned, not simply as a performance is learned, an operation or a given activity like creating a database or compiling a set of accounts, but as a capacity to make judgments is learned, so that activities and operations are at our disposal to call on as they are needed in the service of the principles and aims of the work we engage in. In acquiring the practice we acquire the power to exercise reasonable discretion, based on understanding and experience. Good work is distinguished from routine labor precisely by its practices, which guarantee the freedom of the work—not a freedom to do as we like, but a freedom to act on our best judgment of what the work demands.

There is a sad tale often told of the impact of evolving technology upon human working practices. It goes back to the first wave of the industrial revolution: long-developed skills made useless, whole trades disappearing overnight, work reduced to technical operations of such limited scope as to make the worker effectively mindless, and so on. In the era of computerization some of this story has been lived through again. Working practices must, of course, change as the circumstances of the work change. But there is change that enriches and change that impoverishes. Good change involves a reflective development of the practices led by those who are skilled in them and understand their logic and value. New working patterns must grow up with the work, not be imposed as a one-size-fits-all pattern from without.

(ii) Work may fail to put us in a satisfactory social relation to others, and afford no real experience of cooperation. Cooperation in work is not simply coordination, which is a mechanical rather than a social idea of how one person's effort fits with another's. As Adam Ferguson saw in the eighteenth century, those who labor can be "made like the parts of an engine to concur to a purpose, without any concert of their own." That is to say, they can lack a sense of their place in the whole, and therefore lack commitment to one another.[18] Work demands stable local settings and cooperative relationships.

Sometimes those who work have too little connection with those who benefit from their work. If this may always have been the case with some kinds of work, with manufacturing insulated from consumers, for example, the problem is more acute in an age of global work and electronic communications, when we are often uncertain whom we are communicating with

---

18. Adam Ferguson, *An Essay on the History of Civil Society* [1767], ed. Duncan Forbes (Edinburgh: Edinburgh University Press, 1966), p. 182.

and where in the world they are. There is a problem we may describe as the "displacement" of work. "Place" is a social and cultural concept, and when work is no longer conceived and carried through in relation to given places, workers and their clients are no longer accessible to each other as members of communities, and the risk of work failing to connect with those it is done for becomes exponentially greater. The sense of displacement is often voiced as a complaint about the all-pervasiveness of the market. But "the market" of contemporary demonology is, like most demons, an abstraction, which has left real markets far behind. Markets were a device to overcome distance between producers and purchasers by designating places of meeting. Market crosses in older urban centers remind us that there were focal sites for surrounding regions, places where goods were assembled, compared, bargained over, bought, and sold. The abstract market of modern economic practice lacks precisely the social coherence that made the traditional market strong. The anonymous electronic placing (and withdrawal) of large investments has become a symbol of what exchange becomes when market-crosses disappear, a flood of instantaneous transactions proceeding in ignorance of one another and in ignorance of their social effects.

A corresponding danger is that work may put people too little in touch with those who work with them. For we cannot work only by ourselves. There are tightly collaborative working relationships, conceived and designed to allow the participation of many people with defined roles in a common enterprise, the typical situation *within* institutions and businesses. And there are more loosely cooperative relationships, sharing expectations, information and understandings among those who work independently—the typical situation *among* institutions and businesses, whether they are competitors in the same field or belong to other sectors with which there is a relation of mutual dependence (as between producers of raw materials, manufacturers and retailers). In relation to these two ideal types the variety of relations that arise in work, and the neglect of them, can be located. The fair trade movement recently taught an important lesson to the food industry, strongly affected by dislocation (remember the difficulty of tracing the provenance of the horsemeat?), an old lesson in need of being relearned: between farmer and retailer there needs to be positive cooperation built on a mutual interest in each other's success. The same abstract market conception causes both types of relation to degenerate, collaboration replaced with short-term or piecework contracts, cooperation with mere buying and selling.

And it can happen, in the third place, that workers are cut off from the social communications which enable them to acquire and develop the working practices they need to draw on. Practices demand communities of training and induction where they can be learned, and such communities can grow up not only around typically collaborative forms of work, but around those pursued individually, even competitively, but need to share understandings of what makes for excellence in the work and how its practices can evolve and be improved. To be denied contact with such community is to lack the resources to work well. At some level all kinds of work require it. One of the most troubling legacies of the industrial past was the complacent acceptance of a distinction between "unskilled" and "skilled" labor.

And is all this traceable to failures of management? There is a danger in assuming that that is so, and to point to it we may lay hold on a term recently coined for specific purposes, *managerialism*—a vice well identified and described by management theorists. When management prudence monopolizes the practical thought of the whole working enterprise and skilled working practices are subordinated to it, those who ought to be masters of their skills become cast in the role of cogs in a productive social machine. The universal diffusion of a management-conceptuality always subverts the exercise of specialized judgments, as when doctors are told that they are not diagnosing enough cases of obesity, university teachers that they are not giving good enough marks to students from minority backgrounds, etc., etc. If it is no longer said as frequently as it used to be that managerialism "puts those who know what they are doing under the control of those who don't," that may simply be because a generation of creeping managerialism has left nobody knowing what he or she is doing. But at the heart of the malfunction there is collusion. Managerialism is not the achievement of managers alone; it feeds on a loss of the sense of role and purpose among those who were not supposed to be managers, but who have compromised their specialist understandings with a varnish of managerial knowingness—a loss of vocation, for which only those to whom the vocation was given as a trust can be held responsible. Upholding a threatened tradition of working practices requires of practitioners both well-founded judgments and a willingness to take risks for them. When it seems easier to communicate about one's work in the general *lingua franca* of product, quality assurance, market, etc., all work ends up looking alike, and the very thing that makes it of interest to us—its capacity to stamp our practical lives with a specific character—disappears.

We should notice a change of nomenclature that has become fashionable in recent years, replacing "management" with "leadership." Properly, "leadership" is a service to a common task rendered by someone *performing* the task, as distinct from the kind of adjunct help one may look to an administrator for. To be a "leader" is to be someone other workers look to for help in doing whatever the community of work does, as when an experienced craftsman guides an apprentice. To apply this notion to the administration of large industrial enterprises is to make a tricky transfer of thought. On the face of it, leadership could not be a specialism of its own. But, as a thousand airport bookstalls reveal, that face of it is not what is perceived. A high degree of abstraction is involved in leadership conceived as a specialist skill to be acquired, and the language of New Management, with its "business plans" and "emerging markets" drawn from commercial enterprise, conceals where the true abstraction lies, which is not in the balance sheet but in the data base. It is our astonishing new capacity to generate records and produce quantified answers to every question that will allow of them, that prevents our asking any question that will not allow of them, and so causes data manipulation to replace the exercise of intuitive "people skills" typical of old-fashioned management at its best. Its inevitable outcome is that under the name of "innovation" restlessness and rootlessness become the ruling principles of the workplace instead of stability and mature growth.

(iii) In the third place, work may fail to provide us with a meaningful justification for the efforts it exacts of us. Work can and should be fulfilling, which means that it can focus for us the good of an active life. It is not the only form that our activity will take, nor necessarily the most important. But it is the paradigm, the form that represents our active powers to us concretely and comprehensibly. It is in entering on formal work that the young can typically learn what it is to have powers of action and to be able to use them in a social way. To think of good work is to think of the acquisition of a certain wisdom about life as a whole. It can teach us how fragmentary and disjointed activities can be drawn together into a coherent enterprise. It can teach us how our efforts may be depended on by others. It can teach virtues of routine, of imagination, of persistence, of channeling energy, of collaboration. It can teach us of growth in capacity, as work that occupies our whole attention today becomes the preliminary to more challenging and adventurous work tomorrow. It can teach all this—and it may fail to teach it.

That we should not always be satisfied with our working experience is, perhaps, nothing remarkable; a certain restlessness in work may simply reflect its constantly receding horizon as a dimension of our calling to be ourselves. Dissatisfaction can be the springboard for development. But work can fail us in much more radical ways: it can destroy our health, cease to offer opportunities for learning and insight, even be designed to exclude the use of intelligence and initiative. Technology tends to harden our consciences to the wrong of boring work. Daily we pass the check-out counters in the supermarket, where modestly gifted people spend all their working hours flashing barcodes before a scanner, and we get cross when they hold us up by chatting—as though the work they are doing should be absorbing enough for them!

We have mentioned the sad narrative and the recurrent fear of the loss of learned working practices, whether driven out of existence by economic or other external pressures or corroded from within. With their loss we fear a greying of the world, a shrinkage of its meaning. We have recognized an element of collusion that may often contribute to the loss: practices and their wisdoms disappear rather than develop because those who possess them cannot make the effort to defend them and to teach them, keeping their wisdom accessible to new generations. But in order to learn and communicate working practices *stability* is of decisive importance. The economic gains of short-term and part-time employment contracts are never more than short-term and part-time gains, undermining the foundations of a committed and imaginative workforce. No one can invest energy and imagination in work if it seems entirely transitory. Fear of unemployment or underemployment is a destructively alienating force, producing an approach to work like that of the day-laborer of antiquity (regarded by competent observers at the time as worse off than a domestic slave), with no command of the means of production, no power to imagine his work, no expectation of advancing his position by working well.

The Sanctification of Work

The fulfillment that work should offer, and often does not, brings us back to the questions of justification and sanctification. In Saint Paul's famous formulation, we are justified "by faith and not by works of the law" (Rom. 3:28). The gracious blessing of God is directed to the subjective root of action, to give life; it anticipates, it does not wait upon, the objective fruit. And yet "works," too, become the object of his blessing, as he employs them to reflect his glory in the world: "that they may see your good works" as Jesus taught, "and glorify your Father which is in heaven" (Matt. 5:16). The plural "works" points to the various accomplishments, successful and unsuccessful, that have become objectified within the past. The blessing on our works is *for others*. We cannot look back on our works, not even if they were to all appearances highly successful, and find in them the blessing of

God *on ourselves*. As living agents, we can look for blessing only by looking ahead to our "work," in the singular: "Prosper thou the work of our hands upon us, O prosper thou our handiwork!" (Ps. 90:17) That blessing has to be received in naked humility and dependence on the one and unique blessing pronounced on human agency in Christ. Yet so received, that blessing will reconnect us with our works, extending to invest the brute facticity of all the different things we have done with the glory of the divine purpose. Our agency is justified solely within Christ's agency, our accomplishments sanctified in the all-embracing scope of Christ's accomplishments. Situated in time, the working tasks we have completed, successfully or unsuccessfully, are left behind us and will pass away; yet by his grace they may, in their day, be charged with messages of his goodness that others can receive, and so be granted to carry God's ultimate purpose forward. This is how the eschatological dimensions of work must be spoken of, as a promise that our works may be granted an ultimate meaning that they cannot have in themselves. In that sense our works may "accompany" us when we rest from our labors (Rev. 14:13). So accompanied we may be given the "new name" which no one can know but the one to whom it is given (Rev. 2:17); we may become a "someone."

Christ's work accomplished and finished is a theme Saint John's Gospel often touches on. The "food" on which Jesus lived was to complete the work God had given him to do (John 4:34). The works Jesus performed were those the Father had given him to complete, the demonstration that the Father sent him (John 5:36). On the threshold of the passion he could declare that the work was completed and the Father glorified (John 17:4). And all that before the great cry from the cross, "It is finished" (John 19:30). The passion completes his work, which was to extend faithful action in service to the very suffering of death itself, turning the brute facticity of death into a testimony to the Father's righteousness. The material effect of his work is the empty tomb, a hole punched in the logic of facts, liberating us from the "dead works," the meaningless facticity of the past into which our exertions must otherwise drain away.

And because it is in the accomplished work of Jesus that we are justified, God sanctifies our work by calling us to a service *of* Christ, in which he works "alongside" us (as the longer ending of Saint Mark puts it, 16:20). Human work is sanctified by being drawn into this service, its failings and its impermanence overcome by the coherence, sociality, and effectiveness of the purpose it has been given to serve. The limited horizons of human work—economic viability, productive effectiveness—always lie before a further horizon of more ultimate purposes, but whereas in the general discourse of ends this further horizon ("happiness") is no more than an unfocused aspiration, it acquires a sharp focus through the representative resurrection of Christ and the call to Christian discipleship and witness. "Serving the Lord Christ" becomes the framework within which whatever service may be required by earthly employers can now be given a definite purpose and a clear effectiveness (Col. 3:23).

And those who do not work for earthly employers, those who to a superficial judgment seem to be *without* work, whether in need of it or not, are now enabled to *find* work. A range of activities that would never have struck the imagination of the world as possible work are appropriated to the service of Christ. It was perceptive of De Quincey to identify, as one of the greatest Christian points of impact upon politics, "the expansion of voluntary charitable societies." It was in evidence in the very earliest days of the church in the work of the "deacons." *Diakonia* ("household service") is a constant theme in the New Testament church, and Jesus was remembered as saying that his role was that of a *diakonos* (Luke 22:27).

Today a vast range of activities are treated as work that were once not considered such. The secular world has no way of distinguishing work from any other activity apart from its capacity to find a market and support itself, with the result that a great deal of frivolous and sometimes corrupting activity is dignified with the title of "industry." The ancient world, by contrast, had a narrow conception of work as terminating in the material end of action, the provision of food, shelter, or whatever. Though it was recalled that in rural simplicity every human being had to work—"to him (as farmer) the provision of food, to her (as weaver and spinner) the provision of clothing"—in the urban centers of power work belonged to the inferior social classes, to slaves and hired laborers, artisans, and tradesmen, who collectively made up "the poor," a term understood by John Chrysostom to include all who had to work to stay alive.[19] Public activities were not work, but exercises of personal dignity, terminating in effective social presence; intellectual work, on the other hand, was simply *scholē*, leisure.

It was the life of the church that created the impulse for the massive expansion of the scope of work. *Diakonia* was a matter of doing whatever needed doing in the life of the community, an executive competence of expansive comprehensiveness, the very opposite of the role-bound conceptions of Christian ministry that became normal when the church adapted itself to

---

19. Chrysostom, *Homilies on 1 Corinthians* 34.

the role-consciousness of feudal Europe. It could break beyond the bounds of traditional work to discover new work where it was not looked for, creating structures that enabled it to run in new channels—monasteries, societies, scholarship, etc., etc.—affording a cure for men's boredom and idleness and an opening to uncharted paths of social usefulness. And as the stream of work ran into wider and more divergent channels, not only in works of direct material service but in works of wisdom, praise, encouragement, it allowed the disciple greater freedom to find work, since the coherence of a life did not depend on occupying just one status or fulfilling just one career. Christian work accommodated the exploratory and adventurous spirit, open to the missionary leading of the Spirit. The memory of Stephen, among the first deacons appointed to "serve tables" who became, and met his death as, a Christian controversialist and apologist, is the archetype, perhaps, of later Christian opportunists who passed from one task to the next and so built connections of fruitful importance for those who followed them.

Of the equalizing and liberating power of good work, emphasized in the parable of the laborers, there is a strong echo in the counsel given to household slaves in the New Testament letters. Regardless of how they are viewed by their employers they must assume responsibility for their own standards of work, "not . . . as men-pleasers, but as servants of Christ" (Eph. 6:6 RSV; cf. Col. 3:22). Their route to freedom is free service. This is an embarrassment to the modern imagination, which has been inclined to follow Nietzsche in thinking of it as a sullen compensatory mechanism for those who were impotent to challenge structures. In fact this counsel takes us to the heart of the Christian revaluation of work, which allowed the socially neglected to find themselves the recipients of a high vocation that passed through and transformed the menial tasks they confronted on a daily basis. The reorganization of society around this conviction worked out from the monasteries, where Benedict's *ora et labora* made the saint and the serf one and the same. If we wish to applaud Nietzsche's judgment rather than that of Christian history on this point, we should at least appreciate the implication of doing so, for he certainly appreciated it himself: it is to agree with the ancient world that there is such a thing as "demeaning" work, and to accept that society must be stratified into mean and noble classes. But as Christians understood nobility, menial work was a royal road to dignity of the highest order. As for the legal conception of the slave as a piece of property, that, for them, was a fiction, a joke in bad taste, which only fools could take at its face value![20]

20. Gregory of Nyssa, *Homily in Ecclesiastes* 4.

The Communication of Work

Equalizing and liberating, but not equalizing *without* liberating to a mutual service of one another. The slave and his master are to understand one another as "brothers" in the Lord, just as all Christians do. But the term "brother" implies for Saint Paul a further expression of equal participation in Christian community, that of "collaborators," *synergoi*.

Paul occasionally links the term *adelphos* with *synergos* (Phil. 2:25; 1 Thess. 3:2, if the traditional text is right) and once, with much the same force, passes from *agapētos* to *synergos* (Philem. 1) The same connection is made with *syndoulos* (Col. 1:7; 4:7; cf. Rev. 6:11). In addition to being a "dear friend" and a "brother," someone is also a "fellow-worker." What does that imply? Qualified by a personal pronoun, it usually designates active involvement in Paul's mission, and may be translated "colleague," or in the plural, "team." Such is the case with Prisca and Aquila (Rom. 16:3); Urbanus (16:9); Timothy (Rom. 16:21); Titus (2 Cor. 8:23); Epaphroditus (Phil. 2:25); Aristarchus, Marcus, and Jesus Justus (Col. 4:11); Marcus, Aristarchus, Demas, and Lucas (Philem. 24); and possibly Philemon himself (Philem. 1). This sense is very clear at 1 Corinthians 16:16 where the church is asked to be obedient "to every fellow-worker," i.e., clergy and missionaries. The metaphor "fellow-soldier" is used in the same way of Epaphroditus (Phil. 2:25) and Archippus (Philem. 2), as is that of "fellow-servant" (*syndoulos*) of Epaphras and Tychicus (Col. 1:7; 4:7).

But once the term was in currency referring to a "team" of missionaries, it invited further thought, and in the course of Paul's arguments new applications appear. At 1 Corinthians 3:9, emphasizing the irrelevance of which minister claims credit for which piece of work, Paul declares, "We are *synergoi*—of God!" And following an obvious logic, he represents *all* faithful Christians as his "fellow-workers." Two passages in 2 Corinthians pursue this logic, both of them concerned with the contested question of the missionaries' authority. At 1:24 Paul insists that they do not "lord it," but are "*synergoi* of your joy," a complex expression suggesting that they "work for" the joy of the Corinthian Christians but are also bound together with them in their work. In 5:20–6:1 Paul allows that there has been an authoritative tone to the missionaries' evangelistic appeal—as Christ's representatives through whom God speaks, they *urge* the Corinthians to be reconciled to God—and yet, speaking to them as Christians who have received the grace of God, they speak as collaborative partners (*synergountes*), who *exhort* the church. Again, the prefix *syn-* points to the missionaries' relation to the Christians of Corinth.[21] Outside the limits

---

21. The common interpretation "fellow-workers with God," influenced by 1 Corinthians 3:9, is a misunderstanding prompted by a false chapter division.

of the Pauline correspondence this vocabulary does not have a clerical sense: John the Elder applies *synergoi* to the (lay) ministry of offering hospitality to traveling missionaries (3 John 8), while John the Seer applies it to the martyrs (Rev. 6:11). The *syn-* prefix is applied to other verbs of exertion, and here again the clerical use is not in evidence. In Philippians 4:3 (a text as full of *syn-* compounds as could be imagined), though the unnamed "yokefellow" may be an elder, there is no reason at all to suppose that Euodia and Syntychē (or Syntychēs) have any formal ministerial role, nor even that "Clement and the other *synergoi*" did.[22]

The essence of this collaboration is that one person's call to work may strengthen others specifically in relation to *their* work. The "higher way" of Saint Paul is the way that goes beyond an interest in one's own vocation, to include an interest in others' exercise of their vocations. Hence the virtues of deference and restraint which are, as we have noticed earlier, hallmarks of his praise of *agapē*. More important even than the *giving* of work is the *allowing* of work, the receptiveness to what *they* have to contribute to the whole, which makes what *we* have to contribute a more effective service to them.

In an age when industry was largely the enterprise of small household-businesses reinforced by servants who could well have the legal status of slaves, the apostolic church laid its redemptive emphasis on the re-imagination of working relations as the collaboration of a team of fellow-servants in mutually supportive service. Today we have to learn how to bring the same perspective to our very different working structures, contractual in principle but frequently enslaving in practice. A collaborative equilibrium in which the specific skills and authority of each contributing sector are appreciated as an indispensable element in the whole, is not easy, and can never be taken for granted. It requires the sanctifying of our purposes in work, subordinating the exercise of our own skills and practices to the purposes of God for his world. (Subordinating it, that is, *in our own mature appreciation of the work*, not merely because someone who could deprive us of work instructs us to do so.) It requires a clear sight of the work of other people and a lively sense of our dependence on it, overcoming our instinctive sense that our contribution is the real heartbeat of the common enterprise. The sanctification of work may begin to dawn, perhaps, when everyone in a large corporation from the humblest secretary to the newly appointed CEO is given a week's

---

22. The verb "wrestling together" (συνήθλησαν) does not imply otherwise, but is used of the whole church earlier in the letter, 1:27, just as "competing together" (συναγωνίσθαι) is used of the whole Roman church in its prayers, Rom. 15:30.

induction-course consisting of sitting in on the work of each department and listening to its own account of what it is supposed to do and how it tries to do it.

Which is why we should not neglect to pray for the fruitfulness and sustainability of our work, the healthy evolution of working practices and the cooperative endeavors they give rise to. In the Collect for Trinity XVII in the *Book of Common Prayer* we are invited to pray that God's grace may "prevent and follow us," in order that we may "continually be given to all good works."[23] Every word in that prayer is worth pondering. The "we" means not just "each of us separately," but society as a whole, the only context in which work can be undertaken and effected. That our society may be continually "given *to*" its work—not merely given it—it is necessary that the works be "good," well conceived, well fitted to their circumstance, broadly and wisely designed, successfully carried through, and that we be fit to attend to "all" good works, not only those fashionable ones which carry *éclat* or put us at the cutting edge of progress. And that can be so only if they call not only on the strength of labor they require to execute but also on the wisdom they need to plan them well, for which we must ask the "grace" of God. God's activity not only "accompanies," as the scholastic phrase had it, but "precedes," and "follows." It is required not merely in the execution, but in the imagination of good works and their successful outcome. Not only the rewards of work, but the opportunities for it are the gift of a generous master; is that not the heart of the principle of the equality of workers, as asserted in the parable of the vineyard (Matt. 20:1–16)? If we are wise, then, we pray for work, and especially, since "good works" are a cultural gift of vast importance, easily lost by forgetfulness and negligence, that we may be "continually" given to them.

In the extraordinary expansion of the scope of work as it came to be practiced in Christian civilization, we should not overlook the distinctive contribution of more reflective and isolated forms of work which, in the monastic crucible, enjoyed equal status with active and administrative work, doubtless exacting as great a penalty of physical pain and exhaustion, the scholarship and artistry that achieved the preservation of literary legacies from the ancient world for our appreciation today. That we can recognize such activities as painting, creative writing, and scholarship as work owes everything to the fact that medieval monasteries encouraged them, knowing,

---

23. Cranmer's beautiful translation of the equivalent collect from the Gregorian Sacramentary adds the word "all." "Given to" is his expressive rendering of *intentos*, "attentive to."

as Saint Paul did, that among the variety of the Spirit's gifts there were some that served directly the community's need for spiritual enlightenment.

It is not that point, however, that the spotlight falls on in the story of Martha and Mary in Saint Luke's Gospel, where Jesus contrasts a preoccupation with "many things" with the essential "need for one" (10:41–42). A later tradition, drawing on the classical tradition of the active and contemplative lives, interpreted the story as a justification of the monastic division of tasks into manual and intellectual. In doing so, it forgot the hesitation that earlier Christian thinkers had felt about the distinction of the active and contemplative, wishing to say (with Augustine, a monk and founder of monasteries) that the duality of active and contemplative must be embodied in every working vocation.[24] What the story invites us to consider is not the elevation of a certain *kind* of work (contemplative, or intellectual) over or alongside another kind (active, or manual), but the transforming moment of rest which must accompany *all* work. Rest is focused upon one point, "hearing," which is the only thing Mary is credited with doing; she does not "prophesy," she does not "teach." The better part she has chosen is *not* the exercise of a special gift or the engagement with a special form of work. It is the "higher way" reaching above the variety of gifts and conditioning the way we exercise it, the love that listens and defers before it acts. Here, if anywhere, we may see the point of the strange insistence of the patristic church on the shifting of the day of rest from the sabbath, the seventh day, to the "Lord's Day." The sanctification of work follows the same law that governs the structure of justification itself: hearing governs activity. Attentive listening to Christ in worship provides the coherence with which the variety of our working undertakings can be grasped together as a service.

---

24. Augustine, *City of God* 19.20.

CHAPTER 6

The Communication of Friendship

Coexistence

To think unsentimentally, without idealism or moralism, about the "higher way" of love, we need to take bearings from the lower way, the way of those perfectly ordinary loves that constitute our various communities. Human nature is created social; the only rest available to it lies in communication. It communicates in material goods, it communicates in meanings, and it also communicates, in some cases predominantly, in personal presence. Our ends of action involve being together, without which material goods become dully functional, speech becomes abstractly impersonal. "It is not good that man should be alone" (Gen. 2:18).

We take a point of reference in the term "friendship," which has the widest range of possible applications; it is used of sympathy, of political alliances, of partnerships in life. But not every form of being together is friendship. Human interactions frequently occur on an occasional basis in which neither party knows the other personally; each respects the other's right to be there, and may even desire the other's presence; each wants the encounter to be conducted and concluded on a basis satisfactory to both; neither envisages a continuing connection. So it is, for example, with the electrician we summon to our house when the lights have gone out. There is no "friendship" there, though we may intelligibly speak of "friendliness." To be friendly is not to be a friend; it is merely to conduct an encounter in a manner intended to be comfortable. Commercial transactions are often friendly, as are casual relations struck up among those who stand in a queue, or even—a contact so restricted that we think of it as no more than "politeness"—among those who pass one another considerately on the street, paying the necessary minimum of respect. The "neighbor" is here reduced to his elementary meaning, as the person "next" to us.

Jean-Yves Lacoste thinks that these minimal encounters throw the clearest light on human sociality, in which "we treat the other person as we treat ourselves, and what we are to ourselves we are to the other." Existence is coexistence; it involves minimal but real "concern" (*sollicitude*) or "caring about" (*se soucier de*) the other. There is nothing inevitable about such concern, for sometimes we do not bother with people at all. "'Bothering with' and 'caring about' are moves that recognize the other for what he or she is. They can be forms of giving, . . . as when I care about a hungry person by offering something to eat; they can be dramatic moves, as when I show my care for someone who is sick by visiting. But they can also be moves so discreet as to be barely perceptible. When I jostle someone in the crowd in a distracted moment, I might as easily, still without a moment's thought, have stepped aside to let him pass."[1] The language of "concern," "caring about" "bothering with" and "coexistence" is not a moral language, Lacoste insists. That is to say, concern and coexistence is a fact of our humanity, not something we have to decide to make happen. Yet we may reflect upon the fact, and if we decide to make it go on happening, that is a moral decision. To which we may add the qualification that such a reflection itself could only be the exercise of a moral attitude. But that does not affect Lacoste's primary contention that "even in the ordinary passing encounters of those who coexist (unvirtuously) in peace there is a kind of "promise."[2]

Here he discerns a paradox. Promise is "not written into the everyday logic of existence," yet "if concern is always-already familiar to us, we are right to expect it."[3] Hobbes's "war of all against all" cannot be faulted for misreading the elementary conditions of human existence, but there is a view of existence that it has failed to see. "Concern throws light on existence, and refusal to care throws existence into shadow."[4] We could express this in a different idiom by saying that neighborhood is an "immanent end" of individual human nature. We are truest to the terms of our existence when we promise, and presume on, peaceful coexistence. "A broken promise is, or was, no less a promise for having not been kept; it was perfectly appropriate

---

1. Lacoste, *La Phénoménalité de Dieu* (Paris: Cerf, 2008), pp. 160-61.
2. Lacoste, *La Phénoménalité de Dieu*, p. 162.
3. Lacoste, *La Phénoménalité de Dieu*, p. 165.
4. Lacoste, *La Phénoménalité de Dieu*, p. 166.

to count on it. . . . Even in war it is a misunderstanding to suppose that the enemy is bound to be an enemy for ever, to refuse to admit that he, too, could be included in the economy of promise."

The neighbor, the self's equal and opposite, is the fulfillment of the self. And yet, as we have insisted earlier, the discovery of our calling to be agent-selves is one that the neighbor cannot provide for us. We make it apart from the neighbor in encounter with God alone, and the radical failure of agency at that level is a peril we cannot rule out. But by communion with the neighbor and participation in a common world agency achieves concreteness. God offers us our self, God offers us our neighbor, and the two gifts may be distinguishable, but not separable. The self is destined by God to be a neighbored self, not only to "have" a neighbor, as one might "have" a relation to property, but to *be* a neighbor, realizing itself in neighborhood. The self can be unneighborly and unneighbored only at the cost of self-loss. The neighbor is "as" self, offering the *I* an access to a *we* where it belongs, offering him- or herself as the co-agent with whom agency may realize itself in communion.

It is worth pausing over the small change of these slight social encounters before we press on to speak of deeper things. Is being together a real communication by itself—not doing something materially useful for one another, not explaining or interpreting anything? Or is presence merely a condition for the real communications of a material and intellectual kind? The small social phenomena have the virtue of abstracting from wider contexts and focusing on the bare reality of presence. The person I pass in the street is *not* the merchant from whom I hope to purchase vegetables, *not* the lawyer from whom I seek advice. Take away the materially useful, take away the informative, and what is left in that meeting which might still be valued? The "peace" which Lacoste discerns is a rather minimal relation.

An answer could start from the fact that *loneliness* is an existential problem entirely comparable to that of worklessness and loss of meaning. And though one may be lonely in a crowd, being in a crowd is at least a curb on loneliness. Sometimes we would be glad to see a single living soul. Jeremiah's vision of the undoing of creation (4:23–26), with the absence of the human at its center, has an irresistible terror:

> I looked on the earth, and lo, it was waste and void;
>   and to the heavens, and they had no light.
> I looked on the mountains, and lo, they were quaking,
>   and all the hills moved to and fro.
> I looked, and lo there was no man,

>   and all the birds of the air had fled.
> I looked, and lo, the fruitful land was a desert,
>   and all its cities were laid in ruins.

The curious polarity of "wilderness" and "civilization" that runs so deep in the human imagination, sheds light upon our fear of loneliness. Those who occupy heavily populated regions of the earth find that wilderness exercises a great fascination. We want to experience it, to look around us and see nobody and, if the longing has a deep hold on us, to see no trace of human presence there. Even those who never have visited the South Pole and never will, can be moved to give money and sign petitions to keep industrial exploitation far away from it. Deserts, mountains, tundras, the open sea, and in future, perhaps, outer space lure people to solitary adventures and solitary deaths. Solitude is a boundary we feel we must test. We carry the battle against loneliness onto its home ground, stretching self-awareness, rediscovering the self in its reduction to the persona of a Robinson Crusoe. But the testing is strictly limited. Experiment will teach us that our capacity for solitude runs out. The aim is to know the snapping-point, and to return to civilization better instructed about ourselves, ready to resume our social avocations with renewed enthusiasm.

Together with the ambivalent attitude to solitude, consider another common feeling, the love that many people, especially the young, have for big cities. People are drawn there for many reasons: work, instruction, impressive architecture, valuable purchases, and valuable sales and services, opportunities to develop wide and interesting circles of acquaintance. They are drawn by what they call "the buzz." Some are eager to be in a large crowd with a common project—a football match, a political demonstration, or whatever—and even those who shun such an immersion in the mass can feel a quickening of the pulse as they step off the bus or train in the center of a city and absorb the first appearance of its intense goings and comings. The dullest and most familiar town, with nothing about it to catch the eye, can shake us out of a lethargy if we walk down the high street when business is afoot, experiencing our natural connectedness with the world.

The Commitment of Friendship

We return to Lacoste's talk of presence as a "promise" which casts a line of expectation forward in time from the moment of encounter to future experiences. He uses the word in its weakest sense, simply as a ground of justified anticipation, and the line it casts may often be a very short one. As I approach a stranger on a crowded street, all I can be thought to "promise" is that in the next moment I shall not jostle her and push her off the pavement. Even in this minimal instance human presence binds me to a steady course of action, a course on which the stranger reasonably counts as she makes her way towards me. Yet the "promise" I give entirely without thinking has made no demand upon my freedom. To exercise freedom I must be able to commit myself, whether for a moment, a day, a year, or a lifetime. By giving and receiving promises intentionally, we conduct ourselves as agents, sustaining in relation to others a self-continuity of which agency is capable. Without promises intentionally given or received, we could not fulfill our agent-identities, recalling who we are given to be and laying claim to be that person in action. And here, at last, we may focus our attention on friendship.

There is a great deal included in the peaceful economy of promise that could not by any stretch of the imagination be described as friendship: not only the courteous passing of strangers in the street, but the wide variety of business transactions, the interactions of private persons with officials, the cooperation of those who are engaged in the same work, and so on. Friendship is distinguished from all these polite or friendly encounters precisely by its ambitions to endure as a particular relation. A stranger is recognized as a human being, another self, or whatever, but a friend is recognized as one whom we have known before and hope to know again, not only as "what" she is, but as "who," an identity established in our memory and forming part of our world. If the elementary recognition of the neighbor is instinctive, not articulate—I do not often say to myself, "There goes a fellow human being!"—the more developed recognition of a friend can only be conscious. We cannot know someone to be a friend without being conscious of knowing her, and without knowing that we are supposed to indicate our conscious knowledge by calling her by her name. To make a friend we need not have done anything deliberate. Friends may be thrust on us by circumstances, as happens to children "brought round to play" with other children. Yet the recognition of friendship brings with it an implied decision about how, or whether, we shall carry it forward and deepen it. Her name is Sandy and we chatted pleasantly in a queue at the bank the other day; now, in the street, I must decide whether to claim the acquaintance or, if she claims it first, how warmly to acknowledge it. Friendship may be sown by the wind of circumstance, but it needs the soil of moral commitment to grow. And given our finite capacity for attention, we cannot offer that commitment to everybody.

We may be friendly to all, but we cannot be a friend to all. We select our friends. Classical texts on friendship made a great deal of this, and of the need to do it early and well.

The Western view of friendship was importantly influenced by these few influential writings from Greece and Rome, of which the two most important were Cicero's *Laelius* (otherwise, *De Amicitia*) and, behind it, Aristotle's discussion of friendship in the *Nicomachean Ethics*.[5] Aristotle wrote in response to Plato's formative discussions of both love (*erōs*) and friendship (*philia*), but where Plato invested love with the heavier philosophical freight, Aristotle's preference for *philia* was significant. It permitted him to concentrate on the objective presentations: friendship as a social form, rather than as a feeling. Following his typical method of surveying what was commonly included in a term and then narrowing his focus to describe the ideal type, he came to rest on what he saw as friendship's highest and most stable form, the friendship of the virtuous within the city-state. Later discussions tended to start where Aristotle left off, with the heroic loyalties of exceptional pairs of friends, which gives an idealistic tone to most ancient talk of friendship. Cicero and Plutarch celebrate the exclusive friendships of the virtuous, and are more than doubtful of the many friendships of the ordinary. Hence the urgency of the advice to choose the right friend—and no more than one!

The objections made against the conception are familiar: it sacrifices the spontaneity of "hitting it off" to calculating prudence; it makes friendship the province of the morally strong, with no sense of its importance to the morally weak; it prioritizes what the friend can give over what one can give the friend. In its defense two points are worth making. First, in relation to one special form of friendship, that of marriage, we usually have no hesitation in allowing a role for prudence alongside the more intuitive and spontaneous affections. The two are not incompatible, though they may sometimes be felt as in tension. Second, "choosing the right friends" is not a bad description of what we actually do in practice, though we may be reluctant to admit it. Our uneasy conscience has the effect, as Cicero was quick to point out, that we make our choices later than we need to, and so end up "dropping" friends who have disappointed us.[6]

Friendship needs a beginning, and not only an accomplished maturity;

---

5. *Ethica Nicomachea*, books 8–9. To this leading pair of texts Plutarch's essay "On Having Many Friends" (*Moralia* 93–96) offers a valuable complement.

6. *De amicitia* 22.85.

its beginning must be voluntary and selective. That is what makes it different from family affection, given with the facticities of blood-connection and upbringing. A parent loves a child, a child (more uncertainly but no more selectively) loves a parent, irrespective of his or her virtues. We want to be proud of our children and our parents, and we shall talk about their virtues endlessly if it is possible for us to do so, and if it is not, experience shame. Yet shame does not make the bond of parent and child disappear. With friendship, on the other hand, choice makes the connection an evaluative one from the outset. We want a friend we can think well of, and who will think well of us. While classical texts may speak too calculatingly, they are surely not wrong to think that what we see in our friends is something of what we aspire to be in ourselves.

Yet a sense of tragedy hangs over the classical discourse of friendship: an ideal so rarely realized, and realizable only at the cost of pruning back the prolific bush of friendship to a single leading shoot. It never resolved the problem of combining the ideas of perfection and universality. In the absence of a sense of God's purposes in redemption, friendship could not be seen as an aspect of moral self-development, and so could not point both backwards to the ordinary social needs of mankind and forwards to mankind's perfection. It had an ambivalent, even disdainful view of "vulgar friendship," and an elitist and restrictive idea of "true friendship." It was as though it were searching for a gospel about friendship, a reason for believing this blessing to be open to all who share a common human nature, and yet at the same time a proof of man's glory—or glorification.

Christians of the first millennium spoke more extensively of love than of friendship; yet they had more to say about friendship than one might suppose, and were impressed enough by Aristotle's and Cicero's discussions.[7] To Augustine, who thought about friendship continually, the lesson to be learned from it was that friendship was elusive and uncertain.[8] Yet this was not to disagree with the more optimistic claim of Ambrose, who devoted the closing sections of his treatise on morality, *De officiis*, to a piecemeal reworking of the major Ciceronian themes. Christian friendship, he thought, was the only possible realization of the ideal, for in that context faith could act as the guarantee of virtue. The most notable innovation on the classical

---

7. See Carolinne White, *Christian Friendship in the Fourth Century* (Cambridge: Cambridge University Press, 1992).

8. Augustine, *Epistola* 130.2.4: "*Ita in quibuslibet rebus humanis nihil est homini amicum sine homine amico. Sed quotusquisque talis inuenitur de cuius animo et moribus sit in hac uita certa securitas?*"

view, more assumed than asserted, was that marriage was a field of friendship between husband and wife. But a decisive Christian review of Cicero's *De amicitia* had to wait for the clearer view formed by the twelfth-century English monk, Aelred of Rievaulx. Cicero had not resolved the tension between friendship as a universal tendency of human nature and the exclusive, and rare, phenomenon of "true" friendship. Aelred deals with the problem by drawing friendship into a Christian understanding of pilgrimage, growth, and final attainment, allowing its beginning, development, and perfection to contribute to moral and spiritual growth, and especially associating friendship with wisdom.[9] Cicero's "true" friendship—the occasional partnership of a Patroclus and an Achilles—becomes a "spiritual" friendship, and Cicero's definition of friendship as "agreement on divine and human matters with love and goodwill" can, with the addition of the single word "supreme," be fitted in at the top rung of a four-step ladder of friendship.[10] So while Aelred could admit that friendships are comparatively few on our earthly pilgrimage, he could also, unlike the classical writers, urge us to have as many of them as we can find, and, indeed, could present himself as a much-befriended man. This is all due to a confident hope for universal friendship in the eschaton. Friendship in this life, therefore, takes its place as a means of moral growth towards the goal, both by acquisition of new friendships and through deepening of old ones.[11]

This allows Aelred to situate friendship, as a wholly selective relationship, in relation to universal love (*caritas*). Under the influence of his friend Bernard of Clairvaux he insists that *caritas*, which in Cicero meant simply "affection," should bear its full Christian moral weight as demanded in respect of all, including those we find odious. Love thus becomes the wider category, within which friendship can be situated as a special form, applied only to those to whom we are able to reveal ourselves intimately, suspending differences of social order in the freedom of mutual confidence.[12] So friend-

---

9. Aelred, *De spiritali amicitia* 1.66: "*Si ea quae de amicitia dicta sunt diligenter aduertas, inuenies eam sapientiae sic uicinam uel infertam, ut pene dixerim amicitiam nihil aliud esse quam sapientiam.*" Cf. 1.67: "*Cum igitur in amicitia et aeternitas uigeat, et ueritas luceat, et caritas dulcescat, utrum nomen sapientiae tribus his debeas abrogare, tu uideris.*"

10. 3.8: "*Cernitis ergo quatuor gradus quibus ad amicitiae perfectionem conscenditur; quorum primus est electio, secundus probatio, tertius admissio, quartus rerum diuinarum et humanarum cum quadam caritate et beneuolentia summa consensio.*"

11. 3.80: "*Haec est uera et aeterna amicitia quae hic inchoatur, ibi perficitur, quae paucorum hic est ubi pauci boni, ibi omnium ubi omnes boni.*"

12. 1.31: "*Ergone inter amicitiam et caritatem nihil distare arbitramur? Immo pluri-*

ship is a handhold on the ascent of love, an assistance in the development of perfecting our devotion to God and our service of others. Friendship, which in Cicero is certainly *giving*, thus becomes also *forgiving*, capable of enduring some variable behavior on the friend's part, such as bad-tempered language, periods of coolness, headstrong resistance to good advice or contrary opinion, even the hasty drawing of a sword.[13] Here, perhaps, Aelred found an answer to the problem of the friendship of the non-virtuous. It may be that we love our friend for one virtue only; in the light of the promise of growth and perfection that is enough. If the contingency and changeableness of friendship is due in some measure to our unsettled relation to ourselves, our discomfort with what we have been and our desire to leave it behind and overcome past misjudgments, the most loyal friend is likely to be the one who feels his existence justified, does not need to feel embarrassed by the attachment of a friend with obvious weaknesses.

"Think where man's glory most begins and ends," the poet wrote, "And say, my glory was I had such friends."[14] It is not self-evident that we should tie glory to friendship like this. We might reasonably say that human glory begins and ends with God's judgment of each according to his *works*. Yet works, even those of a poet, come to fruition only in a social setting, and Yeats was not mistaken in thinking that his own work owed much of its depth to those who had lived with him through cultural and political revolution. Work is the fruit of influence, if not of collaboration; solitary work is the fruit of influences close enough to feed the imagination. The acquisition of friends has everything to do with the shaping of our work and the realizing of our calling. This does not mean that friendship must be a working partnership; there are friends who are helpful precisely because their work is different from our own. Yet friendship is not remote from work; there is always a shared engagement in the tasks of life as a whole, and a friend is

---

mum. Multo enim plures gremio caritatis quam amicitiae amplexibus recipiendos diuina sanxit auctoritas. Non enim amicos solum sed et inimicos sinu dilectionis excipere caritatis lege compellimur. Amicos autem eos solos dicimus quibus cor nostrum et quidquid in illo est committere non formidamus. . . ." Cf. 2.19: *"Ex caritatis igitur perfectione plerosque diligimus qui nobis oneri sunt et dolori, quibus licet honeste non ficte, non simulate sed uere uoluntarieque consulimus, ad secreta tamen eos amicitiae nostrae non admittimus."*

13. 3.22: *"Si forte ira praeuentus amicus eduxerit gladium uel si uerbum protulerit triste, si quasi non amans ad tempus tibi sese subtraxerit, si tuo suum aliquando praetulerit consilium, si a te in aliqua sententia uel disputatione dissenserit, non his amicitiam aestimes dissoluendam."*

14. W. B. Yeats, "The Municipal Gallery Revisited," in *Collected Poems* (London: Macmillan, 1950), p. 370.

someone who can be relied on. There is a thesis in need of contradiction here, which is that friendship has nothing to do with "ethical impulses" proper to marriage, work, state, and church, but belongs with the "free" forms of community "which develop independently within the sphere of autonomous culture."[15] Yet the thesis has this much to be said in its favor: friendship is not itself cooperation, but a sabbath-rest that comes to fruition in the moment of pause, in between cooperation and cooperation, a moment at which we can reflect on our mutual services and look forward to them. We value as friends those whom we know value our cooperation as highly as we do theirs.

Cooperation makes friendships equal. It is possible to misunderstand this equality. The classical tradition emphasized the common outlook and common expectations to the point of under-appreciating the contrasts of temperament that often go to make good friendships. But cooperation is what is at stake both in sameness and difference, pulling in the same direction and complementing each other's strengths and weaknesses. The differences which cause moderns most anxiety to think about, those of social weight, between older and younger, richer and poorer, powerful and dependent, can also be brought to equilibrium in a cooperation more profound than they are, and, indeed, making it possible to enjoy them rather than finding them a hindrance. The importance of equality, the ancients understood, is precisely to allow frank speaking and mutual truth-telling. Friendship is a sphere where criticism can be free within the confidence of mutual goodwill, while flattery is the sign that confidence has been broken. The equal candor of friends is a kind of rehearsal of what we know we owe to others but cannot give to others; in it equality is built on an affectionate relation which is strong enough to bear the weight of difference.

With the setting of friendship in the wider context of the love which is due to friend and enemy alike, we can admit that friendship is not an exclusive relationship, but part of a series of concentric circles that allows of greater and lesser proximity. And with this we can take note of the wider penumbra reaching out beyond friendship towards what we call "friendliness," more than the polite civility but less than commitment to mutual interest for the indefinite future. To be friendly is to conduct an encounter with no prospect of familiarity beyond its conclusion, but to conduct it in a manner that might be appropriate if it did have such a prospect. That we

---

15. Emil Brunner, *The Divine Imperative*, trans. O. Wyon (Philadelphia: Westminster, 1937), p. 517.

The Communication of Friendship

can be friendly to all but not a friend to all, does not separate friendliness off from friendship altogether. Friendliness acknowledges a connection with friendship, for friendships are rooted in the manifold openings to other people that arise in the course of daily encounters. In these openings we see friendship unrealized, held back from developing further simply by the constraints of finitude. In being friendly to the taxi driver or the postman we say, in effect, "I am not your friend, nor you mine, nor in this life are we ever likely to become friends; yet in God's eternity, and even in this life if it should so transpire, a friendship between us will be no bad thing."

The effect of friendliness on friendship is to prevent its closing in on itself. A constant alertness to openings for new friendship is a token of the self-transcendence that friends need if they are to avoid becoming stuck in ruts of jealousy and possessiveness. Loyalty is an important element in friendship, to be sure, but loyalty in friendship is not a matter of imposing restrictions on the scope and reach of friendly overtures. Friendship has to be lived as befits a pilgrimage, a constantly expansive readiness for presence and promise. It must be open to the making of new friends, for its tally is never full.

But the limits of our attention mean that old friendships slip back from the foreground of our lives. Friendships are generated by the successive enterprises of our lives, and become identified with our reminiscences of them. An evolution in our work or a change in our location involves a reordering of friendships, the making of new ones, and the relegation of some old ones to the reserve of our memories, a truth that Gregory of Nazianzus found it hard to accept, as he reproached Basil for attending to the duties of his bishopric rather than the claims of old friendship. But we should not see disloyalty in such a development. Even in the background of the mind friendships remain alive, a theme of gratitude, reflection, and common discussion, and may re-emerge, as occasion offers, into the foreground again. And precisely by remaining alive and in the background old friendships keep us open to a wider network of affection and goodwill, so that we are not always concentrating on our latest favorite. The question of disloyalty can only arise when the call to help is ignored.

And here the distinction between marriage and other forms of friendship comes into high relief. It is often said that the ancient world projected upon its ideal of friendship some of the expectations we have of marriage—exclusiveness, permanent fidelity, the sharing of intimate secrets, and so on. Christians of the early centuries, for their part, came to understand the highest value of marriage as that of friendship. Over the long term this worked to raise the general esteem in which marriage was held, and particularly the esteem for married women, though the sharpness of the ascetic resistance in the fourth century is a well-known story. Some of what strike us as odder features of the patristic view of marriage arise precisely from their emphasis on its potential to be friendship. Older married couples who, with parental duties safely behind them, could separate their sleeping arrangements and share a home in enduring harmonious affection, earned a respect similar to that accorded to those who had taken religious vows.[16]

Yet the inclusion of marriage under the heading of friendship could never be more than partial. The commitment to exclusivity, and the commitment to make that exclusivity lifelong, generate a different logic. Marriage does not share in what we have called the expansive dynamics of friendship, its openness to the new; it does not correlate, as friendships do, to enterprises and episodes within our lives. We may see the difference, first of all, in the gravity of the act of decision involved. More is promised and demanded in marriage than when one makes a friend. But that "more" may also be "less." The marriage relationship is tied to bodily proximity. The married couple not only precludes all rivals; it precludes, as far as circumstances allow, distance in space. Friendships can be maintained over a distance, but marriage needs its proximity, and finds long separations difficult. A shared sense of life's larger purposes and possibilities, which is the strength of friendship, may be highly desirable in marriage, too, but marriage can survive without it. It can even survive differences of temper and interest that would destroy any friendship. Marriage is focused on the daily continuity of life. It draws away from the further stretches of anticipation and stays close to the immediate past and future horizons, the realm of identity rather than the realm of possibility. Hence springs Jesus' teaching about the eschatological supersession of marriage, a destiny predicted for no other social form. *This* friendship is dedicated to being the ground on which we stand as mortal beings, a company-keeping of souls engaged in the service of mortal body to mortal body.

---

16. Cf. Paulinus Nolensis, *Epistola* 44.4: "*Manetis ecce iidem coniuges qui fuistis, sed non ita coniuges ut fuistis; estis ipsi, nec ipsi: et sicut Christum ita et uosmetipsos iam secundum carnem non nostis.*" The treatment of this theme in Peter Brown, *The Body in Society* (London: Faber, 1989), is memorable.

The Communication of Friendship

The Wrongs of Hostility

With friendship, as with work, false developments take on a systemic character. Unfriendliness is not only a personal failing; there are also unfriendly social environments, unfriendly structures of society, where the good of friendship becomes distorted or inaccessible. These are not constituted by assembling the most naturally unfriendly people, but by conditions of work and responsibility which make naturally friendly people behave in unfriendly ways. The immediate pursuits of friendship must often be suspended in contexts of work and public responsibility. The justice of the public sphere maintains an impersonal universality against all preferential understandings. The office girls must put aside laughing over their selfies when there are customers at the desk; the political organization must make its decisions in open and procedured ways, not by cronies putting their heads together. Yet the negative way in which we construct the universality of public justice by sieving out particular and familiar relationships tends to deprive us of what is essential to human existence—essential even to good public engagements. A purely formal conception of justice, denied the undergirding of special relations, is prey to the dynamics of suspicion and hostility that spring up unbidden where opposition is not mitigated by trust. The public, too, is dependent on a network of confiding relationships built from experiences of friendship. "Political friendship," the name derived from Aristotle, is not itself friendship except in the loosest of senses, but it is certainly dependent on friendship. And without it it is hard to see how political life can be other than the perpetual brawl that it increasingly becomes.

We may find ourselves denied the possibility of friendship from either of two angles: denied the possibility of *forming* it or denied the possibility of *sustaining* it. Exclusion and betrayal are the two complaints that echo through the Psalter, highlighting the implications of failure on the one hand and on the other: "those who hate me without a cause" (Ps. 35:19; 69:4); "Even my familiar friend in whom I trusted . . . has lifted his heel against me" (Ps. 41:9; cf. Ps. 55:20).

(i) "Exclusion" is the term we use to describe associates who define themselves purely negatively against those outside them. Friendship, confined within the existing group, is denied its natural tendency to replicate itself and expand. Group identity then feeds on suspicious oppositions. Small and well-defined groups (the "little platoons" of Burke's famous phrase) have a positive role in evoking binding political loyalties; but those loyalties are constructive only as they succeed in mediating larger and more comprehensive identities. To be from Yorkshire must be a way of being English; to be Scottish must be a way of being British. If the platoons cultivate xenophobia as a necessity of their existence, they will bring the perception of threat to undermine the positive links they have to the outside world. Exclusion thus generates conflict. Conflicts there always are, and always must be. The test of their good faith is whether they have responded to perceptions of threat to the common good a posteriori, rather than anticipated them a priori simply on the basis of distinct identities.

A certain tension between old and new friends is natural enough. It belongs to existence in time to be at once true to our past and open to our future, and this distension in time is essentially creative for us, making us alert to life's demands. It should certainly not be dissolved preemptively, as it was by the classical doctrine that we should always favor the old friend in preference to the new. To cherish old friendships and treat loyalty as a virtue is a fine thing; but to close ourselves off against new friendships for any cause, including loyalty to old ones, is destructive of time's dialectic. Taken in its full rigor, the classical doctrine would deny friendship a place on the horizon of ends of action, relegating it to the underpinning of achieved identities. But friendship cannot bear the weight of too much identity-conferral; that is the respect in which it differs from family relations. It needs openness to exploration and discovery, and if it loses that quality, old friendships are cheated, too, for they need to be able to move onto new ground and respond to new experiences, especially to those involving pain and loss.

To install old friendships against all comers is to embed them in the social structures that support our identities, and they then lose the capacity to stand independently of those structures. So when classical discussion posed the question of conflict between friendship and political structures, there was only one answer it could give: the *patria*, the more encompassing structure, takes priority over friendship. E. M. Forster's protest against this answer is often quoted: "I hate the idea of causes, and if I had to choose between betraying my country and betraying my friend, I hope I should have the guts to betray my country."[17] Does this do more than answer a demoralized thesis with a demoralized antithesis? Are we offered, in place of the fatherland as the supreme friendship, the friend as the most precious "cause"?

Forster's novels characteristically present friendships as adventurous, mold-breaking affinities that transgress accepted social and political bound-

---

17. Forster, "What I Believe" [1939], in *Two Cheers for Democracy* (London: Arnold, 1951), p. 78.

aries. They have a kind of moral ideality, for rare souls who find themselves at odds with a social world that is content to stick in its molds, pointing the way to a wider cultural self-transcendence. Yet they also have an obsessive, even willfully destructive character; and create internal and external chaos, even ending by destroying their object. The triumph of friendship is at best partial, and at worst thoroughly ambiguous. The reconciliation scene with which *A Passage to India* concludes is so uncertain of what has been accomplished as almost to threaten the novel's coherence. And what of traditioned loyalties, like those of the home? The most satisfying of his novels, *Howard's End*, has made space for the moral power of these, too. Forster the novelist displayed a more subtle insight into the complex forms and limited powers of friendship than Forster the later essayist and man-of-opinions. By the measure of Forster's own greatest writings the question of whether friend trumps country or country trumps friend is a pseudo-question susceptible only of pseudo-answers.

Frank O'Connor's famous story of the three Irish soldiers in the War of Independence ordered to execute two British hostages with whom they have become intimate, could be read as a commentary from ten years before on Forster's declaration.[18] Their dilemma is never presented in abstract terms; the words "friendship" and "country" do not appear in either narrative or dialogue, while "nation" appears only once, ironically, in the title. Otherwise there is simply "your side" and "our side," and there is "duty." They view each other, in the English soldiers' argot, as "chums," a word the strangeness of which the narrator draws attention to more than once, as though to warn us against supposing we know what it means. When the story reaches the climax at which the two hostages are made aware of their fate, one of the victims comes out with a hysterical bluster of Forster-type arguments. "Why should we want to shoot him?" the narrator reports. "What had he done to us? Weren't we chums (the word lingers painfully in my memory)? Weren't we? Didn't we understand him and didn't he understand us? Did either of us imagine for an instant that he'd shoot us for all the so-and-so brigadiers in the so-and-so British Army?" The second victim reacts differently. Asked to agree that "It's not so much our doing, it's our duty, so to speak," he replies: "I never could make out what duty was, myself... but I think you're all good lads, if that's what you mean." This is not outright skepticism about "duty," simply a confession of the bewilderment they all share at the opacity of its

---

18. O'Connor, "Guests of the Nation" [1929], in *The Best of Frank O'Connor*, ed. Julian Barnes (New York: Knopf, 2009), pp. 5–15.

appalling demands. Never does the story allow the suggestion that the fatal orders could be evaded; that is its own abstraction, focusing attention on what makes the situation different from a "dilemma," where one must (and can) "choose" between betraying one's country and betraying one's friend. All parties are *en prise* to the logic of the structures from which they derive their identities, and their friendship cannot outbid their respective "duties." Yet in extending his appreciation to the men who are about to kill him, the British soldier demonstrates that friendship can at least hold its six square inches of ground, and express itself even at the moment when an alien duty overwhelms it.

The larger-scale loyalty, the "cause" that unites us with those outside our circle of acquaintance, does not have prescriptive rights over the smaller-scale one, but neither can the little circle of personal acquaintance wrap itself in a cloak of moral invulnerability against the claims of the larger-scale one. What needs to be asked is how the criteria of *good* friendship and *good* patriotism (or internationalism, or corporatism, or political consciousness, or public-spiritedness in general) may interpret each in such a way that the other has enough room to flourish. We may gladly entertain the suggestion that public-spiritedness may not depend solely on a legal or corporate structure, but may need a kind of "political friendship" to support it. But *what* friendship? Where shall we find a friendship which, in validating the particular relations in which our own particular life has been set, can lift its sight-line high enough to observe the wider universe of claims and demands?

(ii) Let us describe *betrayal*, on the other hand, as an extension of the logic of competition into a general condition of society. If exclusion turns the dynamics of friendship against itself, freezing the relations of friends where they are and denying them expansiveness and initiative, betrayal confronts friendship with a principle directly hostile to it: the thought that being-against is more fundamental than being-with, and can always trump friendship and set it aside. "They hate me without a cause," the Psalmist complains, recognizing the arbitrariness of friendship's limits. Hostility pleads no justifying cause because it thinks it needs none. It has become the default position.

Outright conflict is a struggle which one wins and one loses, totally and decisively. But it is an ideal, not a condition that has ever obtained in history. In history there is no total winning or losing, only an adjustment of the relative disadvantages and advantages, and there are many historical conflicts in which both sides have lost much more than either can have ever hoped to win. *Decisive* winning and losing can enter historical conflict only through conventional agreements. In ancient warfare the institution of the single combat is the earliest and simplest agreed procedure for bringing conflicts to a conclusion, ruling that the defeat of a single champion would be regarded on both sides as the defeat of his army. Competitive games brought this procedure into the conduct of social life in peacetime, channeling the destructive forces of competing honor into rule-governed confrontations that allowed a victory of honor without loss of life. The essence of competition is a twofold limit: it has a conclusion, making ordinary life possible again afterwards; it is constituted by its rules of conduct, positive and negative. The positive rules describe the performance competitors must accomplish, the negative exclude the influence of external relations upon the equality from which the competitors begin: "You must get round the post at the far end!" "You must not fall deliberately in front of another competitor to help your kinsman!" These rules, abstracting from all concrete relations of honor or affection that obtain *outside* the competition, exclusively determine what winning shall mean. "A competitor cannot be crowned if he does not compete according to the rules" (2 Tim. 2:5). Which is to say: the first and last rule of any competition is, *thus* you shall win, and not otherwise!

But when the principle of competition seeps beyond the formalized and restricted arena with its regulated procedures, and enters the lifeblood of society, the first of the two limits is defeated. There can be no end to strife when there is no moment at which victory is declared and honor awarded. So if the regime of the formal rule continues to prevail, it is without the idea of a conclusion, and therefore without a defined performance. The constitutive rule that remains is wholly negative: no practical engagement may be qualified by special relationships; every engagement is to be conducted on the same understanding, and all parties to the engagement are in a strictly equal position, which is to say, compelled to be rivals. Competition is thus the purest expression of an abstract universal justice stripped of all the special relations that make society interesting and valuable. What is being described here, of course, is no more than an imaginative construction of society, and especially justice, interpreted negatively as the exclusion of relations and associations that make one life different from another. It is not an actual social development, nor could it ever become one. But simply as an imagination it exercises powerful fascination over late-modern man and shapes his capacities decisively. Whole cultures are determined by it, and individuals who lack the freedom to live outside its sway are reduced, at best, to trying to qualify its grip on the conduct of their lives. It requires no particular will of mine for me to see myself as locked in rivalry with others. All it needs is for them to behave towards me on that assumption.

Most importantly, this imaginative construction limits the seriousness with which we can *recognize* and *promise*, which is to say, it limits our capacity to act under the influence of memory and anticipation. The Hobbesian "compact" was conceived as a device to establish binding commitments in a world imagined simply as rivalry. But the compact can never be more than hypothetical, for the logic of the negative view of society is to hold all contracts soluble when the purposes for which they were formed no longer seem important. Nothing in the conditions of rivalry could allow the participants to make agreements that were unbreachable in principle, and that fact keeps the ultimate opposition of "him or me" on the horizon of every particular policy or decision. Friendship in a world constituted as rivalry, especially a world in which economic rivalry is deliberately heightened as a device to encourage production, can be no more than a provisional truce in a war of annihilation. To recognize that I am bound to someone by a promise, and to anticipate that a promise someone made me will be kept, are strategies that may keep friendliness on the road for the moment, but they must ultimately pose the question, which of us is *finally* to win? If final justice is not reserved for God and the absolute future, every moment is a final judgment. It is not that the *beginnings* of friendship have no place: we may ooze friendliness from every pore, as aggressive marketers have long learned to do, appropriating the familiar "Hi!" and the use of the automatic Christian name. But these beginnings have no way of growing to become serious or lasting, and how can friendliness be other than hollow when every suggestion of further possibilities is stripped away from it? Time with its life-constituting continuities disappears into the wings, and the present becomes an eternity without past or future.

Friendship, then, as a commitment to presence through time, is excluded from view when time is denied its rights. The betrayal of the familiar friend is an abandonment of time, an abandonment of fond memories and reasonable anticipations, and therefore also an abandonment of ourselves. The "familiar" is the repository of our own past experience, and the betrayal of the familiar friend is at the same time self-betrayal. Ambitions for future time are ambitions for ourselves over time, and investing these in friendship we invest them in a stability that will enable our growth and enrichment. To live as a rival is to have no ends, merely to act in response to the empty but all-controlling rule of competition: *thus* you shall win!

The Communication of Friendship

The Sanctification of Friendship

Is there to be found, then, a universal that can embrace the perfecting influence of friendship? That is the question posed and left unanswered by the classical discourse of friendship. In answer Christians turned to the friendship offered by Christ to his disciples. There is a difference we should not miss between speaking of friendship with Christ and friendship with God. Friendship with God was a concept not unknown in pagan antiquity, on which both Jews and Christians drew freely.[19] It is the opposite of friendship with pleasure, as the Pythagoreans had said, or of friendship with the world, as Saint James had it (4:4). Friendship with God is a moral orientation, a direction of love towards the transcendent good. Friendship with Christ, however, is a moment of fulfillment, a concrete, material encounter. Such an idea could only be conceived in the context of the resurrection, the supreme justifying and sanctifying act of God set in the middle of history, which gives Christ back to his friends in real and personal presence.

Friendship with Christ is not a concept widely deployed in the New Testament; it is unique to Saint John, but is introduced by him at a point of great structural importance in his text, at the center of the farewell discourses. These form a section of the Gospel in which Jesus prepares his disciples for the time of his exaltation, corresponding to the forty days' teaching before the ascension spoken of by Saint Luke (Acts 1:3). Framed by the drama of the upper room (John 13:1–30) and the prayer of self-committal (chap. 17), the discourses begin with the command that is to govern the whole period of his departure: to love one another, as he has loved them (13:31–35). They contain two major blocks of teaching on the coming gift of the Holy Spirit (14:15–31; 15:26–16:15), between which, at the very center, there comes the section on Jesus' friendship (15:1–25). In this section the reference to the Spirit is suspended as Jesus reflects upon the permanent relation of the disciples to his own person. The absence implied in his exaltation is not to be a total absence, but one sustained by a vital relation of friendship, which draws its strength from memory and anticipation, the highest form of love in its capacity to motivate sacrifice (15:13). It is, indeed, Jesus' own sacrifice that has made this enduring friendship possible. It is not that the disciples enter

---

19. *The Philo Index* reports 48 instances of the adjective φιλόθεος in the works of Philo of Alexandria. On the tendency of medieval theology to transform love of God into friendship see, notably, John M. Rist, *Augustine Deformed* (Cambridge: Cambridge University Press, 2014).

the circle of friendship by sacrificing themselves, though that possibility is raised in commentary elsewhere (1 John 3:16). This is not a circle of initiates associated only negatively by martyrdom. Their friendship is constituted by joyful adherence to Jesus' teaching, and supremely to the command of mutual love.

The teaching on friendship opens with the last of the Johannine "I am" parables, a depiction of the relation between Jesus and his friends as a living organism, a vine in which the life of the trunk flows out into the branches and permits the growth of fruit. Together with the trunk and the branches there is a further figure in the parable, the viniculturist, God the Father, whose purpose shapes the growth of the vine and makes decisions about its care. The life of the vine is continuous with the care of the viniculturist, so that his love bestowed on the vine is continuous with the love flowing out from the trunk to the branches. The life of the vine thus becomes the sole glory with which the divine viniculturist surrounds himself (15:8). The life to which the parable points is a life at once divine and human, articulated on an ascending scale as joy, mutual love, and sacrificial friendship (vv. 11–13). There are echoes here of the classical understanding of friendship as the highest form of affection: selective, cooperative, and sharing the secrets of the heart. Yet there is also a feature that is not at all classical: command and obedience. The friends are not born equal (v. 16), but are drawn into equality as the disciples enter the mind of the teacher. The language of friendship frees the idea of command from its suggestion of subservience. The friend cooperates precisely because he or she has been allowed to understand, has been made party to the great purpose, which is not the purpose of the vine alone, but of the viniculturist (vv. 14–15). The command is summed up again as mutual love (v. 17, recalling v. 12 and 13:34), to keep which is to enter fully into the purpose, with an understanding given only to friends. This allows them confidence in making requests, which implies the freedom to take initiatives and to act (v. 16).

How does this true and universal friendship overcome the limited and restricted friendships of the exclusive group? Throughout the New Testament we find that the redemptive community has the effect of radicalizing the resistance of human evil in order to bring it to judgment. Here we see the exclusive group, associated in refusal, radicalized into "the world"—the horizon of human society set over against the horizon of Jesus' redeeming friendship. The little platoons have not preserved either their identities or their littleness, but have been swallowed up in the principle of refusal, now elevated onto the cosmic scale. "The world," as a conceptual horizon rather than a concrete body of people, is constituted by the same train of thought that constitutes exclusive bodies of people, namely, the rejection of a universal friendship offered by the Lord of history. The arbitrariness that underlay the self-definition of the closed group here reaches its clearest expression: "they hated me without a cause" (v. 25). Rejection and hostility, no longer the accidental attributes of a positive local identity, have become in themselves the sole identity available in opposition to friendship.

The reader of John's Gospel is surely intended to remember all this when coming to the last discussion between Jesus and Peter by the lake of Galilee (21:15–17). There is no greater love than sacrificial friendship, we have been told. "Friendship" is the narrower and more specific term, naming the special form in which "love" attains its fullest expression.[20] That is how Peter understood it when Jesus asked him "Do you love me?" (*agapas*) and he replied, "I am your friend!" (*philō*). The shifting vocabulary in this conversation has perplexed readers who have begun from the assumption that *agapē* represents the gold standard, the uniquely Christian conception of love, and *philia* something rather more common and uninteresting. But Peter is laying claim to the relationship Jesus has taught him to see as most decisive, namely, friendship. When the question is subsequently reworded and Jesus asks, "Are you my friend?" (*phileis*), Peter's offence is understandable: the question has been asked three times, and the words of his own assertion put in question. If *philia* had stood for something less than *agapē*, Peter's answer would have been evasive and Jesus' third question merely accommodating. Peter would have had no ground for offence whatever.

It is to the triumph of Jesus that the category of his friendship directs us. We must accept in principle the point of theologians who insist that this triumph must be conceived as his *presence*, rather than his absence, and the Holy Spirit understood as the mediator of his presence, not as his substitute.[21] The New Testament can certainly present things in that light, from the death of Stephen to the vision of John, though the language of his "going away" must also be respected. The question of how we may know the friendship of Jesus is strictly parallel, then, to the question of how we can know his authority and glory after the cloud has hidden him from the disciples' sight. How may the presence of the risen Christ enter experience

---

20. In the Hebraized koine Greek of the New Testament ἀγάπη is simply the translation of the Hebrew אַהֲבָה.

21. Most recently, Oliver Davies, *Theology of Transformation* (Oxford: Oxford University Press, 2013).

at our juncture of history? Kierkegaard is prepared to issue a *ne plus ultra*. Commenting on the words, "Come unto me," he remarks: "Who is the Inviter? Jesus Christ. Which Jesus Christ? The Jesus Christ who sits in glory at the right hand of the Father? No. From the seat of His glory He has not spoken one word. Therefore it is Jesus Christ in His humiliation, in the state of humiliation, who spoke these words. . . . Is He then not now in glory? Yes indeed; this the Christian *believes*. But it was in the state of humiliation He uttered these words; from the seat of His glory He has not uttered them."[22] Kierkegaard's position is presented under the pseudonym "Anti-Climacus," and to understand what is important in it, we must see what it intended to oppose: a too-easy assimilation of the glorified Christ to our present context, avoiding the threat of criticism on our ways and allowing the concrete historicity of the incarnation to fall out of sight. That, in his view, was an evasion of the "contemporaneity of faith," by which he meant our contemporaneity to the first century, not the contemporaneity of Christ to our nineteenth (or twenty-first). Christ "is and insists upon being the definite historical person He was 1800 years ago . . . , living under the conditions he then lived under."

To a rationalist-idealist tradition of spirituality, such as flourished in the nineteenth century, it appeared that the pastness and futurity of the glorified Christ could simply be dismissed. "Why forward reach or backward look for love that clasps like air?" asked John Greenleaf Whittier. Christ's presence was enough; it vindicated a sense of spiritual apartness from the common world. And as pastness and futurity became nothing, so did the conquest of death: "Death comes, life goes; the asking eye and ear are answerless." In this way Christ's presence became little more than a sustained metaphor for our own most comforting perceptions of the world we live in:

> No dead fact stranded on the shore
>   Of the oblivious years;
> But warm, sweet, tender, even yet
>   A present help is he;
> And faith has still its Olivet,
>   And love its Galilee.[23]

---

22. Søren Kierkegaard, *Training in Christianity*, trans. Walter Lowrie (Princeton: Princeton University Press, 1941), p. 26.

23. John Greenleaf Whittier, *Poetical Works* (London and New York: Ward Lock, ca. 1885), p. 398. Those who cunningly recovered eight out of the thirty-eight stanzas of Whittier's poem "Our Master" to make a rather fine hymn for Protestant hymnbooks were not wrong to think

The Communication of Friendship

Yes, faith *may* have its Olivet and love its Galilee, even yet. But *how* that may be so depends on our openness to the power of past events in historic Galilee. But if we cannot allow the Quaker Whittier his assurance that past and future Jesus, Peter, John, Olivet, and Galilee can all be rendered without loss as present-day states of mind, neither can we allow "Anti-Climacus" to have it all his way in the opposite direction. The past reality of Jesus did not end in humiliation, but in a decisive moment of victorious presence, as essential to the Paschal mystery as the cross itself.

We must go beyond the inarticulate amazement of the empty tomb (Mark 16:8), then, to speak of Christ's risen acts of presence, not universally public, but within the social circle to which he returned as a friend. Friendship is mutual, not one-sided; the narratives of the appearance of the risen Christ demonstrate both sides, inseparable but distinct, played out, as it were, in slow motion. It takes time for the communication of presence to be effective, eliciting recognition and response. We have spoken of the unity-in-difference of justification and sanctification—on the one hand, the gift of accomplished restoration; on the other, the call into active engagement. This same duality is apparent in the motif of delayed recognition. For Mary Magdalene by the empty tomb Jesus' approach appears to be that of a gardener; his repeated questioning, "why do you weep?" "whom do you seek?" is answered each time beside the point. Only at the third exchange, when Jesus calls her name, can she make the response of recognition (John 20:13–16). So, too, with Cleopas and his friend in Emmaus, who benefit from a long walk and a long discourse before the gesture at the table allows them to recognize whom they have been with (Luke 24:31–32). Among the gathering disciples in the upper room the greeting "Peace be with you!" at first elicits confusion and incredulity, only gradually overcome (Luke 24:36–43). As Saint John narrates the same scene, Jesus greets them, shows them his hands and his side, and only then does the joy of recognition dawn (20:19–20). By the lakeside it takes the miracle of the draught of fish to provoke the beloved disciple to cry "It is the Lord!" (21:6–7). In discovering the identity of the risen Lord with their dead rabbi, Jesus' followers are required to come to themselves, to recover a continuity of experience. It is not a new Savior the disciples struggle to receive, but a Savior they already know. The delay arises over the recovery of that past in the context of this present, the act of recollection that can generate the welcome. That is what is meant in Saint John's resurrection narratives by the verb "to believe."

---

of Whittier as an instance of the dictum that a theologian may more often be right in what he asserts than in what he denies.

The Gospel we believe is about Christ's risen presence to us, and to the extent that they focused upon this point, rejecting a Protestant tendency to reduce the Gospel to a *meaning* to be *understood*, the contentions of the Catholic party at the time of the Reformation must claim their measure of justification. But to the extent that the Protestant aim was to speak with appropriate complexity about this presence, to demystify an undialectical location of it in Papal see or consecrated elements, its contentions, too, must be allowed their share of justice. The presence of Christ is suspended over redemptive time, grounded in a definite past and a definite future which alone can give the present moment its meaning. Our present knowledge must begin from the pledge of friendship given in past events. There is space for life in friendship created in the world by the resurrection, and that space is where Christian living begins and ends. We are "followers," not simply as imitators or bearers of his cross, but chronologically, as those who come after that moment of decisive presence and live in the light it has shed. If we do not turn first to the historic resurrection and the community that it formed, we are left supposing, as spiritualist Christians of every stamp have supposed, that death is overcome by romanticizing reflections on the virtue of sacrifice. For the present to be redeemed complete and entire, it needs to recover its past horizon, but also to receive its future. "I am with you—to the end of the age" (Matt. 28:20). The "I am" must become an "I shall be," and with that, indeed, a "you shall be." The gift of Jesus to his disciples is his presence, accomplished in the conquest of death and open to be entered, real and faithful, claiming back the past and claiming the future with it. Our present knowledge of his friendship has the definite expectation of future meeting. We live in the light of the angels' warning and promise on the mount of ascension—not only not gazing into heaven, but expecting the Lord's return. If the resurrection is decisive for history, that is because it shapes history to its end. The entering of the end of history into temporal existence is how a coherent moral reason is made possible. As the moment of resurrection was a moment of presence, so must the future be a *parousia*.

The present of friendship, mediated by the Holy Spirit, a gift rooted in the past of Pentecost and in the future coming of which it is a pledge, is a real presence, but in absence, and to justify that paradox we have to look no further than the phenomenon of mutual exchange and confidence between loyal friends who are kept physically apart but sustain their friendship at a distance. The Spirit is no mere projection of our human spirit. It speaks to us of Christ in such a way as to engage our human spirit, but the Spirit's action is prior to and beyond that engagement, in history and in the church. And in the church it is not only found in the mutual pleasure members may take in one another, but in their outward attention to the world to draw to fellowship with Christ those in whom faith has been quickened. Inward-looking and outward-looking aspects are summed up in the primary movement that characterizes this social unit: gathering. "Where two or three are gathered together in my name, there am I in the midst" (Matt. 18:20). The simplest description of the social entity the friends of Jesus form is a "congregation." As there are many forms of peace other than friendship, so there are many movements which suggest a peaceful presence: stepping aside, passing by, confronting, linking arms, and so on. But this peaceful presence of friendship is expressed by a centripetal movement in which each party is drawn to find fulfillment in congregating with the others. Though in mission the church looks out, the underlying movement of gathering, sustained by the Holy Spirit, is more basic. The lamp on the stand shines "to give light to those who are entering the house" (Luke 11:33).

To be friends with the risen Jesus is to have the same friends as he. The New Testament epistles like to express this thought in a variant, *philadelphia*.[24] This word describes the love that binds Christians together through their relation as *adelphoi*, brothers and sisters, used of a rabbi's disciples and applied to his disciples by Jesus, and ties it together with the designation "friends." It is often used to specify the actuality of the relation Christians have to each other over against other manifestations of love. In its first appearance (1 Thess. 4:9) *philadelphia* is clearly a synonym for "loving one another." But in Romans 12:9–10 it is just one item in a list of dispositions and practices that unfold the meaning of "sincere love": hating evil and holding to good, affectionate *philadelphia*, deference to one another's honor, enthusiastic energy, spiritual excitement. In 1 Peter 1:22 the direction of the unfolding is reversed: "Having sanctified your souls by obedience to the truth and entered a sincere *philadelphia*, love one another with a pure heart fervently"—church friendship being the basis from which a purer and more intense affection may be developed. In Hebrews 13:1, "Let *philadelphia* remain; do not forget hospitality to strangers," the act of hospitality is seen as an expression of *philadelphia*. The community that gathers as a brotherly group gladly receives those that would seek its protection on their journeys. And not only does it receive guests, but it goes out to visit the sick and the

---

24. The history of the term before the New Testament use is an intriguing one. In a strictly literal sense it described the virtue of loyalty between siblings (as in Plutarch's *Peri Philadelphias*). But it also appears as the name of more than one city, a tribute to the popular Ptolemy II of Egypt, ironically nicknamed Philadelphus for his revival of the ancient pharaohs' practice of incest. The New Testament use of the term does not seem to have an obvious precedent.

afflicted who cannot make themselves present without its help (James 1:27; 5:14–15).

The commission of Peter to tend the flock, then, is not an *addition* to the gift of friendship, but a disclosure of its true horizon. It is connected with Peter's unique role in the early church, to be sure, and in that sense unique to him. Yet it is a commission that can only be discharged in the context of a company of friends that care for one another, and who need to make the congregation visible and local. It is at once an advantage and a disadvantage for the church to be visible, not only in its historicity but in its present institutional organizations. It is the paradox of revelation itself that the eschatological Bride of the Lamb, the community of disciples in whom he will be eternally present, is both disclosed and concealed by the familial congregation that presents it. To common understanding "the church" refers to an institution, a more or less voluntary body of people constituted by certain officers and laws. This is, of course, a double misunderstanding. The institution is not constituted primarily by its officers and laws (which, of course, it must have), but by its practices and proclamation, by word and sacrament. The second and deeper layer of misunderstanding concerns the sense in which the church "is" its institutional form: looking for the community of Christ's friends is not simply a matter of looking *there*, at the institutional structure, but of looking *through* the institutional structure to discern what God has given it the power to reveal. "We have this treasure in earthernware vessels that the overflowing of power may be seen to be God's, not ours" (2 Cor. 4:7). "Overflowing power," because what it shows, the reality of the friendship of Christ, is not natural to its structure and conduct, but looks eschatologically beyond it. It is with the church as with the sacraments: their material concreteness and presence have to be seen through as we look for the eschatological reality. Balthasar famously commented that the calling of the institutional church was to suffer with its first bishop, Peter, crucified upside down.[25]

Into those institutional forms the Bride of Christ can sometimes disappear, swallowed up by the mediating forms that should have served her

---

25. H. U. von Balthasar, *The Glory of the Lord*, vol. 1, *Seeing the Form*, trans. E. Leiva-Merikakis, ed. J. Fussio and J. Riches (Edinburgh: T & T Clark, 1982), pp. 566-67. This moving passage, which takes Peter as a model of the institutional church, is strikingly successful in reflecting both Catholic convictions of institutional continuity and Protestant awareness of the distance between the institution and the essence of the church: "The Church's institutional aspect also receives the ability to follow Christ and, therefore, to image him to the world, but only, as is made quite clear, after an initial estrangement."

appearance. Is this disappearance objectively real, or merely the function of a subjective point of view? Sometimes the loss of sight affects ourselves alone, sometimes many others. Sometimes it is obviously correlated with our own difficulties in believing, sometimes with failures of belief among others. It is real enough when what causes it is a serious misdirection within the institution and its government. Yet the church's disappearance is not a dissolution. The problem is a matter not of the church's existence, but of its visibility. Which is why our prayer for the church is fittingly concerned with its appearance:

> Show me, dear Christ, thy spouse so bright and clear.

The ecclesiastical institutions of John Donne's day seemed to suffer from one of two alternative disadvantages: they were too obviously successful, or they were too obviously unsuccessful:

> What! Is it she that on the other shore
> Goes rich and painted? Or which robbed and tore
> Laments and mourns in Germany and here?[26]

Both conditions could destroy the conditions of revelation by offering a purely worldly phenomenon in its place: wealth and political power, or the divisive struggle of reform. The bewildering array of narratives of Christian history as defection and revival, as permanent institutional continuity or as scattered plurality, as a church at hand, "established," or as a church in secret, "gathered," all suffered from an attempt to make the church perspicuous, while in fact she still waits to be "betrayed" to faith:

> Sleeps she a thousand, then peeps up one year?
> Is she self truth, and errs? Now new, now outwore?
> Doth she, and did she, and shall she evermore
> On one, on seven, or on no hill appear?
> Dwells she with us, or like adventuring knights
> First travail we to seek and then make love?

If the problem lies in the *seeing* and *being visible* of the spouse of Christ, our response can only be to look for it, which means, to let our own love for

---

26. *The Divine Poems*, ed. Helen Gardner (Oxford: Oxford University Press, 1952, 2011), p. 15.

Christ and for his followers lead us to where we find him and them present. We shall look, of course, where we saw before, for we could have no reason to conclude that institutions sanctified by the presence of Christ had now been deserted by him. Yet the promise made once on the mountain in Galilee, "I am with you" (Matt. 28:20), belongs not to any institution but to the body of disciples as a whole, and we shall find that body wherever it is revealed to us by its confession of its Lord, by its adherence to his teaching and obedience to his universal mission,

> Who is most true, and pleasing to thee, then
> When she is embraced and open to most men.

CHAPTER 7

The Communication of Meaning

Meaning and Reality

We communicate not only in material goods and mutual presence, but in meaning. For other social animals, perhaps (though we had better be agnostic), feeding the young and gathering for protection may be the beginning and end of society. Human beings, however, have a further interest, an interest in knowing who and what and where we are. This is not simply a matter of being capable of language. If someone wishes to say that social animals have a "language," that is a decision we need not quarrel with. They certainly have signals of alarm and affection that indicate presence and evoke cooperation. But, as Jean-Yves Lacoste observes, the distinctive thing that members of the human species do is to *correct* their language.[1] Their shared cognitive interest in reality shapes language to communicate a knowledge of the world. We imagine the language of animals and birds as full of imperatives: "Flee!" "Attack!" "Feed me!" and perhaps, like Levinas's Other, "Do not kill me!" When the seagulls round my house set up a deafening chorus of "Do not kill me!" taking me for a predator as I walk down the path, not one of them, I suppose, pauses to remark to another, "False alarm!" Human language, on the other hand, is built around statements open to verification and correction that refer to what is the case in the world. For the form imposed on communications by this shared interest in reality we use the term "meaning." Meaning is in play, dominantly or subordinately, in all human

---

1. Lacoste, *Recherches sur la Parole* (Louvain: Peeters, 2015), p. 12: "*L'animal qui détient le langage tout en ayant le pouvoir de reformer son langage.*"

communications, and when the meaning we communicate about the world dissolves into unmeaning, it provokes an existential crisis. We no longer know how to settle back comfortably into presence, as Matthew Arnold on Dover Beach rather hoped one might. The loss of meaning threatens us with our annihilation as social beings.

"Reality" is what is independent of ourselves, prior to our communication of it, so that our "meaning" is not something that we bring into being. Only God creates what he means, and even with God we may distinguish the act of creation from the act of reflection, as is done in the ancient narrative that tells how he "saw everything that he had made, and behold, it was very good" (Gen. 1:31). "Saw" it, that is, as something already real, something that now had its own creaturely status. But though we may credit God with reflecting and rejoicing, our ways of reflecting on reality are very different from his. We do not "see" all that God has made in one comprehensive gaze. We need constantly to refer back to one or another aspect of it, and depend on each other to draw our attention to it, to make it accessible to us again, or for the first time. Our communications, furthermore, may be unsuccessful, or only partially successful. Our meanings can be false. Whether intentionally or by accident, they may fail of the reality to which they refer. Yet they are meaningful to the extent that they refer to it, successfully or unsuccessfully.

How does a meaning refer to a reality? The elementary linguistic form for reference to reality is the statement, but it is clearly not the case that our communications of meaning are always formed as statements. Questions can be meaningful, as can commands and wishes, although the primary force of a command or wish is not to provide cognitive access to reality, but to announce an intention, and the primary force of a question is to elicit a communication of reality, not to offer one. Yet if we try to say what makes the difference between meaningful and unmeaningful in questions, commands, and wishes, we are likely to find ourselves coming back to statements. Volitions and questions can have effective meanings only by presupposing some reality, and when we ask about what they presuppose, we are likely to resort to statements. So, in the textbook example, the question, "Have you stopped beating your wife?" has a meaning only if it can be truly stated that you used to beat your wife. The command, "Bring the yellow chair into the sitting room!" could have a meaning only if it could be stated that the yellow chair is presently outside the sitting room. Statements need to be invoked when there is doubt of the meaningfulness of a question, command or wish.

But if it is true that other linguistic forms have meaning only on the presupposition of something that may be stated, it is equally true that a statement is impotent to communicate meaning without an act of volition. The French expression for "meaning," *vouloir-dire*, tells us something of importance. There is no meaning that is not actually meant, *by* somebody *for* somebody. The communication of a meaning *offers* the reference to reality to some determinate audience or readership. Selected out of all possible realities that could be referred to, this item of reality is referred to distinctly, and addressed to a particular recipient in a particular situation. A successful communication must be opportune as well as true, something that this recipient needs to know at this time. Even when the reality referred to is lamentable, the communication is offered as a service: "I have some bad news *for you*," we say.

Bad the news may be, but communicating it will accomplish at least one good: it will establish between speaker and hearer a common reference to a common world. A reality *meant* is a reality *shared*, a reference to truth that is proposed in order to set terms of social coexistence. Not terms of mutual *acquaintance*, since there are meaningful communications that retain their objectivity, limiting the speaker's self-revelation and displaying no interest in the recipient—an article published in a scientific journal would be an example, or an official notice posted for everybody to read. Nor terms of *goodwill*, for we may communicate reality with hostile intent, to hurt, to subjugate, or to disempower. But in communicating a supposed truth we offer terms: *here* lies the world we are to inhabit together; coexistence can proceed on *this* basis of understanding, and no other.

The communication of meaning makes shared labor, on the one hand, and shared friendship, on the other, human in the fullest sense. It shapes them by the empowerment of speech to serve the destiny to which God summoned Adam. Of course, speech is not the whole of human communication. There is non-linguistic or unimportantly linguistic communication. In casual conversation or in danger we may chatter like seagulls, just to let one another know we are there. With more serious cultural ambitions we communicate also through non-linguistic and non-representational arts, which do not need to convey a meaning. A sequence of musical notes, a dance step, an *ensemble* of shapes and colors on a canvas, draw us together in a common perceptual attention that we may become strongly aware of. The "arts," as we call them, are plural because their media (of sound, shape, texture, form, movement, and speech) are various. Elements of communication that appear in combination in everyday life are deployed separately by the arts. Abstract and experimental of their very essence, they explore communicative powers that would otherwise not come to our attention. To the question of the "meaning" of a non-linguistic work of art two types of answer are commonly offered, neither of which is quite right. It is said, on the one hand, that the meaning *is* the work itself, the stippled brushwork in the top right corner, the semiquaver modulating figure in the winds, etc., not something *beyond* these things; it is said, on the other, that the work has as many meanings as there are discursive reflections that can prove a connection to it. It would be better to say that non-linguistic communications have no "meaning" at all. Yet, while they do not convey meaning, there is *something* they convey, which is the power of the forms as such. In their abstractness they bring vividly to bear the emotional force of sound and shape and color and texture.

With the literary arts of drama, poetry, and fiction, and the representative arts of painting and sculpture, the matter is more complicated, since they are not exclusively formal. A literary work is "about" something, a picture is "of" something. Goethe's *Werther* is about the self-destructiveness of the erotic sensibility, Holbein's *Henry VIII* portrays a man who exercises supreme power through a weighty presence and a none-too-benevolent countenance. Yet in drawing these meanings out of them we risk robbing the works of nine-tenths of their interest. *The Sorrows of Young Werther* is a good novel if and only if it interests us in Werther, not simply in general truths about erotic sensibility; *Henry VIII* is a good portrait if and only if it interests us in King Henry, not simply in the generalities of power. They may very well suggest general reflections, but to succeed in their aim they must immerse us in a concrete world of the imagination, a world where Werther suffers or Henry reigns. These worlds are not the real world that we now inhabit, yet in greater or lesser respects they are parallel to it. High story telling, according to one expert practitioner of the art, communicates "verisimilitude"; within the terms of its form it accomplishes a fitting reflection on the realities of the world.[2] This verisimilitude is not descriptive or factual accuracy, and has nothing to do with the "saving of appearances" that successful descriptions in philosophy, history, and science achieve. For it is the privilege of artistic forms to shape their own appearances, composing representations that lead our imaginations out of this world into another, which then offers them a new reflective view on the actual appearances of this world, which they come to understand the better for taking leave of it. The good that readers draw from literature or representative painting is not simply that of having some topic to think about, but that of having the world represented to them with a sharper vision, its forms romanticized, its follies

---

2. Frank O'Connor, *The Lonely Voice* (London: Macmillan, 1963), p. 1.

satirized, its pretensions punctured. The form, simply *as* form, is the means that accomplishes this, and for the work of art to succeed, its form must be right. It is never an excuse for an unconvincing story or a weakly composed painting that, after all, things may look just like that in real life.

Let us consider a very different example of literary art, the effect of which is almost wholly dependent on its form, the ancient Hebrew poem which appears in our Psalter as number 119 (Septuagint 118). It takes the form of an alphabet—*aleph, beth, gimel,* etc.—and while it is not the only Hebrew poem that does so, it is the most developed and self-conscious. An alphabet by itself does not constitute a poem, but it can be made into one; here it is done by allowing each successive letter of the alphabet to generate eight words of which it is the initial letter; each of those words then generating a line of poetry of five or six stresses of which it is the initial word. What are those lines about? They are mainly about words, about poems made out of words, about experiences whose moods are suggested by the sounds of the letters, about words that provide rules to governing the leading of life, about journeys through experience as through the letters of the alphabet. The alphabetic design with which the poet confronts his Hebrew readers serves as a reflecting mirror for the poem's existential content. It is not the alphabetic design *as such* that constitutes its form, but the *correspondence* of the design to the meaning of the lines. That is what makes it a subtle work of art, and perhaps it is simply a heightened example of something all high poetry tries to achieve, a formal presentation that perfectly fits the semantic communication. In that case the insuperable problems this poem presents to its translators are an exquisite example of the problems every poem in every language presents to translation. But since no translator has ever succeeded, or will succeed, in reconstructing the form of this poem in another language, do we, when reading it in our maimed translations, understand its meaning? We understand its *meaning* perfectly well. Yet we cannot *receive the communication* as the poet intended to give it to us. For what it intended to communicate about life, language, and God resided only very partially in the meaning of its statements (which a translation can get close to); it resided in the form, which, founded on the meaning, was greater than the meaning and could not be translated.[3]

What this example shows us is that there is another "meaning" to be

---

3. It was an impressive achievement of the Septuagint translator to place the first Hebrew word of each line in the same position in his Greek, and in this the Latin translator of the Vulgate version followed him. The alphabetic structure itself, however, was lost, as it always will be.

reckoned with besides that of the linguistic utterance, the meaning of the account that can be given of the artwork's form. If I were so foolish as to claim to have explained "the real meaning" of this poem, I should have to face the very proper objection that the poem says nothing of the kind about itself. Its meaning is plain; it protests an earnest desire to walk according to the path, the law, the way, the specifications of Yhwh, and begs for help, for deliverance and for life. My commentary on its form has a meaning, but it is my meaning, not the poet's. If asked to justify it, I shall point to what the poet has done (and for the sake of argument let us suppose that that will be sufficient), but what the poet has *done* is not the same as what the poet has *said*, and what *I have said* is not identical either with what the poet has done or with what he has said. The poet has accomplished a "work," and the point of a work is to make a difference. With Jean-Yves Lacoste we can describe that difference as "unveiling."[4] It facilitates our seeing something. A great literary work can effect an unveiling from which there will flow a wondering reception and reflective commentary. If our limitations in relation to this poem are that we can understand its meaning without seeing all that it has to unveil to us, commentary can help to overcome them to a degree. The comment is a communication of meaning uttered by one who is struck with wonder, and the Long Psalm has proved effective if it has given rise to my comments, and will vindicate them. But even when vindicated, they are no more than my comments—or perhaps Origen's, whose interpretation pointed in that direction nineteen hundred years ago, or those of the rabbis that Origen used to consult.

To every object of wonder its appropriate commentary. The object generates comment, and affords the only criterion of the comment's adequacy. The object is not itself the comment. And what can be said about technical commentary on literary objects applies just as well to non-technical commentary on non-literary objects. "I think that I shall never see a poem lovely as a tree" observed someone with pretensions, at least, to compose poems.[5] The difficulty in making a comment fit its object is known to anyone who has ever looked carefully at anything, not only to poets looking carefully at trees. I think that I shall never see a musicological analysis as sonorous as a string quartet. I think that I shall never see a geological survey as brilliant as

---

4. *Recherches*, p. 116: "*De la fiction, donc, et avant décider si elle dit vrai en un sens tolérable, nous avons d'abord à dire qu'elle dévoile.*"

5. "Poems are made by fools like me, But only God can make a tree." Joyce Kilmer (1886–1932).

a quartz. I think that I shall never see a theological doctrine as liberating as a Gospel. Yet we should not deny ourselves comment merely because it is not the object it comments on. We may, at a cost, ignore the comments of others on objects that interest us, and content ourselves with our own observations. I may comment on the brilliance of a piece of quartz on my mantelpiece without ever opening a geological survey. Yet the survey is still a testimony of wonder at the object, and if an object were to excite no commentary, we could only suppose that it had excited no wonder, either.

The act of commentary, then, whether on texts, objects, historical events, or sequences of sounds, is an expression of wonder with its own meaning. Does that imply that it is wholly *ad libitum*, governed by no canon of faithfulness to the object other than that of adequate description? If the poet likens a sultry evening in the city to "a patient etherised upon a table," can anyone say him nay?[6] Yet even of poetic images, and certainly of commentary on a text, there is more demanded than a flight of fancy. Someone who reads the novels of Jane Austen as a critique of the Napoleonic wars is less likely to persuade us than someone who reads them as exploring the familial virtues. It is not simply that her narrator and characters have *more to say* about the familial virtues than about the Napoleonic wars, for they have even less to say about divine providence, and providence is actually not remote from the plots of the novels. She writes within a framework of moral understanding greater than the sum of the meanings she gives expression to, yet verifiable, in part from the historical context of her life and letters, in part from the formal devices she employs as a storyteller, as something she might have owned to. The commentary, then, while exceeding the explicit meaning-content of the text, owes a faithfulness to its form, circumstance, and cultural context, bringing to an explicit meaning the text in its totality as a work and as an act of presence.

This touches the debate around what has come to be known as "postmodernism" in literary fields (bracketing out the rather different use of the term in architecture), which attempts to see the text not simply as a series of meanings, but as a total object. An object, of course, it is; yet it is an object created by writing, and its status as writing depends on a demonstrable coherence between its explicit meanings, its formal devices, and its historical setting. There are such things as failed texts, which have little interest for readers or critics precisely because they do not "work" as acts of writing.

---

6. T. S. Eliot, "The Love-Song of J. Alfred Prufrock," in *The Complete Poems and Plays* (London: Faber, 1969), p. 13.

But once we look for this coherence, we know that we cannot accept the exuberant suggestion that a text will justify any commentary that can prove a relation to it. The meaning of a commentary is more than the meaning of the text, for commentary would be mere paraphrase otherwise, but the meaning of the text is an indispensable key to the writing-event that produced it. The successful commentary must therefore be faithful to the meaning of the text if it is to make *that* act of writing—undertaken in *that* context and with *that* form—intelligible. The commentary is validated or invalidated not by the text stripped-down, but by the communicative act of writing in all its dimensions. If we refer to "authorial intent" in this context, that is not to suggest some psychological state that we could never reconstruct, but to point to an intelligibility in the act of composition.

If we believe that the communication of meaning is possible for us, we believe that meaning captures and re-echoes meaning, repeating, reinforcing, and confirming it. No law of logic requires this belief of us. It is possible to imagine an endless succession of articulate cries, each bearing a meaning that no one will ever receive or respond to. One consideration, however, should spare us from reaching that stark conclusion. We experience meaning, as we conceive it and give utterance to it, as a superlative good. And it belongs to the experience of the good that it is received, first of all, as a gift. Our meanings, then, are nested within a meaning originally communicated to us, a meaning which our new meanings echo and respond to, a meaning that originates with the Creator and Redeemer of a meaningful world. And to conceive them as such is to know that responding to meaning with meaning is something that human powers may be equipped for. In offering meaning to others, then, we have some reasonable hope of being understood, and of eliciting further utterances of meaning that faithfully respond to them.

Narrative and Description

Proverbial wisdom urges silence as the condition for effectively formed speech. Language itself, the basis of speech, requires discipline if it is to be formed to communicate meaning by conforming to grammatical and syntactical structures. Speech requires something more by way of discipline; it must give order to the thoughts that charge language with its freight. Disciplines of thought have to do with *history* and *nature*, two complementary matrices of reality, distinct and yet inseparable. The reality open to communication is some *happening* in relation to some *conditions* for its happening. For that is what reality is: some thing emerging out of prior things that were "always" there—"always," since "sufficient" conditions are generic: they are sufficient to make *such* happenings necessary and intelligible *whenever* they occur. The landslide happened not only because it had been raining hard the day before, but because water modifies the viscosity of clay.

To communicate reality is to engage with the dialectic of phenomenon and explanation, and to fall back on the original communicative functions of narrative (of phenomena) and description (of explanation): *this* thing *has happened, such* things *happen*. Neither description nor narrative can convey reality on its own. As soon as we speak seriously about what things are, we are forced to think about what has happened, and *vice versa*. If ever there was a wave-particle paradox, this is it. Narrative presents reality as events in time, description presents it as formal relations. The two depend on each other. Sequences of events are comprehensible only when they exemplify relations with an inherent logic: Werther committed suicide, the novelist relates, and we will believe him only if we think that young men in certain states of emotional excitement are liable to kill themselves. Formal relations are concrete only as manifest in repeated patterns of events: the flower unfolds from the bud, the botanist tells us, and we believe him as we observe each spring that this and that bud opens into flower. Qoheleth, for whom nothing was new, Hegel, for whom the new itself was the necessary working of a dialectical law, found meaning in events by tracing them back to regular patterns. The primeval history with which the book of Genesis opens, on the contrary, expounds the recurrence of natural order through sequential narrative, while the vision of heaven with which the New Testament closes presents the eternal praise of God as a decisive conclusion to world history.[7]

Depending on the project of thought we have in hand, we may be tempted to think one of these two forms of meaning more primitive, less reflective, interpretatively weaker, and the other more complete, more reflective, more ultimately true. Science engages supremely in description; it builds descriptions on narratives of observation and (where possible) makes predictions to verify them, but observations and predictions do not constitute a science, only the inductive leap from event to theoretical description,

---

7. Cf. N. T. Wright, *Paul and the Faithfulness of God* (London: SPCK, 2013), p. 456: "It is a truth insufficiently acknowledged that a sensible worldview, equipped with appropriate symbolic praxis, must be in want of a story." Since I am cited as having questioned Wright's dependence on the concept of story, I should state that, while hesitating over the pretensions of the "worldview," which seems to recast the drama in purely intellectualist terms, I can pick no quarrel with the balance my old friend has here struck between narrative and description.

from what was, or may be, observed, to how things really are. Where would a science of geography be if every attempt to map the relation of North America to Europe and the Atlantic Ocean had to recount Columbus's voyage? From the scientific point of view, narrative is a mere precursor. Philosophy, like science, is descriptive, and though postmodern philosophy has liked to say that all reality is narrative, it has yet to find a narrative way of saying it, avoiding the self-refutation of "All truth is narrative truth." Yet there is certainly a point at which narrative goes beyond description, and philosophy may at least gesture towards it. If description is an art that elicits form from event, narrative, too, may be an art, eliciting sequences from forms. The scientist who draws a theory out of experimental reports is answered by the novelist, who deploys typical situations to bring an individual character to our imaginations, with all the marks of concrete uniqueness that we commonly recognize in one another.

When we talk about just one aspect of reality at a time, which we do most of the time, philosophers call it "reduction"; both narrative and description are "reductions" in that sense. To achieve description we abstract from the contingency of temporal events, to achieve narrative we abstract from the regularity of laws and forms. Both reductions are open to more or less skillful execution, but neither can be successful if it pushes its claims so far as to exclude its opposite. The pure narrative which "recounts" and does not "explain" cannot exist in reality; it is merely a polar point in relation to the magnetic field of explanatory meaning. Narrative, to *be* narrative, has to be *about* something; it must assume some typical behavior or states of things for which it takes no responsibility. When it starts out, "there was a woodcutter who lived in a forest with his only daughter," we are supposed to know about woodcutters, forests and daughters already. (And when it starts out "'Twas brillig, and the slithy tove did gyre and gimble in the wabe . . ." it is just a joke played on us by the separation of narrative literary forms from all known descriptive reference points.[8] We should not take it as a model narrative.) Theoretical description, correspondingly, presumes on actual or possible experiences, and on observations that provide it with sufficient evidence; the joke about medieval arguments over how many angels could dance on the head of a pin was an always pertinent warning against wholly unanchored theory.

Narrative and description, then, are disciplines of thinking. Are they also disciplines of linguistic use and of written form? Trivially, it is clear

---

8. Lewis Carroll, of course: "Jabberwocky" from *Through the Looking-Glass*.

that to be disciplined at the one level requires discipline at the other. If narrative is to be communicated in writing or speech, the appropriate literary and linguistic forms are needed to signal it. And there are literary forms (the "story") and linguistic forms (the statement in the historic past tense) that suggest narrative, while there are others (the theorem, the statement in the present tense) that suggest description. But literary and linguistic forms are both very various, and resist being marshalled into two columns, one for narrative, the other for description. Open a school textbook intended to introduce students to the elements of a foreign language, and you will be introduced to characters with names like Geert and Lise, who have experiences recounted in the simplest narrative style. Yet the function of the literary genre, "textbook," is not narrative but descriptive, to communicate the grammar, vocabulary and syntax of a language. And its narrative style, though simple, will accommodate all the usual linguistic forms: questions, exclamations, commands, etc., not only statements. Open a novel, which has a narrative function, and the same variety will appear: depending on its period, you may find letters, poems, interior monologues, even shopping lists, with all the linguistic constructions that these require. Failure to distinguish levels of communicative structure has encouraged a good deal of nonsense. The word "story" (transplanted from English into other European languages and acquiring curiously exotic overtones in the process) has been used to accomplish the wildest slides from discussion of literary genres to discussion of deep communicative functions.

To recall events in good order, on the one hand, and to discern what things are what, on the other, are both fundamental disciplines without which we could not think straight. Experiences of past happenings do not present themselves to our minds in ready-ordered sequences, while experiences of form do not come duly sorted out into substantial and relational categories. Both kinds of experience need critical sifting before they are ready to be cast into communicative speech. A memory may "haunt" us, disturbing our awareness of the world by looming up in dissociation from the temporal sequence that gave it a place in our present consciousness. An observation, on the other hand, can mislead us, not because we have not observed correctly but because we have drawn the wrong inferences. Reflective communication of reality, then, is a task with two sides to it: to bring remembered pasts together into ordered history, and to bring scattered observations together into ordered *theōria*.

To do either effectively involves doing both. Yet we may start from either pole. We narrate a story, beginning from the contingency of recollected events and searching for the principles that govern their necessity, positing world-time in order to situate proven recollections in sequential order. To test the validity of our recollections we draw on what we know of natural regularities, not letting them impose a veto on narrative testimony, but merely providing the structured context to make it intelligible. (Did Jesus rise from the dead? We know that people generally don't, which does not tell us that *he* did not, but does tell us that if he did, it was an event of such importance that other events and sequences of events must ultimately derive their meaning from it.) We describe reality, starting from the other end with appearances of *necessary implication*, evident rational intuitions of the form that φ entails ψ, and proceeding to look for their instantiations in time, calling on historical records of observations and attestations—not, again, to allow the narratives a veto on what may and may not possibly happen, but using them to refine our grasp of implication. (Do all revolutions arise from pauperized masses? It looks likely, but there are historical cases that should incline us to look for a hypothesis with more complexity.) The past is then used as a repository of recollections that clarify the patterns we think we observe; the anomalies of historical testimony (like the cows with two heads in Livy) we throw back into the ocean of abandoned memories.

As I once heard the adjudicator of an Irish folksong competition say, "Time is as important in singing as it is in music." Music could not survive the expulsion of tone by time or of time by tone; the two must wrestle like Jacob and the angel until the final cadence. It is not a bad illustration of the struggle of narrative and description. The function of narrative in integrating the truth of the world into the records of time is balanced by the role of description (theological, philosophical, psychological etc.) in displaying events as a testimony to the eternal truths of God's dealings. As narrative frames the atemporal discourses of philosophy and law, so it is itself structured from within by the descriptive truths they communicate. Stable categories make the art of narrative possible, defining the events and assigning them their moral significance. The meaning of our world emerges simultaneously in a narratable sequence and a stable recurrent order. Each opens up new dimensions of the other; each tests and vindicates the right of the other.

Theology, Ethics, and Narrative

That our communications include much more than we actually tell one another is not something to surprise any theologian who has wrestled with the concept of revelation. Revelation is not proposition only, but presence. In accounting for the importance of their propositions the apostles referred to "what we have seen and heard, what our hands have touched" (1 John 1:1). The creed is not for the creed's sake alone, but for the sake of the presence it opens us to. Yet theology as a reflective discipline is committed to bringing the acts of God in history to communicable meaning. As we follow the history of Israelite prophecy, beginning with groups of wandering dervishes that fall into ecstasies at the sound of musical instruments, turning into representational mime with brief oral commentary, and finally becoming totally dependent on linguistic forms and assuming a pioneering role in the development of the written book, it is irresistibly brought home to us that the drama of God's encounter with his human creatures is the drama of the uttered word, spoken and written.

In recent years theologians have made much of the deep narrative function in Christian talk about God. Jewish theology grounded on the Exodus, Christian Theology grounded on the life, death, and resurrection of Christ, have to do with the acts of God in history. In theology, therefore, we are bidden to recognize a definite priority of narrative thought over description, "to read," as Gerhard Sauter puts it, "biblical texts—not only stories but also prayers, advice, visions, wisdom-literature, letters—as parts of an overarching *hidden* story."[9] Reacting against neo-scholastic ontotheology on the one side and universalist humanism on the other, late modern Western theology has tended to see narrative as its special line, and the proclamation of event as its primary communication. God has redeemed the world he made and drawn rebel mankind to himself in his Son; all else—philosophy, doctrine, moral exhortation, prediction—comes second to that. So far, so good. As it stands, that does not disturb the claim we have made for a complementarity of narrative and descriptive functions. It simply identifies a narrated event at the center of salvation history as the definitive moment for Christian proclamation. It does not, and it could not, confine Christian communication to narrative, for narrative can never be separated effectively from description. If the proclamation is to be understood and received, its implications for the understanding of world, human life, and action must still be accounted for non-narratively.

It is at this point that the issue over "narrative theology" has been joined in relation to claims for the *continuing* sufficiency of narrative communi-

---

9. Gerhard Sauter, *Protestant Theology at the Crossroads* (Grand Rapids: Eerdmans, 2007), p. 40.

cation. If consciousness of God must take a primarily narrative form, it is argued, so must our consciousness of ourselves. To complete the quotation from Sauter, "To read biblical texts—not only stories but also prayers, advice, visions, wisdom-literature, letters—as parts of an overarching *hidden* story provides the surprise that we find ourselves being read in the story. This is one of the advantages of a sound *narrative theology*." Not only narrative proclamation at the source of theology, then, but narrative *ethics* and narrative *doctrine*. A communication that begins in narrative must be carried through in narrative. That proposal constitutes the theological narrativism of our day.[10]

The program may be more or less radically construed. It does not necessarily go hand in hand with the claim that the *literary form* of Theology and Ethics must be narrative. (It is almost unheard of, in fact, that narrative theologians write narratives, nor should they be expected to, if they are willing to distinguish a primary narrative communication within the church from a secondary intellectual interpretation among the scholars.) Nor does it always go hand in hand with the claim for a predominance of narrative among the *literary forms of Scripture*, though that claim sometimes seems to be implied. The literary forms of Holy Scripture are very varied; a good deal of narrative, both in the Hebrew Scriptures and the New Testament, but a good deal else besides. The rabbis who divided the Hebrew Scriptures into law, prophets and writings (i.e., "creative" writings, as in poetry), found no use for a category of story at all. The tendency of the narrativist claim is to favor a canon within the canon: the Synoptic Gospels, perhaps, or even just the parables of Jesus, which come closer than anything else in Scripture to the ideal of a perfectly pure narrative with no explanations or theories attached. But that suggestion ought to raise an alarm. If the story of God's deeds is "hidden" in scriptural prayers, advice, visions, wisdom literature, letters, etc., might that not, after all, be because those other forms of communication are more effective in allowing certain aspects of the story to

---

10. It should be mentioned *en passant* that we do not find the proposal in this form in the celebrated article of Stanley Hauerwas which more than forty years ago set a generation of Ethics students off in pursuit of a narrative ethic. For all its wider suggestiveness, "The Self as Story" came down clearly, and in my view correctly, in support of a complementarist account of narrative and prescription. See *Vision and Virtue* (Notre Dame: Fides, 1974), p. 89: "Even though moral principles are not sufficient for our moral existence, neither are stories sufficient if they do not generate principles that are morally significant. Stories without principles will have no way of concretely specifying actions and practices consistent with the moral orientation of the story."

make their impact? The notion that we could get behind scriptural prayers, advice, commands, breaking through to the narrative that each of them has concealed, is a bizarre one. Though sometimes apparently implied in some exercises of biblical commentary (as when a law is glossed with the explanation, "the aim of the Deuteronomic program at this point was to achieve a centralization of the cult"), it has nothing to be said for it theologically. We may reasonably say that while it can be a valuable corrective to speculative ontotheology or humanist reflection to stress the role of narrative forms in Scripture, as Hans Frei did memorably in the case of Christology, that does not entitle us to suppress the force of other literary forms. There may be a danger in narrativism of speaking so constantly of the event that we lose sight of what the event is about, which is to say, what it means to predicate historical action *of God*.[11] When we read in Genesis 18 of three men who arrived at Abraham's tent, accepted an invitation to a meal, and then began to speak in the first person singular of what Yhwh planned—Sarah would have a child, Abraham would be the father of nations, Sodom would be destroyed, etc.—any appreciation of that narrative must depend on something *else* we have been told, and told *non-narratively*, about Yhwh, his covenant, his righteousness, and so on.

The proposal that moral reasoning or teaching, or reflective Ethics itself, will most fittingly understand its task as a narrative one, raises yet more basic problems. It is typically approached by way of the suggestion we find in Sauter, that hearers and readers of a narrative may find themselves "read in the story." What can be meant by this phrase, and others like it? Sometimes it is simply that we may understand the bearing of the story on how we live our lives. "If you have been raised with Christ, seek the things that are above" (Col. 3:1). That is a paradigm of theological ethical reasoning, a narrative moment leading on to the prescription of a new moral orientation. But in a great deal that sees itself as "narrative ethics" something more than this is intended, the suggestion that the life I now lead can be construed as *an extension* of the same story, so that I live, as it were, by continual narration. A strange dictum from Walter Benjamin's essay on storytelling captures the idea: "The storyteller is the form in which the righteous man encounters himself."[12]

---

11. On this point the legacy of the late John Webster is eloquent. See, for example, "'Omnia pertractantur in sacra doctrina sub ratione Dei': On the Matter of Christian Theology," in *God without Measure 1: God and the Works of God* (London and New York: Bloomsbury T&T Clark, 2015), pp. 1–10.

12. Quoted from Benjamin, *Illuminationen* (Frankfurt am Main: Suhrkamp, 1977),

To "read myself" in a narrative where I am not mentioned would be to suffer a delusion. Those who are so affected by *The Lord of the Rings* that they dress up as hobbits, or by *Werther* that they commit suicide, are pathological readers in a false relation to the narrative. Narrative is about *those* events, not *these*, those characters (real or fictional) and not ourselves. Narrative is about the past (recalled or imagined), not about the present or the future. Narrative, when cast in the literary form of a story, is brought to a conclusion. Those are its formal constraints. To be sure, artful storytellers (and biblical narrators are no less artful than others) like to "transgress" formal constraints by caesura, inconclusive transitions, historic presents, echoes of realities from outside the story, and so on. In a novel about sixteenth-century England a character is allowed to use a phrase that became politically notorious in 1980s Britain. The anachronism makes a point, but *not* by drawing the reader into the story, but rather by pulling the reader out of it, allowing a moment of distance three hundred and fifty years after the fictional date to compare the one story with another. In a skillful narrative the reader is kept always at a proximate distance, not wholly remote from events but not part of them, either. The narrative, correspondingly, is kept at a proximate distance from the reader's self-consciousness, affecting it, but not taking it over.

There is, of course, one story genre that comes nearer than others to including the reader in the story. We call it the "parable." The parable is not the only meaningful narrative, nor necessarily the *most* meaningful, but it is supremely useful as a device of moral teaching since it places the reader in life situations where he or she may encounter him or herself. Moral teaching has to do with moral order, and so inevitably involves other forms of communication, both descriptive and prescriptive, and yet it may take form as a narrative that captures some aspect of moral order in a typical way. But there is a price to pay for the moral relevance of the parable: the closer the narrative draws to the reader, the less occupied it becomes with the particularity of the story as such, the more with the relations it mirrors, relations obtaining always and for everyone. It loses the historical concreteness which narrative may otherwise achieve. Not all narrative with moral significance is parable. The narrative of the ministry of Jesus is not; the narratives of the resurrection and of the descent of the Spirit at Pentecost are not. I may be morally affected by these narratives, as

---

p. 410, by Hans Ulrich, in "Wie Geschöpfe leben: Zur narrativen Exploration im geschöpflichen Leben. Aspekte einer Ethik des Erzählens," in *Ethik und Erzählung: Theologische und philosophische Beiträge zur narrativen Ethik*, ed. M. Hofheinz, F. Mathwig, and M. Zeindler (Zürich: TVZ, 2009), p. 320.

I am affected by the parable of the prodigal son, but where I can see *myself* as the prodigal, his father, or his elder brother (which is what the parable meant to help me do), I can only very restrictedly see myself as Jesus, Mary Magdalene, or the apostle Peter. Perhaps my situation is like that of Mary here, or like that of Peter there, and I may learn from their actions and reactions something to help me shape my own. But Mary and Peter, unlike the prodigal and his father, are not exhaustively accounted for by whatever moral situations they may have in common with me. They were who they were. I must take what I have learned from them, and turn back enriched by it to my own situation in the world.

We should be very cautious, then, of the language of "continuing" a story which, in the New Testament, has been brought to a decisive conclusion by the ascension of Jesus into heaven, the arrival of the Gospel in Rome, and the pointed declaration of John the Seer that there is no scope for further visions. Storytelling as a form of meaning-giving must reach a close. It has beginnings and endings, not merely in the events of which it speaks but in the opening and shutting of the storyteller's mouth. We cannot prolong our tale forever. The storyteller, as contemporary philosophers of the "opaque self" insist, cannot simply *be part* of the story told, not even if that story tells of his or her own experiences. "The one story that the 'I' cannot tell is the story of its own emergence as an 'I' who not only speaks but comes to give an account of itself."[13] A story is just one communication of narrative meaning, and narrative is just one form of the communication of meaning. The category suffers an aneurysm if it is made to cover all functions and forms of communicated meaning. Then we end up reading of "stories" which have no events in them, a drearier entertainment by far, one might think, than the books Alice complained of for having no pictures and no conversations!

On the other hand, the task of acting and living, both in general and in any particular moment, is one that needs careful *description*, which cannot be replaced by storytelling. The world we must live and act in is a world delivered over to us (to ourselves, that is, who ask about it) at a certain moment, a "now" where we have to understand it. When we have learned to see it as won for us by the redemptive act of God in the past, we face questions about its future horizon. And when we have learned to hope that the promise of the Kingdom of God will illuminate that horizon for us, it still remains *our* now, with its own past and future horizons. We must learn to give an account of it. We are not Israelite nomad conquerors or Greek sophists or Galilean fishermen. We are

---

13. Judith Butler, *Giving an Account of Oneself* (New York: Fordham University Press, 2005), p. 66.

Christian disciples who, by virtue of a narrative and a promise given us, can frame our engagement with our present moral challenges by a "formerly" and a "hereafter." The Gospel narrative instructs us as we seek to act not by including our "now" in its narrative, but by casting light on the achieved realities that opened the way for our "now" to arise in history. If we allow ourselves to forget the narrative and the promise, we may quickly take our "now" for an absolute, subjecting all things past, present, and future to its perspectives; but if we allow the narrative to block out the present of action, we become enthusiasts (in the bad sense), who do not know how to look around us.

And yet it may be replied that the story of God's action in history is not, in a final sense, closed. It is a story of the redemption of the universe, and the universe is finally redeemed only at "the" end. If the particular story of Jesus and his disciples is closed, that is only in order that a further and longer phase in the larger story may be opened to our view and our participation. Why, then, should the reader's present life and actions, and those of the present-day community of faith, not be told as the logical sequel, a continuation of the story which, its crisis passed, is now confidently heading towards its foreordained completion? At which point many theologians have been attracted by a dramaturgical analogy.[14] Drama seems to allow the combination of a conclusive narrative destiny prescribed by the dramatist, on the one hand, with human performance on the other. Even while the characters are negotiating the pitfalls of Act Three before our eyes, we know that the great reconciliation of Act Five is waiting to be given us. But does this analogy allow enough for the freedom and responsibility of action? In order to enable it to do so, recourse is often had to the model of dramatic improvisation.

---

14. Hans Urs von Balthasar's great *Theodrama* must take credit for the ecumenical reach of this model. Yet its advocates are aware of adding a new element to his conception. So Kevin Vanhoozer, at the opening of his ambitious and rewarding exposition of doctrinal theology on this model, *The Drama of Doctrine* (Louisville: Westminster John Knox Press, 2005), claims to focus "not simply on the dramatic nature of the content of Christian doctrine, but on the dramatic nature of Christian doctrine itself" (p. 18). The analogy allows Vanhoozer two further steps, which he treats as one: (i) a dramatic process of biblical interpretation in doctrine; (ii) a dramatic character to the Christian life as a whole, for "the proper end of the drama of doctrine is wisdom: lived knowledge, a performance of the truth" (p. 21). The Bible is to be viewed as "a script that calls for faithful yet creative performance" (p. 22), while the church is a "theater of the Gospel," in which the gospel is rendered public by leading lives in creative imitation of Christ (pp. 32–33). We should not object to the characterization of the hermeneutic task as practical. But it is a different matter to subsume all practical reason under hermeneutics. Practice is not exclusively a communication of meaning, and to represent it as such is to impose the gravest constraints on freedom and responsibility in action.

The Communication of Meaning

The first reply to this must be that the authorial indications—the dialogue, the stage directions etc., which constitute this text as a story to be played by actors—may present a narrative *to the audience*, but *to the actors* they are prescriptions as to how they should fulfill their task. When we went to the theater all those years ago and saw Robert Bolt's *A Man for All Seasons*, we saw Paul Scofield "play" Thomas More. That meant that whenever Bolt wrote "Enter More," Scofield stepped onto the stage, and whenever lines were assigned to More, Scofield spoke them. In so doing Scofield obeyed Bolt's directions; nothing determined his entry at this or that moment other than the requirements of the script and his engagement to perform it. That engagement did not in any way detract from Paul Scofield's freedom. He had to get himself to the theater each night, put on the make-up and the costume, and perform. Moreover, obedient performance allowed him a great deal of creative discretion: the gestures, the inflections of his voice, the timing all earned him his reputation as a towering "interpreter" of the part, capable of grasping imaginatively what the author's written instructions intended to make possible. Had Bolt written his play in *avant-gardiste* style, Scofield might also have had to "improvise" lines of his own, but that would have made no difference in principle, for these, too, would simply have been interpretations of the author's intentions.

So much for Scofield; but what of Thomas More—the dramatic character, that is, leaving correspondence to the historical More aside? When Bolt wrote "Enter More," More did not step onstage in the theater, but stepped into the hall of his house at Chelsea; he did not obey Robert Bolt, but Henry VIII (not, alas, to that arbitrary monarch's satisfaction). More had no free engagement with the dramatist and producer, but was their *presentation*. His performance was not that of a free agent, simply what the dramatist and players conspired to make it. He had no room for interpretation or improvisation. Yet the drama played was More's drama, and the destiny More's destiny, not that of Paul Scofield, who would never clash with the king and never die by the headsman's axe. Here, then, there is a dysfunction in the dramaturgical analogy, and to my mind it is quite fatal. For as an analogue to our agency it offers *indistinguishably* the performances of Thomas More and Paul Scofield. We are supposed to be *at once* the character destined by the dramatic narrative *and* the actor who is free to improvise on the author's directions. It takes two to make a dramatic representation, actor and character; the freedom is the actor's, the narrative destiny the character's. One cannot play oneself—not, that is, oneself as the free agent one presently is.

There are, of course, reflective as well as prospective perspectives on the life we lead. We may reflectively imagine salvation history as a narrative drama in five acts and we may imagine our situation within that drama. That perspective may continue to orient us when we turn prospectively to face the tasks of living. But we cannot deliberate on and recognize our present tasks reflectively, only prospectively. To believe that there is a story (in God's mind) that will include the life I am now leading is one thing; to undertake to perform that story is quite another. I can only pray for it to be formed around faithful action. The guidance we need for that is prescriptive, validated explicitly or implicitly on the basis of descriptive, rather than narrative, meaning. The danger of our seeing future decisions and actions as a script to be played is that the lives we have to live, the decisions we have to make are viewed as though they were lived and made already—shirking the responsibility for living and making them, like Macbeth.[15] And "interpretation," rather than "improvisation" is the category we need to describe how we apply our minds to the guidance we receive. "Improvisation" suggests a *lacuna* in the guidance, a space left bare to allow the performer to take over from the dramatist. But the interpretative relation between the text and its performer is constant. And that is why the collapse of the analogy is, in the end, harmless. It was trying to solve the old problem of how we may act within the embracing whole of God's action, but on the false assumption that God's freedom of action necessarily excludes ours. The "God of the gaps" has as its corollary an "agency of the gaps," which can only be realized in a vacancy of other agencies.

Neither narrative nor description has any direct reach into the future—that is the point to which we must come back. Here it is Augustine who witnesses to one aspect of the opacity of the self, namely, that the self's privileged self-access vanishes into thin air when it turns to confront its future in action: "no one is so known to another as each person is known to himself, and yet no one is so known to himself as to be sure of his conduct tomorrow."[16] The communication of meaning is a cognitive communication of reality, and there is no reality of the future that is open to direct cognition. From the moment prophecy appeared in Israel, it was contested. And prophecy today, of which there is a very great deal, remains contested. That is simply a reflection of the fragmentary epistemic access which we have to the future: not one future, but many, some ontologically weighty, some weightless, some near, some far, some subjective, some objective, and the discipline we have to learn is to measure these many anticipated futures, deciding

---

15. See *Finding and Seeking*, p. 156.
16. Augustine, *Epistula* 130.2.4: "*Nam sicut sibi quisque nemo alter alteri notus est, et tamen nec sibi quisque ita notus est ut sit de sua crastina conversatione securus.*"

which we should attend to. When we think about the future, as we necessarily do in the exercise of practical reason, we think about it indirectly; it is reflected off descriptions of present realities and narrative accounts of past realities. The two forms in which we achieve quasi-knowledge of the future, as we described them in *Finding and Seeking*, are anticipation and hope.[17] Knowledge by anticipation is a projection from the careful description of present regularities; hope bases itself on the promise which the narrative of saving history communicates to us. What together they show us is enough to evoke considerate and faithful action. If the default position of the modern imagination is to think of the future as history in a mirror image, a narrative for which the evidence is yet to be gathered, just like the past except that we have not heard the news yet, practical reason needs no future narrative. It needs good enough understanding of constant regularities to predict the relation of an act to its end of action. It needs a word of promise sufficient to identify a last end of human endeavor as a reality and not a chimerical ideal. A famous passage in the Deuteronomic law code (18:18–22) declares that the only possible test of prophecy is its fulfillment. In order to be fully validated, a prophecy must have ceased to be a prophecy and become a narrative, the prophesied events having transpired and become past. Which is not to undermine prophecy, but to insist on the continuity of prophecy with law and covenant-history as the basis for the claims it makes on our trust. The true prophet, in speaking of the future, will always speak "like Moses," out of the past of God's deeds and the present of God's law.

The Wrongs of Falsehood

In communicating "reality" in its double aspect of happening and conditions, do we communicate "truth"? No, for we communicate a reference to the truth, and truth is not a reality, but the condition for any reality. The truth cannot be an object of communication, because the truth cannot be represented. The transcendence of truth over fact is suggested by the theological assertion that the truth is personal—"I am . . . the truth, the life"—the source of our true communications, not the object of them. The truth we may ask about in our own communications is a quality internal to them, a success they may have in representing reality communally. The thing we communicate is this or that; the truth with which we communicate it is the aptness

---

17. *Finding and Seeking*, pp. 145–66.

of our speech or writing to represent this or that to others. To the extent that we are incapable of communicating truly, we fail to communicate, even if the syntactical forms of our language are unimpaired; and to the extent that we fail to communicate, we fail to engage in and renew community. For creatures endowed with speech can know no level of community that is not formed by communications of truth. We may say that truth is the criterion distinguishing what is "well meant" from what is "ill meant." But those phrases commonly have a different sense, suggesting not truth but benevolence and malevolence; hence the need for quotation marks. And on that difference hangs the great question of falsehood: can benevolence and malevolence be effective independently of truth?

There is a fundamental theological proposition to begin from: God who is life, and therefore love, is also truth. And there is a second proposition to follow: the saving destiny to which humankind is called is nothing other than participation in the unity of truth and love. "Joy in the truth," *gaudium de veritate*, is the existential determination of our human community.[18] Presence alone cannot create human community. Presence may have many moods, threatening, bewildering, oppressive, and undermining as well as strengthening and enlightening. Presence can realize human community only through the sharing of meaning. There can be no holding common without some thing to be held in common, a something that is not communicated illusorily, but in truth, able to be relied on as only reality can be.[19]

That foundational link between community and truth is also fundamental, then, for what must be said about lying. From one angle, lying is *the* offence, embodying all offences. Lying was the sin of the serpent in Eden, and the Devil is called the "father of lies." If there appears to be a dissonance between claiming this foundational status for lying and claiming the sovereignty in human action for love, that appearance comes merely from the confusion of protology with eschatology. The lie that opens the door to sin does so as the original expression of hatred; the love that puts an end to sin is essentially cognitive, recognizing the human brother and sister as a partner

---

18. The celebrated phrase is from Augustine, *Confessions* 10.23.33.

19. Cf. Jean-Yves Lacoste, *Recherches sur la Parole* (Louvain: Peeters, 2015), pp. 151–52: "Nous ne pouvons comprendre le mode d'être de l'étant que nous sommes sans apercevoir que nous sommes voués, non pas à utiliser le langage en général, mais à l'utiliser pour dire le vrai. . . . Autrui a droit à ma sollicitude. Il a droit à celle-ci sous une forme 'authentique', qui est la bienveillance. Ipso facto il a droit à ce que je lui dise la vérité, dans la mesure où j'en suis capable. Et ce droit répond à un besoin: s'il faut dire la vérité, c'est parce qu'autrui en manque, de même qu'il faut nourrir l'affamé parce qu'il manque de nourriture."

in meaningful communication. All the meals and nursing care we need, with never a word of truth, is a denial of partnership in the human world, and thus a proud refusal of love. It is what people find archetypally frightening in the way they imagine care-homes for the elderly. Truth-telling, on the other hand, as we have said, is not simply a function of a true statement or proposition, but an interpersonal act directed towards somebody, a venture upon the capacity of the other to enter a partnership of shared understanding. This creates a series of complexities.

(i) There is no direct correlation between the truth *of a statement* and the communication of truth which makes use of that statement. On the one hand falsities in statements may be quite accidental and unimportant, mere matters of "precision," in the context of a real attempt to convey the truth to another. "You will feel so much better!" we say to a loved one before a difficult medical or surgical procedure. There is good reason to hope so, of course, but the statement necessarily over-simplifies. What of the likely side effects, or possible complications? It is reasonable to answer that the time for mentioning those is not now, when their frightening possibilities might crowd out the more important aspect of the question. On the other hand the truest statement in the world may convey, in some contexts, a *suggestio falsi*. The skilled liar, as we learn from spy fiction, tells as much truth as he can, to launch his deception floating on the sea of likelihood and plausibility.

(ii) Still in the realm of matching speech with reception, we add that the *linguistic means* by which truth is communicated are enormously various. Fiction, poetic imagery, philosophical paradox, joking, all are communicative language forms. Silence itself, in certain contexts, is truthful utterance. Truth-telling is not confined to the factual statement, and departing from the canons of factual truth may not even be a *prima facie* wrong of communicated meaning. Yet the variety of communicative means which creates a constant possibility of miscommunication—the joke not received as such, the silence misinterpreted—creates a sphere of ambiguity which may be used as a protection against the often terrifying burden of communication. The flippant person who turns each observation into a joke is over-weighted with the burden of speaking truth, and seeks refuge in the ambiguities of wit to evade responsibility.

(iii) Since truth-telling is an act, its success must be measured by its *circumstantial reference* to its life-context, not only by the immediate content of what it said. Communication of meaning is an undertaking with fitting occasions and forms. We are not bound to communicate everything to everybody all the time, nor could we imagine doing so, for though truth is the nourishment of human community, our appetite for it is quickly sated; giving and receiving it is hard work, and it exhausts us. To direct meanings successfully to their recipients we must sometimes *not* express them, must even withhold them when a communication is demanded inopportunely. We share a personal secret to cement a particular friendship; if anyone is to have the power of using personal secrets in this way, we must all learn not to confide secrets to everybody all the time. Withholding truths where the demand for truth is "impertinent," as we say, or is made by someone apparently incapable of receiving it well, is not even a *prima facie* wrong of false meaning. Yet the *disciplina arcani*, however justified in principle, can be misjudged. Over-concerned about the right moment and manner of approach, we may fail to share what we know, even when our hearer has a real interest in knowing it. Alternatively, the patient attentiveness required for reception of the truth may be lacking. Ill-judged expectations and misinterpretation of the rhythms of speech and silence can lead to false conclusions. The framing of communication may be misunderstood, the hearer's assumptions or the social context working to block off the meaning intended. Failures to receive, as well as failures to give communications, are failures of truth.

(iv) We must go on to observe that "truth" is *not simply an assembling of truths*. The pursuit and communication of truth involves the discernment of relationships of truth statements of major and minor importance. We may be too easily content with communicating fragments that seem to offer a point of rest, rather than allowing ourselves to develop a description of the form of the truth. The platitude and the truism are thus substitutes for a truth pursued carefully and articulately; they are bite-sized fragments of truth which, shorn of their dialectical connections and logical implications, can create no more than an illusion of truth. "John behaved badly"; "John responded badly to severe provocation"; "John failed to anticipate the strength of feeling in the opposition and how it would provoke him," etc., etc. Each may be true in its turn, but the first statement leaves a question to be answered by the second, the second a question to be answered by the third, and so on.

(v) What I communicate may simply be false, not because I intend it to be so but because *I am ignorant*. As we have had occasion to see already in *Self, World, and Time*, the notion of a pure and innocent ignorance is a notion of a trivial ignorance. At a certain level of gravity to speak in ignorance, not about the time of the next train but about the time for repentance or the permissibility of breaking one's word, is as such a moral failure. We need to know what we need to know. Perhaps the most common case of culpable misstatement is where we have a vague idea of something that may be true, but have not troubled to clarify it. We don't know what we are talking about—which is different from *sheer* ignorance. To grasp the truth in a form fit for communication may require hard struggle, and we may fail with the best intentions if the right language is not at our disposal or if we have not formed a sufficiently wide view of the matter. Experiences are given in succession, dialectically, complementing, succeeding, challenging one another for possession of our minds and control of our understandings. Are they men coming down upon the city from the mountains, or merely shadows cast by the mountains in the early morning light (cf. Judg. 9:36)? To grasp a truth worth communicating involves a synthesis of experiences, and we may often feel the compulsion to speak before the work of synthesis is adequately done.

(vi) Reticence, error, thoughtlessness, incomprehension enter into our communications to confuse and frustrate them at every point. These failures of truth must be taken into consideration before we can grapple with the paradigm case of *falsification* of the truth, the deliberate lie. That I can solemnly assure someone of something I know not to be the case looks like absolute arbitrariness, a simple abandonment of practical rationality on my part, for which it may seem that no account whatever can be given. That strategies of deception can be rational, and lies in their service tactical, is possible only because the context of ambiguity and misunderstanding is so pervasive that it seems to establish the possibility of an alternative reality. Lying can be a response to failed communications as well as a cause of them. To stop a disagreement in its tracks or prevent a quarrel, I say something I do not believe, simply because the other party won't be quiet until I say it. Lying is, to be sure, a new departure, a special case of false-speaking. It is reflective, as other failures of truth-telling are not. The unfitness of humanity to hear the truth, in general or in particular, prompts us to try to control the situation with a parade of truthful communication that seeks to neutralize the difficulty of truth ill-received, because illusion seems to be the only "truth" that will actually fit the situation.

It is possible to try to absorb this special case within the paradigm of the more familiar cases. So Plato doubted that falsehood in speech was vicious apart from falsehood "in the soul," i.e., the mind, which is to say that the ultimate diagnosis of the intentional untruth must be exceptional moral blindness. But that does not explain how very *easy* it is for us to lie—and not only for those whose souls are obviously blind, but for those whose general moral principles favor candor. Those of us who would never steal by inadvertence or commit rape by inadvertence will often tell falsehoods by inadvertence, knowing that what we say is not the truth but not *attending* to the falsehood as a serious consideration until, in retrospect, we have the opportunity to reevaluate it and perhaps repent of it. Children lie without being taught, and have to be taught to tell the truth. We may be right to see this as an evidence (more potent than anything in the sexual realm!) of mankind's generic sinfulness. But that is to treat the lie not as one particularly grave sin among others, but as an archetype of sin, a special clue to the ways in which communications of true meaning are socially perverted, their failures built into the way in which society constructs itself. Augustine ventured an original interpretation of the lie as duplicity, which is to say, a double mind, a mind occupied with two distinct and conflicting meanings: what the truth of the matter is as I tell it to myself, and what I intend the hearer to accept as the truth.[20] That these two aspects of meaning have fallen apart is the essential phenomenology of the lie. However much nonsense I talk, what I usually want (i.e., when I am not lying) is for my hearers to believe what I believe. The lie is the revelation of an underlying tension, a splitting apart between the dynamics of action and communication which reflects the divided soul within.

I relate to my hearer in more than one way, as to a partner in communication within a community of meanings, and as to a project of action, an object to be maneuvered and manipulated through control of his or her beliefs. At one level I offer communication, at another I withhold it. I *can* tell the truth; if I could not, I could certainly not lie. Yet in these particular circumstances I *cannot* tell the truth—to the satisfaction of my practical ambitions, at least. The result of attempting to tell it, it seems to me, will be a miscommunication of disastrous proportions. What is it, then, that apparently prevents my doing what at another level I apparently can do? The prevailing structure of communications, which makes it *seem* impossible that *this* truth should be communicated to *this* person. But that perception is not evident to the one who is expecting the truth from me. In some professional contexts the excuse "I am not at liberty to tell you that" is readily understood and accepted, but in most life settings such professional protections are not in service. The capacity of society to group and regroup its communications around successive undertakings puts us in a position to say "Yes" and "No" at the same time to someone who thinks we are in a community of truth with him. We *are* in community, or we *have been* in

---

20. On the distinctiveness of Augustine's conception see Paul J. Griffiths, *Lying: An Augustinian Theology of Duplicity* (Grand Rapids: Brazos, 2004).

community with him, but other communities may now have claimed us. Or he or she may have entered a community with some third party, modifying the possibilities of the two of us being confidential with each other. Was Zebul allied with Gaal or Abimelech? First with Gaal, then with Abimelech; it was the moment of political transition that made him a lying counselor to Gaal. There is a meaning I communicate with the one I deceive; there is a meaning I have entertained in my mind *about* the one I deceive, which has caused me to withdraw my confidence and become a deceiver. Not first communicating, then withdrawing, but communicating and withdrawing at the same time, making the communication serve the act of withdrawal—that is the dynamic of duplicitous communication. Is it, as such, betrayal? Or can we envisage duplicity as sometimes valid, even necessary to the service of communication overall?

Augustine's early exploration of the question produced one of the most creative, and at the same time most confusing works of his youth, the *De Mendacio*, which turns around two dialectically related propositions: first, that communication of true meaning is itself a supreme good, a service of love, not merely an instrument to secure other goods; and second, that speech, as an action, must be ordered to serve the whole range of goods that moral reflection can learn to value. Those who say that we must frame our speech to promote real goods and avert real evils are not wrong to say so, he thinks. (There is a major sub-plot to this discussion, namely, his prolonged attempt to persuade his contemporaries that to be the victim of rape—something that might befall either men or women in his violent times—is not a real degradation, such as could justify whatever we might need to do or say to avert it.) On the other hand, those who say that it is never a sin to refuse to tell a lie are not wrong to say so—though he is well aware that it can sometimes be a sin to tell the truth—inopportunely, or with hostile intent. This leaves him with a carefully constructed gradation of lies from the most excusable to the most inexcusable, the gravity relating to the content of the falsified communication. Just as truthful speech has everything to do with the truthful assessment of what is *most* important to communicate, so the malice of lying has everything to do with a failure to comprehend the order of communicative values. Scripture, Augustine concludes, condemns all lying, but it does not condemn all lies equally. Ultimate reality must never be denied, so that the lie in religion is the most wholly detestable. Lies designed to avert the wicked from their wickedness are the most pardonable. We need not suffer too terrible a self-reproach in misleading the would-be rapist about his victim's whereabouts or telling the compulsive drinker that the bars are closed. Yet if we *can* find a way of gaining the point by evasion, is it not better? Moreover—and here Augustine draws his *ne plus ultra*—God's invitation to all mankind to enter a community of truth is so fundamental to our relations as human beings, that to place it above other considerations and to refuse to lie irrespective of what may be lost by refusing, is such a witness to the transcendent unity of truth and love, that though we may understand, and perhaps condone, a decision to lie in difficult circumstances, we can never impugn a decision *not* to tell a lie.

It is a curious conclusion, not wholly typical of Augustine's other treatments of sin. It caused him some discomfort when he reread it later in life, and yet he resisted his initial impulse to suppress the work, since behind the strange schema of more and less tolerable lies there is a wide-ranging perception of social constraints on true speech. Sin breeds sin; behind the pardonable sin of misinforming the rapist lies the sin of the rapist's violent lust. The impertinent question thrust threateningly upon us, leaving no room to refuse an answer, forces us, it seems, to back into a lie. Speech is the medium of society, and fragmentation, unclarity, partiality, collusion, falsification, and threat are woven into social existence as such. Augustine's early treatment of lying may be far from entirely satisfying as it stands, but it achieves some stature by refusing to discuss the sin of false speech simply as "a" serious sin, like murder or rape. To avoid a given sin it is normally enough to resist temptation, but with falsehood we are implicated already through a chain of social communications constructed to evade the first truth, communications we did not originate but have somehow to plot our path through as faithfully as we can. Augustine never came closer than this, perhaps, to the Lutheran conviction of a necessary involvement in guilt. When he frames his question about lying as duplicity, we are not to assume that the blameworthy falsehood *begins and ends* with deliberate lying. In allowing the widest discretion to modes of essentially truthful speech—non-culpable error, fiction, joking, reticence, irony, etc.—he does not imply that these can never be means of deception, merely that they do not have to be. Yet in concentrating on the wrong of deliberate lying he attempts to draw attention to our underlying *Tendenz* towards the evasion of truth, bringing it into the open day of conscious duplicity.

With the best will and in the best circumstances it is easy to speak falsehood. Not only because the whole truth of anything is indefinite, and one can explain and qualify for ever; not only because we have to judge a proposed speech by its relevance, and the truth about x as bearing upon y needs to be *selected* from the whole range of truths, so that we can say too much or too little, or too much in one regard and too little in another. The greatest pressure is imposed by the social constitution of speech. Communicative language refers to realities, things that are so, out there in the world. But it does so while being subject all the time to the push and pull of material and personal communication, for speech is deployed in the course of living life. To maintain a purity of reference under high-tensile conditions of communication, that is what faithful truth-telling, as it may be granted to us as a virtue, means. There is so often a need to say *anything*. The need to achieve a personal presence, to make contact or to attract attention, can prompt us to pour out unsifted information or to frame complex events in well-worn and easily recognized patterns, irrespective of their appropriateness. This is the problem with gossip, reflected on a large scale in the news media, always reaching for stereotypes that will make the new familiar. Sometimes—and this problem is not far removed from the other—it is the need to elicit a response we will be able to control, for rhetorical manipulation offers itself as a means to control things. And there is the need to make a positive, rather than a negative contribution to the situation, to avert evil and to cause good to flourish. Our very sense of responsibility leads us constantly into falsehood. The clash between truth and benevolence fascinates Augustine because it brings him as close as can be imagined to an absolute clash of principles, the situation of the Manichaean worldview, in overcoming which he asserts that the gift of truth-telling is central to benevolence. The benevolent lie must ultimately fail to be benevolent, though it may, in confronting acute hostility, make a pardonable mistake, showing good will to a victim in a way that fails to express the *root* of good will in God's gift of truth to mankind.

Falsehood is a peril in politics, because collective action depends on representation, which requires planning action in ways not known to everybody and open to subversion. If we think democratic politics is more duplicitous than most, it is simply that it raises higher expectations of confidence and "transparency," which will never be fully reconciled with the formulation of policies and the planning of action. These perils we can, in the course of political life, learn conventional ways of handling in normal circumstances and with moderate conscientiousness. If we hold secrets, we can learn how not to spill them; if we are talking to someone whose duties include holding secrets, we can stop ourselves demanding to be told too much. Yet there is no stable *modus vivendi*. The presence of falsity lurking in our social conventions can turn virulent at the drop of a hat, when solidarity closes its ranks at the scent of danger and declares some truths unacceptable—truths that expose the lies that conceal the truths we would have wished to tell if we could only have found the concepts and words to convey them. Falsity is not eliminated. Yet it is de-potentiated by the occupation of human speech with a new truth-telling.

The Sanctification of Meaning

In communicating meaning we communicate a world; but the world has been made diaphanous to the self-disclosing working of God in raising Jesus from the dead. Our mouths are filled with laughing speech; for there is news to rejoice in together. Our routine practices of communication can be sanctified to "declare the wonderful deeds of him who called you out of darkness into his marvelous light" (1 Pet. 2:9). Each of the complete resurrection narratives (i.e., excluding Mark) includes a command to the disciples to tell one another, and subsequently to proclaim the message universally. Human speech is to be filled with the news of the resurrection. He is raised "for our justification"—for the justification, among other things, of our human power to give and receive meanings. The world is given back to us together with its Lord as a world where many meanings now combine to confirm one meaning, the praises of God who has rescued his fallen creation.

We have spoken of the resurrection as the giving-back of Jesus to the verifications of sense and affection. Verification begins through contact with physical realities: the satisfaction of the senses' proper need for evidence, as in the empty tomb, the invitation to touch his risen body, the consuming of a meal. In addition there is recognition of the presence of the human form, the cry "Rabboni!" or "It is the Lord!" and the exchange of words and greetings: "Peace be unto you!" But for the happening to be verified, it must, as such, be intelligible. Is it the Lord in flesh and blood, or is it a ghost? The wholly unprecedented can be expounded only through narration, description, and prophecy: situating the unique happening within a logic of events that can be followed; accounting for it as a demonstration of the truth and glory of God in the world; anticipating the fulfillment of God's purposes in history. Which is why the risen Lord spoke to the disciples on the road to Emmaus, and to others in the course of the forty days, about history as a whole and its destiny to reach that very moment the disciples were living through. It was a declaration of how the sense of the world itself was revealed in that moment ("All power is given to me in heaven on earth"), and it was a promise of the world's fulfillment drawn near ("I ascend to your Father and my Father"). The resurrection was given not only to proof and not only to affection, but to belief.

The Communication of Meaning

By "belief" we mean the understanding that faith both seeks and achieves, the agent's advance to a comprehension of the world, the primary instance of "faith working through love." A message received in belief is intelligible, and so open to communication. As our communications are justified by being made the bearers of such a message, so they are sanctified to the task of proclaiming it. Proclamation is not merely sharing news, which may attract interest but will leave us essentially as it found us. The authorization to communicate is an authorization to change the shape of human living, to allow the Gospel to confer a meaning upon contexts of life yet to unfold. If the unprecedented invasion of the world by God's working in a particular person and particular circumstances of one time and place is at the heart of the message to be proclaimed, that heart is a living and working heart: it distributes the transcendent life of the Spirit throughout the world and the ages, enabling our own life circumstances and action to be revalued. The communication does not stop short with narration; it points the way for us to "follow." And that is the source of the authority conferred on the apostles to "loose and to bind," i.e., to determine the ways in which life may be lived in the new age. It is not an exercise of administrative or governing authority, but the setting loose of the authority of the Gospel itself, which liberates us for the freedom of obedience, or, if it is met with unbelief, binds us to our enslaving self-involvement. A work of ongoing reinterpretation of the world and its life is set in hand, an interpretation in which there will be decisive partings of the way.

The message entrusted to the church was understood, from the first, as a *moral* message consequent on the proclamation of the Easter miracle. Alongside the prayer for the community's sanctification, "body, soul, and spirit" (1 Thess. 5:23), which we have taken as our guide in this exploration, we may illuminatingly set another threefold statement about the empowering of the Holy Spirit: "God has not given us a spirit of cowardice, but of power, of love and of moral instruction" (2 Tim. 1:7). Which is to say, the Holy Spirit empowers the community to withstand pressure from opposition; he draws the community together in mutual identification; he confers the linguistic communication by which its members are made wise in life and action. With this remark we are taken to the core of the Pastoral Epistles' concern, which was to guard against a type of teaching that was essentially speculative and mythic, practical only in the pursuit of an ascetic technique of speculation, diverging to one side and the other of a witness to the coherence of Gospel and common life. The Christian message is at once a *didaskalia*, a teaching, and a *parangelia*, an encouragement or exhortation, the goal of which is love

(1 Tim. 1:5). There may and must be narration, description, and prophetic expectation within the content of the church's teaching, but whichever occupies the foreground at any given moment, it must carry prescriptive overtones, offering direction for living life on the part of one whose own life is deeply engaged in the redemptive work of God for the community. The witness speaks out of ongoing lived experience, whether as an eye-witness that has seen the form of the Word of Life in Jesus, or as one who has subsequently come to experience life restored within the community, and who summons others, believers or unbelievers, to experience "how one must conduct life in the household of God." And that because the church is "pillar and bulwark of the truth" (1 Tim. 3:15). No true truth is only contemplated or only talked about; the truth is proved true in the living of it.

My translation of the third of the three characteristics of the Spirit in 2 Timothy 1:7, *sôphronismou*, is not one of the customary ones, which have varied between "wisdom" or "prudence" on the one hand and the now predominant "self-discipline," "self-control," on the other. But the Western translation tradition, which was founded on two early Latin renderings, *mens sana* and *sobrietas*, was born of a misunderstanding. *Sôphronismos* referred in first-century Greek to a certain type of speech: instruction, warning, and correction, intended to make its hearers *sôphrones*, i.e., intelligent and discerning agents. The early Latin translators did not grasp this sense, though the early Syriac translators did.[21] Timothy does not need more discretion; he needs to be more forthright and outspoken. The immediate context of the saying is an exhortation about Timothy's "gift", i.e., the special ministry committed to him by ordination, which he must "rekindle" (v. 6). It requires him "not to be ashamed" of bearing witness to the Lord (v. 8), nor of his association with Paul in prison, but to "take a share of the abuse" to which the Gospel, as the public disclosure of God's saving power demonstrated in Christ, is inevitably exposed. Timothy, as a minister, must expect to suffer what the "herald, apostle and teacher" has endured (v. 11), and to derive the model for how he teaches from the way Paul has taught (v. 13). To emerge from his low-profile stance and assume a more prominent and exposed position, he must recognize that "God has not given us a spirit of cowardice, but of power, of love, and of moral instruction." The instruction that the

---

21. A fuller account of the philological arguments will be presented in my forthcoming article "Neither Sober nor of Sound Mind: Timothy's Spirit of Σωφρονισμός," to appear in *One God, One People, One Future*, ed. John Anthony Dunne and Eric Lewellen (London: SPCK, 2018).

church needs is the instruction the Spirit confers, the Spirit given to "*us*" and who dwells "*in us*" (v. 14), i.e., in the church of which Timothy is ordained a minister. The Spirit who guards the deposit of the apostolic Gospel (v. 12) is the Spirit who will enable Timothy, too, to guard it (v. 14).

The communication is entrusted to the church as a whole, not only to a class within the church. There is no member of the body who may not from time to time be privileged to take it in his mouth to speak it to another person, believer or unbeliever. But the chief concern of the Pastoral Epistles is the ordained ministry, which has special responsibilities for speaking. It has to be *didaktikos*, "capable of teaching" (1 Tim. 3:2; 2 Tim. 2:24); it has to be engaged in the communication "in season and out of season" (2 Tim. 4:2), ensuring that it is always current in the church and never lost sight of. And to that extent the ministers are engaged immediately in the articulation of the meaning by which all live, they are the more exposed to its judgment. At Shiloh Eli teaches Samuel, Samuel condemns Eli; Eli calls Samuel to maturity, Samuel calls Eli to judgment, a paradigm of the relationship of pastor to disciples. In speaking a word to help another attend to God and live before God, the pastor is exposed to the judgment of the word God speaks: judgment for inadequate teaching, judgment for lives that do not echo and amplify the teaching, judgment for a contented compromise that avoids the necessary confrontations with the values of the world. "Let not many be teachers," James warns, "for . . . we who teach shall be judged with greater strictness" (James 3:1).

The degeneration of the so-called "pastoral" ministry in our own time—"pastoral" improperly opposed to "theological"—into a profession that neither can nor will give moral guidance and instruction to Christian people on how they may conduct themselves within the household of God, must cause us endless grief. Serious heart-searching is needed on the part of those whose chief business in life, like mine, has been with theological education. If to a degree we did succeed in putting behind us the naïve ambitions of mid-twentieth-century theology to drive a wedge between faith and learning, we did not succeed in addressing the fitness of theological learning to equip its students for thought and judgment.[22] We were too content with the fissuring of theology into its separate fiefdoms, which placed unnecessary stumbling-blocks in the way of serious students. Yet while accepting the reproach we deserve, we should comment also on the determination of the

---

22. Cf. Vanhoozer, *Drama*, p. 2: "Theological competence is ultimately a matter of being able to make judgments that display the mind of Christ."

major Western churches to economize on preparing candidates for ministry, with exactly the results that were foreseen: as the task has grown harder in a society less and less vestigially Christian, it has been approached with less preparation, less time for prayer, study, and thought, a fatal economy that has marched in step with the churches' numerical decline.

Let us be clear about one thing: within the traditional churches of the West (I speak of what I know, and make no comment on the style of the new independent and Pentecostal churches) there is little reason to be terrified of the perils of moralistic teaching. "Moralism" is the mistake of safeguarding a pattern of life while losing sight of the proclamation that gives it joyful significance. It may be merely negative, accusing those who fail, or it may be positive, giving detailed instructions for the living of life, and in either case it is an offence to the Gospel since it posits the righteous life as an autonomous enterprise, apart from the sacrifice and triumph of Christ and the indwelling of the Holy Spirit. Moralism does, however, suppose a certain coherence in its vision of the righteous life, and it may even achieve a stern dignity in the expectations of self-mastery that it extends to serious men and women. Even in its inadequacy it may have been a preparation for the Gospel, such as Luther described as the "first use of the law." By contrast, the impotent *Sturm und Drang* of preaching about justice and humanity with which we are so weary today has neither the coherence of clear moral vision nor the dignity of high expectations. It thrives on empty pathos, pointing in no direction whatever, and though it may frequently employ the tones of accusation and reproach, it directs them against abstractions without a concrete focus, hurling its weapons of denunciation from a great distance, with a pious gesture towards the news media as containing all that we could ever need to inform them. There might have been a time when moralistic preaching could have been helpfully corrected by an emphasis on narrative, but we are far beyond the help of such a remedy now. If the clergy are to learn once again what it could mean to give direction to the Christian faithful, they must begin afresh from the moral categories and forms of moral speech that we encounter in the evangelists and apostles.

We turn our eyes also on the lay ministries of the church, which lie chiefly in the sphere of service and care. How do these functions of the church's life relate to communication of meaning? We can identify two aspects of this question. (i) The first is that there is no human communication that does not participate in some way in all three levels of communication, through body, soul, and spirit. We cannot think of material and social communication as self-contained or independent of the meaning-giving of teaching, any more than we can think of teaching as insulated from the community of work and assembly. In this threefold cord it is the spoken witness to Christ that is determinative in confirming service rendered in other ways as offered in Christ and sanctified by God. This is not to say that activities of service and care are merely instrumental means to assist preaching and teaching. They are consecrated by God with evangelical power *as such*; the Christian hospital bears witness by being a hospital, the offering of friendship by being an offering of friendship. Where God has sanctified them, their meaning will be plain, independently of whatever discourse may or may not accompany them. They can refer to the Easter event simply by what they are. Yet meaning, however given and received, needs to be given and received *somehow*. The authenticity of Christian ministry to the sick, comforting the sorrowful, etc., cannot survive a lack of will to receive and give communications of what God has done in Christ. Evangelical meaning cannot be enshrined in institutions by a founding document, a clause in the constitution, or whatever. Either the service is sanctified as a witness, or it is not so sanctified. And if the evangelical meaning of what is done is not consciously and gladly accepted by those who serve in them, they cannot bear witness, and the God who sanctified the works of their predecessors to his service proves himself, as so often, a God who can pull down what he has built, and sanctifies them no more. The church has more or less disappeared from many institutions of former Christendom that were founded to extend its reach (we can start a list with the ancient universities, and continue *ad infinitum* through children's homes, schools, hospitals, organizations for famine relief, etc.). These are testimonies to the fact that meaning, like manna, cannot be stored from one day to the next.

So while acts of service and fellowship may be authentic witnesses in their own right and on their own terms, they are known as such by their resonance and connection with the witness of speech and instruction. Here still we may learn from the relics of Christendom: Christian meaning has been best preserved where the practice of Christian *worship* has been maintained to accompany forms of service and assembly. The charitable institutions of the wealthy aldermen of the City had and maintained their annual acts of worship. The Christian school with a chapel has retained its character better than a school with a pious founder and no more, even though not everything done in such chapels may have afforded a good model of worship. The preaching of the true word of God and the celebration of the sacraments was the Reformation criterion of the church's visible presence. (Not a *definition* of the church, which would have to refer to Christ's body, and not a *description* of the church, which would have to say more about the variety of things the church does, and fails to do, but a *criterion*, well-focused for its purpose, by which among the proliferation of services and assemblies we may identify the presence of the resurrection community.) Liturgy of word and sacrament is the anchor of evangelical meaning, enabling the multiplicity and variety of witnessing vocations to flourish in authentic freedom.

(ii) The second point, however, is that we cannot understand the logic of witness without understanding the hidden and independent ways in which God works to bear witness to himself. The story of Christian witness is a story of Christian culture, and the story of Christian culture is precisely a story of how the effects of the church's witness may fall outside the church's control, and even its cognizance. The scattering of the seed of meaning on the soil of culture is always, from the church's point of view, an uneconomic business; it is bound to fall wide, and is subject to the relentless wastage of the parable of the sower. The lack of an obvious yield may be, and often is, disheartening. But God uses what he has done in quite another way and context. We may think (to make amends for what may seem a persistent discourtesy on my part!) of those who translated and published the Scriptures in modern languages, largely ignored and sometimes actually harassed, and the deep impact their work made on the culture of the West. Only in retrospect and from a distance can we discern what God did by his chosen means and in his chosen contexts. Any dictionary of quotations bears witness to it. In a smaller way, I do not forget an encounter I had as a young man when holidaying in the Scottish Highlands, when in the course of a lonely walk on a Sunday I came across a tent pitched far away from anywhere. What caused me to approach and risk a greeting I cannot now remember, but within it I found a young man of my own age or less, not a holidaymaker but a wandering farm laborer whose tent was his home, deeply engaged in reading the Bible, an old King James. The story should have ended, no doubt, with my explaining to him what he was reading or baptizing him, but God does not lightly repeat himself. The point of the encounter was my education: on the one hand I learned that my strange friend made a regular practice of his Sunday reading, and on the other that he had never set foot in a church in his life.

There is education here, too, for a church surrounded by the relics of Christendom. While our immediate reflection on the disappearance of the church from its institutions may be that the salt which has lost its savor is fit for nothing but to be thrown out and trampled underfoot, that may not be God's own last word. A rediscovery of their original dedication to Christian understanding and practice can—if only for one person or a few, who come to appreciate their significance—be an occasion for a renewal of meaning. It is an argument not to dismiss too quickly the scattered institutional relics of Christendom that remain in our time. Here an oath required in God's name, there a practice of saying prayers, practices long viewed as archaeological curiosities, may focus new questions suddenly with significance and power. The other logic that governs the sowing of the seed of the word is, "Unless a grain of wheat falls into the earth and dies . . ." (John 12:24). Yet any rediscovery must be premised on an understanding of the loss. If God gives back in another form what he has judged and taken away, does that make his judgment impotent? If a once-Christian institution loses its Christian meaning, that cannot be an indifferent fact of history. The mind of man abhors a vacuum of meaning, and where the meaning of mankind's redemption is driven out, the meanings of a bureaucratic and anti-human age are waiting to take it over.

CHAPTER 8

The Endurance of Love

The Bewilderment of Love

On the riverbank at Inverness, the most northerly but not the least pleasant of Britain's smaller cities, is placed an imposing group of statuary representing Faith, Hope, and Charity. Carved in 1865 in the romantic style of the period by a minor local sculptor, Andrew Davidson, it adopts traditional iconographical conventions. The theological virtues are represented as women. Faith steps forward, looking straight ahead with a Bible clutched to her breast, Hope just behind her to the left, leaning slightly outwards upon her anchor but erect, eyes set on a trajectory that intersects, where the observer stands, with the gaze of Faith. Charity stands to Faith's right, also slightly behind. The eldest of the three, she looks down at a child to the right, her right hand touching his head with maternal solicitude, her left pouring a drink from an unwieldy amphora. These representations were well-established in the sculptor's day, but his composition poses an interesting interpretative question to the tradition in which it stands: is it inevitable that Faith's forward movement is *held back* by the postures of Hope and Charity? Hope, to be sure, merely adds a certain stabilizing balance, a support to ensure that Faith will not stumble. But Love is so distracted from the direction in which the other two are looking, so engaged with looking about her and making herself useful, that the group seems to run the risk of falling apart with the tension.

In the context of Victorian Christendom two alternative accounts of this suggest themselves, between which we may find, and are perhaps meant to find, our judgment evenly balanced. One account speaks for an anti-revolutionary progressivism: Charity is the humanizing accompaniment to the forward movement of history. The intimate emotions, care lavished on the weak and dependent, do not have to be cruelly sacrificed to progress, but can be sustained *en marche*. The other account, which speaks for a more skeptical conservatism, will see Charity as correcting and redirecting the concerns of Faith and Hope away from the distant horizon to the needs at hand. If the real point of the group lies in the contrast of youth and age, the ideality that fires the younger virtues finally comes to rest in the nurturing outreach of the older one. Transcendent and visionary moments are proper in their time, but they must be grown out of; they are no more than a religious and metaphysical prolegomenon to the practice of care, which comprises the good of human society. Either of these two interpretations should leave us theologically troubled. On either of them Charity lacks transcendence. At home in the world, she exercises her generous rule with nearsighted focus to the exclusion of a world to come. She cares, but without the vision that would enable her to see beyond the immediate objects of her care. Either she must be carried along, despite herself, by the need of Faith and Hope to engage the future, or she must bring action to a halt by tarrying along the way.

Love makes a home in the world. In caring for the needs around her she envisages a stable world, governed by stable dynamics of need and its satisfaction: thirst quenched with a drink, vulnerability sheltered by a gesture of protection. Cognitively her world is constructed on past experiences, emotionally on the concentration of felt presence. Love is rich in sorrow and joy that resonate with worldly sorrows and joys. Love therefore exercises a certain restraint on faith and hope. She offers them their only possible cognitive and emotional foundation for human action in the world, but, by the same token, imposes limits on their range of vision. She offers a practical purchase on the world, yet acts as a drag-weight. Of herself love cannot look into the future. Yet time is an essential determinant of existence in the world, and there is nothing more certain than that time will prevail, whether faith and hope can grasp it or not, and that it will abolish every state of the world that has come to exist. The maternal figure will lose contact with the dependent child, dragged forward in the wake of time. We must anticipate, as surely as we can anticipate anything, the "bewilderment" of love, the loss of the cognitive-emotional world she has constructed around her. "Will the dust praise you?" the Psalmist pleaded (30:9), since the praise of God itself presupposes a world ordered and made lovely through God's action—the very opposite of the swirling dust that has lost its material structure. And love's bewilderment is the point at which human action fails altogether, since we can never act on the basis of faith and hope alone, in a worldless vacuum.

"Love never fails," are the climactic words of Saint Paul's description of love (1 Cor. 13:8). To give intelligible substance to them, we must show how love can overcome her bewilderment, can "bear all things . . . endure all things," which is to say, take into herself the futureward movement of faith and hope: "love believes all things, hopes all things" (1 Cor. 13:7). What is this bewilderment that has to be overcome? It has two aspects: first, the inability to accommodate intrusive realities that do not "fit," that make no "sense" in relation to the cognitive-emotional world of love and action; second, the inability to envisage cessation, the ending of that world for the cognitive subject, and the ending of the cognitive subject for the world. Love is bewildered in the face of suffering, and bewildered in the face of death.

Ethics must be content to remain where the logic of worldly action prevails. Its competence is bounded by the program, "find and you will seek," accompanying the search for a path of obedience, tracing the journeys of practical reason between the past and future horizons, interrogating ends of action that we commonly propose to ourselves. To the extent that it is instructed by the proclamation of the Gospel, it can identify ends of action sanctified as purchases for the sole of our foot, but of a final resting-place it cannot speak, for eschatology is not a projection of practical reason, but issues from the prophetic word of promise. Yet Ethics can speak, at least, of life in the world as *determined* by the end that lies beyond it. Across the valley of the shadow of death Ethics cannot look, but it can accompany the human agent to the lip of the valley. Suffering and dying, then, are themes that belong with the concern of Ethics for life and action. Suffering and dying are ways in which agents come right up against the limits of their active life, in the midst of life or at its end, and Ethics may probe the extent to which those limits are permeable to hope and faith, and so to a love that will take hope and faith into its own cognitive-emotional framework.

Suffering

We experience suffering as impotence, as the frustration and termination of our agency. To be unable to act, to be powerless to help ourselves, to want and to need to do something and not to be capable of doing it, these are the elements that constitute suffering in its essential character. We experience suffering, furthermore, as an event that overtakes us in life. Impotence, if it has always been a factor and we have always reckoned with it, is not a cause of suffering. If we have never flown, or planned to fly, it is no suffering to be unable to fly; if flying has been the great undertaking of our life, to be told we cannot fly is to suffer. Suffering is experienced when resources fail us, when physical or mental capacities which we counted on are withdrawn. John Milton's sonnet on his blindness famously gave voice to the suffering of an agency frustrated: "Doth God exact day-labor, light denied?" The idea does not make sense of itself. To know ourselves framed for the service of God in general, endowed for some special service in particular, and then to find that the powers we need for that service are taken from us, is an existential contradiction.

Suffering goes beyond sorrow. The two may fade into each other imperceptibly, but sorrow as such has not reached the point where love is simply bewildered of the world it once knew. Sorrow can appreciate goods that have not been realized, or were realized and are now lost; it can cherish absent goods as possibilities the world contained. In loving something that "might have been," sorrow can love the world. Sorrow is constructed with an "at . . ." or a "that. . . ." It has an object, which it knows even in its absence; what the absent good is, and why it is a good, are perfectly clear to the sorrow that mourns it. Sorrow reveals the world in its temporal processes and its inherent imperfectibility, and knows how to value the world in which good things pass away. Suffering, on the other hand, leaves the loveliness of the world inaccessible, makes us unable to inhabit it. It drains the world's goods, real and ideal, of their value for us, so that we cannot love what is present to be loved, and cannot act in faith and hope towards what is possible.

Types of suffering differ in their immediacy. At one end of the scale is the suffering of acute pain, an experience that imposes on us a single, irresistible focus of attention, occupying all conscious horizons, disabling attention to any other thing. With practice, we may get used to suffering weakness and incapacity, or, since frustration remains as a constant element of experience, "get used to not getting used," in Thomas Mann's luminous phrase. But acute pain brings us to a crisis that we cannot ever get used to not getting used to. The typical reaction to acute pain is, "I can't bear it another moment!" which is strange, as it suggests that there is an actual struggle going on in which we are exerting ourselves. Pain simply happens to us. We may hold out against the urge to scream or the desire to complain, but pain itself is not "borne" like a burden; it leaves no room for "can" or "can't." And, paradoxically, the moment when we conceive the feeling of pain as a kind of exertion is the moment when we conceive the exertion as giving out. "Can" arises only when "can't" takes control, when we feel some destructive change taking charge of us inexorably. We feel our very physical existence tottering on the verge of collapse. Pain presents us with the immediate prospect of our physical constitution dissolving.

At the other end of the scale of immediacy there is the suffering of diffuse depression, where there is no one focus that threatens to overthrow agency, but the world as a whole becomes simply unreceptive to it, just an *ensemble* of accidents with no logic, of judgments with no sense, of human stupidity and inhuman chance. We seem to exist as a last island of helpless agency among the rising waters of meaninglessness. And perhaps more terrible than this (for it is possible to cultivate an *insouciant* sense of the self afloat on an ocean of nothingness involving nothing more solemn than a light-headed self-dramatization, designated, perhaps, as "irony"), is an experience where it is not the world that dissolves into meaninglessness, but ourselves. The very goodness of the world can impose itself oppressively, making us aware of our own inability to respond in an emotionally fitting way, leaving us isolated, beyond its sphere of influence, without a point of entry. So Job thought he was being taunted by the friends who encouraged him to consider the goodness of providence, since there was no route open to him to engage himself with that goodness, no advocate to bring him into its presence. When Christian reflection used to speculate about the soul that believed itself "cast away," it intended to explore a condition it knew to be both possible and perilous, a mind that confronted the ultimate summons of the good and found itself incapable of response. What was important about the speculations was not whether anyone could know as a matter of fact that he or she was rejected, but that someone might so *feel* the possibility of divine rejection that no response seemed possible but that of Satan, turning in hostility against what is lovely, blaspheming (in Jesus' words) against the Holy Spirit.[1] The impression of exclusion from grace was not something one could simply correct, as one might correct a "silly" mistake about oneself. It did not derive merely from doubtful dogmatic premises, within Calvinist theology or elsewhere. In fact it was an experience that survived the collapse of the dogmatic framework and became a staple of the Romantic age, as in *The Sorrows of Young Werther*, the first of many explorations of a subjectivity

---

1. Thomas Cranmer, with his usual insight, saw this as the real issue in the question of predestination: "So for curious and carnall persones lacking the Spirite of Christ to haue continuallie before their yies the sentence of Goddes predestination, is a moste daungerous dounefalle, whereby the Deuill maie thrust them either into desperation, or into a rechielesnesse of most vncleane liuing, no lesse perilous than desperation" (*Articles of Religion* 17).

that looks in upon the pursuits and fulfillments of the ordinary world and believes itself eternally banished from them. Is this a form of madness? We may say so, but only if we allow that some madness has its own ontologically weighty disclosure to give. A sense of the judgment of God is a sense of the ultimate horror of one's own inadequacy to the good of the universe. That is not simple illusion, though it is not an aspect of reality we can look at for very long. To sense it is to sense the disintegration of the self overwhelmed by objectivity, the self that has lost hold on its agency.

Suffering is the antithesis of action, yet it is woven into our active lives from the beginning to the end. It weaves its way through it in a variety of forms, sometimes absent long enough for us to think of ourselves as happy and to be thankful, sometimes relentlessly persistent in its attentions, but never further away than the horizon. Indeed, when it does not force itself upon us, we may perversely go in search of it, looking for grounds of unhappiness in circumstances that need not provide them, as though something told us that suffering was due to arrive, and that we could not be complete without it. We may prevent particular sufferings by action, as when we fight disease, but it is as impossible to think of living altogether without suffering as it is to think about acting without limits to our action. The strategy of action in relation to suffering as a whole cannot, then, be one of prevention. It must be to draw suffering into the scope of reflective action, to find ways of "bearing" suffering, undertaking actively what must be undergone passively. For the antithesis of suffering and action is a dialectical one. We know that suffering brings to life a practical impulse in resistance to it. A newborn can do nothing before it cries, and its crying is a hopeful sign of its energy for life. We may say afterwards that we are glad that suffering happened. It draws attention to our limits, and forces us to make important decisions. In closing down possibilities of satisfaction, it directs us to possibilities of development. A paralyzed patient who expends every ounce of energy in the effort to reassert control of a limb, turns an otherwise commonplace operation into a dramatic achievement. A child who suffers the loss of a parent or a lover who is abandoned is in some sense freed from emotional ties and allowed an opportunity to realize a life of his or her own. Ethics has to speak, then, of what tradition called the "uses" of suffering, which would better be described as the conversion of suffering into action, the wresting of articulacy and meaning out of frustration.

We master suffering most effectively when we see it as implied in an enterprise of great importance to us. We can then accept it as expressing our commitment to the goal: it is what we are willing to put out in order to purchase the treasure hidden in the field. The relation between commitment and suffering was symbolized in the antique discipline of fasting, now out of favor. The renunciation of goods we rightly value and enjoy, but find to be competing with our greater purpose of discipleship, canceling out multiple possibilities in order to realize that one possibility, is the elementary form in which a serious decision is made. We may even say that there is no practical enterprise of any value that does not imply suffering. Yet suffering embraced in pursuit of an overridingly important goal is not the typical case of suffering. Taken by storm that way, suffering is deprived of much of its bitterness, for we have ourselves determined what we shall suffer, what powers we shall forego, and we have determined it in purposing what we are to do. We may suffer, and experience our impotence to do what we would have liked to do, but only on the front line of action; behind the line we have a fortress of well-defined purpose to fall back on, which gives us overall control of the field of action. In the typical case of suffering, on the other hand, we are ourselves taken by storm, our purposes disrupted in a way that is unanticipated and unwelcome.

Suffering welcomed for the sake of achievement affords a simple model of what it means to appropriate suffering to active purposes. Applying it to the more typical case of unwelcome suffering is not a straightforward matter, yet the model is still illuminating. Stepping back from our suffering, we may recognize it as an opportunity for a further step on our pilgrimage, experiencing what we have not experienced, deprived of what we have not hitherto been deprived of, focusing attention upon aspects of God's will on which we have not focused it before. Jesus' summons to a disciple was not simply to "follow me," but to "deny himself and take up his cross and follow" (Mark 8:34). Suffering that is not embraced *a priori* as part of a planned purpose may be embraced *a posteriori* if we have learned to understand the living of our lives as governed by the following of the master's teaching and example. Not every cross that we encounter will be as undeserved, as clearly undertaken, as his cross, and yet if our responses are in pursuit of that overarching goal, there is no pain, not even the pain we know we have brought on ourselves by our own folly, which we cannot turn to that purpose and make to serve that use.

The answer Milton received to his question was so striking that it has entered the language as a proverb: "They also serve who only stand and wait."[2] There is an opening for active self-disposal, even when what we un-

---

2. Milton, "Sonnet XIX," in *Poetical Works*, ed. Douglas Bush (Oxford: Oxford University Press, 1966), p. 190.

derstood as action has become an impossibility. Because agents are what we are and consciously remain, there is a possibility not taken away when other possibilities are taken away, which is that of attention to the original giver of our agency, motionless concentration on the master's will. The waiting servant stands ready and focused for the task which the circumstance does not allow. Milton was prepared to think that such a disposition was, in itself, a necessary part in the service of a God who had so much more active service at his disposal than we could imagine. "Thousands at his bidding speed And post o'er Land and Ocean without rest." It demands stillness as a complement. The blindness of the smitten body becomes an occasion for the will of the master to be the total object of attention—an achievement for the embodied human spirit which can only be regarded as a gift. The meaning of Milton's discovery is that agency remains, even when its powers are withdrawn, and persists in its disposition of glorifying God when the power to give active expression to it has been taken away.

Death

If talk of the cross has an ongoing and continual meaning in relation to our active life, it has another meaning also, which is that of final ending. The intermittent increase and decrease of strength, which we experience in action and suffering, is evident wherever there is life subject to changes in time. But it is only where life is focused in individuated units, as in the life of animals, that temporal increase and decrease have an absolute beginning and ending in birth and death. We are called not only to take up our cross to follow Christ, but to die with him. That is the vocation to which we are sacramentally sealed in baptism. If it expresses itself in numberless moments of renunciation, which shape effective action, and in the patient response to sickness, ill-fortune, and misery of every kind, it achieves its sharpest focus in the approaches to death, where suffering extends its reach to drive our powers of self-disposal to their final stand. Dying with Christ is, by definition, not the last word of the Gospel. For if death is not ordered towards *rising* with Christ, it is not dying *with Christ*. It was by his rising that his death was revealed as unique in itself, and unique in what it offered the world. But dying is the last word for which Christian Ethics, which is neither prophecy nor Dogmatics, can take responsibility. And it can do so because Christ's dying is not merely something that happened to him, but his supreme act, the completion of a faithful witness offered in obedient worship to the Father.

Have we any right to call dying an act? Suffering in general may be brought within the logic of action, since we encounter it before the horizon of future self-disposal and action. Courage in the face of suffering has a meaning for all Ethics, and all Ethics understands it as focusing on possibilities for active life beyond the suffering, whether small or great. But is dying not another question entirely? Does the very term "dying" perhaps conceal under the form of a verb what in reality can never be an action, merely a fate that befalls agents? Death is wholly antagonistic to our purposes and ends. It offers no ground on which the soles of our feet can stand. When, circumstantially, we are given the privilege of hoping that our deaths will achieve something—a witness to the truth, a defeat of the enemy, or whatever—no certain knowledge of that achievement is granted us. Death offers no object for practical reason to focus on, but simply terminates practical reason, and is therefore capable of blocking from view any horizon beyond itself, reducing us in our last anticipations to the inert object that our body will certainly become. Though the physiological processes that result in death take a longer or a shorter time, existentially death is a point without dimensions. While we live, we live, still on the approach, and when we are dead we are dead. Unpredictable and unscheduled—unless we die by a deliberate act, our own or someone else's—it offers not much of a stage for accomplishment.

For that reason some have thought it the course both of wisdom and of comfort to exclude our own death from practical consideration altogether. Epicurus believed that by rejecting the natural immortality of the soul he could consign death to the status of birth, treating it as a mere framing event, which never impinged upon the life we actually lived. *Within* the space cleared between birth and death we form purposes, conceive of ends of action and realize them, and we do so wisely and contentedly if we take careful measure of the framework in which we live. But the framework itself can be neither an end of action nor the frustration of an end of action. It can never be *looked towards* directly. "When I am gone," like "before I was born," lies outside the range of deliberation. No one is in a position to be bothered about it. For the living, being dead is neither a good to be desired nor an evil to be feared; it is a state to which the categories of good-for-me and bad-for-me have no application. To one who has died, on the other hand, it is, like everything else, a matter of indifference.

But in speaking only of "death," and not of "dying," this proposal for our wisdom and comfort attempts a transparent sleight of hand. The inescapable meaning of dying as the *ending of life* is simply passed over unmentioned. As the ending-in-time of our being-in-time, dying stands in the closest connection to the possibilities for living. Our beginnings, too, affect our possibilities, but because we live forward in time, not backward, we can forget our beginnings most of the time, reflecting on them only when it is useful to do so. Endings are not like beginnings in that respect. We may relegate the knowledge of our end-in-time to the edges of consciousness, if we wish to, but it will always be there. Deliberation faces the future, and so faces the time of our ending; our ends of action, reaching indefinitely forwards, find themselves entangled with the anticipation of our temporal end, suspended on the hypothesis, "If we live. . . ." We can, and do, weigh the prospects of our dying. We can see it coming, and can guess at how near it may be; we can fear it, just as we can fear any future mishap, since it will put an end to our living. Not only in prospect, but also in event, our death determines in important ways (though not entirely) what our lives will have achieved in relation to what we hoped they would achieve. I can end worthily or unworthily of what I have been. I can, in common estimation, die "too soon," and live "too long." Deaths are judged as better or worse, not only in terms of what it might be to suffer them, but also in terms of the shape they impose upon the lives they terminate. It has not been left to theologians, then, to insist on the importance of thinking towards death as part of thinking towards living our lives. Anciently, the recommendation of the practice of death as a philosophical task was attributed to Socrates.[3] In modernity, making death "our ownmost" was asserted by Heidegger as the "authentic" way of existence. Death as an event cannot be turned into a deed, but by anticipating and approaching events, we appropriate them to our life of action. In some measure, then, we may undertake what we must undergo.

But from what point of purchase can we undertake it? Death cannot be taken into our ends of action. Or, if we accept that the act of suicide may embrace death as an end and not only as a means, it cannot be integrated *among* our ends, but can appear among them only as a counter-end to subvert all other ends. To pursue that end is to refuse to pursue our ends any further. And only that, for death cannot even be imagined; our foreknowledge of the *fact* that we shall end as all living things end does not convey what that might mean *for the self*. Heidegger's "anticipatory resolve," then, looks like a practical disposition, but seems to lack purchase on any imagined future. Are we not exposed to another sleight of hand when we are told that the main thing is to confront death with our eyes open—as if that were not precisely the difficulty? An essential condition for a stable practical stance is hope.

---

3. Plato, *Phaedo* 64a.

The question put to us as human agents, then, is how we may locate a hope in the face of our death, which will allow us to resist its pretensions to bring the whole significance of our active life to nothing.

By virtue of the role death plays in the moral characterization of a life, and by virtue of our need to think about approaching death, moral thought is driven to look for a point of vantage beyond death from which life may appear as a moral unity, and its end as a rounding-off and a completion. Even Heidegger can be accused of "speaking from beyond the grave," as though "death had already occurred, and the narrative had come together in complete coherence."[4] We have referred already to Iris Murdoch's character who craved to look over the Recording Angel's shoulder, in order to "understand it all." It is possible for people to live with their eyes on what future generations will say about them, a crutch with no solid ground to rest on. When a robust Jewish and Christian monotheism proclaimed that God would judge every man according to his works, its message addressed this unresolved antinomy of moral reason, the need for a retrospective point of view from which to look on life as a whole. That point of view existed, not in our imaginations but in the purposes of God. And God's judgment on a life must be his judgment on the life's end, too: "Precious in the sight of Yнwн is the death of his saints" (Ps. 116:15). The lives of the "saints" allow their deaths, too, to be understood positively, as their completion. From which we reach the dictum of Ambrose of Milan, that "from every point of view death is a good."[5] A good conscience will permit us to look forward to death as the confirmation of life's purpose, the beginning of a higher existence and not only the cessation of a trial. Judgment is already partly given, and perhaps in our favor, in the way death itself is encountered.

Yet as the promise of coming judgment cannot be the last word on redemption, so neither can talk of the "good" of death be the last word about dying. Judgment has already been given in the raising of Christ from the dead. To speak of dying with Christ, who was given up for our sins and raised for our justification, is to speak not merely of dying as we have lived, as the last consistent act of our lives, but of dying *in order to* live. Such a dying, though subject to the annihilation of human will and action that all death involves, still belongs to the logic of action restored by God for the

---

4. We take the occasion for a last quotation from the philosopher who has opened a path for us at a number of points in this study, Jean-Yves Lacoste, *Être en Danger* (Paris: du Cerf, 2011), p. 181.

5. Ambrose, *De bono mortis* 4.15 (PL 14.547): "*Omnifariam igitur mors est bonum.*"

world's redemption. The martyrs of the church were called "witnesses," their deaths were not merely a suffering but a testimony, conformed to the death of Christ himself, the first witness to the resurrection of the dead. It is possible, Augustine believed in reacting against Ambrose, to rest too quietly in the assurance of a "good death." Sometimes deplored as "pessimism" on account of its emphasis on the link between death and sin, Augustine's account of the evil of death is essentially an assertion of bodily resurrection. Living implies the hope of its own continuance—and that, for him, is a principle that governs not only the biological phenomenon of life as a whole, but the personal phenomenon of each individual life. Death, then, on Augustine's account, is profoundly unnatural. The death that ends our lives is not our final ending but only a provisional one, the contingent result of sin. It is the "first death," overcome by the resurrection. The "second death," which is eternal, cannot be a natural death, but can only be the outcome, like eternal life, of God's judgment.[6]

To this debate conducted in the ancient world modernity has added its own distinctive preoccupations. Though individual life seeks its own continuance, it need not seek its own continuance forever. So far as life in this world is concerned, indeed, it does not do so. The idea of indefinitely prolonged life is an idea of an ever-increasing burden, as the myth of Tithonus taught the ancient Greeks. Nobody can face that burden, and everybody wants to be assured that they will be allowed to die—in the end, though not just yet! This raises the stakes very high in the struggle between belief and unbelief. Does belief imply the idea of an "immortality," which for practical purposes is unimaginable, at least in terms of continuing in time as we know it? "When we've been there ten thousand years, bright shining as the sun, there's no less days . . ." sounds crude in modern believers' ears, for whom the thought of thousands upon thousands of succeeding years does not adequately convey what it might mean to enter the Kingdom of God. The Kingdom of Heaven has become more of a "last thing," less a "next world." Unbelief in a "last thing" does not have it any easier, for endless time is as indispensible to it theoretically as it is unimaginable practically. The "end of time" does not belong to the universe. The only end that could possibly be imposed on time, it would seem, is the subjective end we may impose on it by mastering our stubborn unwillingness to die right now. The technical quest for means of prolonging life and the legal-administrative quest for the right to end one's

---

6. Augustine, *City of God* 13. On the development between Ambrose and Augustine, see David Albert Jones, *Approaching the End* (Oxford: Oxford University Press, 2007).

life go hand in hand together, and in many ways imply one another. The aim of both enterprises is to exercise control over the lifespan, to preempt death by action, even to the point of teaching ourselves what nature persistently refuses to teach us, namely, to decide to die.

That aim is not a coherent one. Though we form ends of action *around* death—by providing for the administrative circumstances that will confront our mourners (who are likely to thank us for it), by the routine business of disposing constructively of our assets in making a will, buying a plot in the cemetery, etc., dying itself cannot be made an end of action. This is not sentimental reluctance; it is written into the logic of practical action that life seeks to perpetuate itself, and we can kill ourselves only as we refuse to think directly about what we are doing. The project of control over lifespan has not been thought through, and especially in relation to the problem of an ever-increasing population. A generation with unconstrained choice of when to die has unconstrained choice of when and how to permit its successor-generation to mature and assume control. And since most of the time we believe that the right time to die is not yet, the elder generation will believe, most of the time, that the right time for the next generation to take over is not yet, either. The elder generation controls the social space (not merely the surface areas of this or some other planet, but the room to make contributions to society) which the younger generation needs to be able to enter if it is to live. Two alternative outcomes suggest themselves: on the one hand, unconstrained choice may have to be taken out of the hands of individuals and put at the disposal of the same administrative-legal system that made it possible, so that the whole effect will have been to transfer to political authorities the power that was formerly exercised quite naturally and unprejudicially by physical weakness; alternatively, we shall exercise our right to die on behalf of the race, i.e., we shall bring it about by our refusal to die that we shall have no successors. Public discussion of the mastery of death ends up in incoherence, not "joined up" to the population and climate debates. Yet there is no lack of individual voices to suggest that willingness to end the human species altogether, "inhuman" as it may appear, does not lie very far beyond the reach of ordinary human beings. It has, after all, been a constant trait of our species to be willing to do without thinking what we are not willing to think about doing.

The modern aspirations for the control of death are a manifestation of the perennial wish to deny what cannot be denied, that in dying we ultimately become wholly passive, so that we cannot conduct ourselves as the agents we have been. The theological statement, then, is not complete when we have asserted, with Christ's resurrection, the possibility of approaching death in faith, hope, and love, making it the challenge of a responsible moral life. It has to do justice to the corresponding truth, that we endure death as helpless victims. It is not enough to say that Christ died and rose again; we must say that he *suffered* death. There has been too little sympathy for the sense of exhaustion with the world's repetitive circles which the Pietists, in particular, expressed in their reflections upon death.[7] In the twenty-first century we are not likely to sing, "World, adieu! Of thee I'm weary! I seek only Jesus now!" We may rather, if we are theologically inclined, flatter ourselves that a stern insistence on everyone's professing to enjoy life to the last moment somehow protects "incarnation"! It is, of course, true that there is a false world-weariness, born of the rejection of God's creative purposes. It is a strain that runs through Romanticism, which Denis de Rougemont derived from Manichaeism, and it goes with an aesthetic fascination with suicide. The line dividing the one world-weariness from another, the world-weariness that marshals its remaining powers to say "I seek only Jesus now!" and the sullen "Doomsday may thunder and lighten, And little 'twill matter to one!" is a fine one.[8] And that is quite as we would expect, for at the last moment of human experience hope and hopelessness both lack a mediating relation to the world, and so have no "thickness" to measure the difference by. We still-worldly beings, looking on at this transaction that almost bypasses the world, may not see the difference, but the difference is infinite.

And here we must remember the double reference of the word "world."[9] The world that becomes a cognitive burden, a series of demands of which we lose the power to keep track, is the world we constantly need to "constitute" in our imaginations around our own life and actions. The demand to be free of the world is a demand to be relieved of the cognitive burden laid on Adam summoned to name the creatures that God had made. It does not reject God's creation, but shares in its "groaning" for regeneration and rebirth. And the point of connection between the two worlds, the world of our making and the world of God's giving, is Jesus, ascended to the right hand of God in the risen flesh through which the world is given back, ready to appear. The world, too, obeys the logic of the grain of wheat in Jesus' parable, that it

---

7. In this charge of lack of sympathy I must include myself, I am afraid, in what I wrote in "Keeping Body and Soul Together," in *Covenants of Life*, ed. Kenneth L. Vaux, Sarah Vaux, and Mark Stenberg (Dordrecht: Kluwer, 2002), pp. 35–56. French trans. by M.-B. Mesnet: "Ne pas séparer l'âme du corps," *Éthique* 11 (1994): 64–89.

8. A. E. Housman, "Clun," in *Collected Poems* (London: Cape, 1939), p. 75.

9. Cf. *Finding and Seeking*, pp. 72–77.

must fall into the earth and die. Love itself must die and be reborn, for love is mediated through loveliness, and requires a lovely world, this world or the next, to irradiate; only hope can pierce through the blank wall at the end of the world and insist that where nature has no alternative but to let everything go, the summons to follow Jesus need not be let go.

That farewell to the world reminds us of the complementarity of the end of life with the end of all things. Objectively we can anticipate that the world will continue when we are no longer part of it. Yet not denying the objectivity of world and time, we are bound, as those for whom the world is not an object to be observed but a context of living, to see the end of our presence to the world as the end of the world's presence to us. There are two complementary deaths: "the world is crucified to me and I to the world" (Gal. 6:14). That is how the promise of the Kingdom of Heaven meets our need with an end in which God will be all in all, an end which is at once an end *for our agency* and *for the world*. (And if that simultaneity creates difficulties over future time in *this* world, which we shall not be present to experience, we must remember that futurity is not univocal.) This importantly qualifies the conception of death as departing "from the world." The fulfillment of our time to which action looks forward, the fulfillment of world-time located indefinitely beyond our action, belong inescapably together. The fulfillment of time is a point of rest from both points of view. Hence the dual imagery of eschatological prediction, in which the ultimate future is seen both as a battle, resolving the moral contradictions of world-time, and as a city in which the presence of one to another will finally be universalized.

The Sanctification of Temporality

As creatures in a world subject to the passage of time, ourselves subject to ending in time, how may we comprehend and acknowledge the time-bound character of our existence? We may do so by acknowledging our aging: "I have been young and now am old" (Ps. 37:25). That acknowledgment is not reversible; there is no way that we can say we have been old and now are young. Which implies, if we are to make it in full cognizance of what we are saying, that we must first qualify to do so by enduring time. It is an acknowledgment that has its own privileged position within our lifetime, towards its latter end. We do not, of course, have to wait that long to know *that* the passing of time and the succession of generations is a fact of human existence. From the very beginning of our existence we have been determined by the poles of youth and age, with their contrasting modes of presence and their contrasting powers, as fundamental to human coexistence as the poles of male and female, and in a similar way, both narrowly focused in the family and widely diffused throughout society. Our temporality has always framed us, and we have always known that it did. Yet to have lived the time from youth to age is to have acquired an experience of temporality for which youth has no equivalent. One might say, perhaps, that for youth time is elusive, a horizon of opportunity that lies hidden behind the solid forms of beckoning possibilities, revealing itself only through delay, in refusing to deliver opportunities straightaway into hands stretched out to grasp them. By contrast, the experience of age is to be *en prise* to time, gripped in its resolute motion, carried on with the impetus of an irreversible past towards an inevitable ending. Old age *has suffered* time:

> Headlong, the down night train rushes on with us,
> Screams through the stations . . . how many more? Is it
>   Time soon to think of taking down one's
>   Case from the rack? Are we nearly there now?[10]

Modernity is often accused of eliminating every non-interchangeable relation from the field of vision. We may certainly suspect it of trying to make the relation of old and young disappear, just as it makes the relation of male and female disappear. And whether or not our modern political ideologies do that, modern moral philosophy certainly does it, and does it as a matter of principle. It is understood as a condition of moral thought that the location of any given subject in relation to the temporal polarities of human existence must be irrelevant to moral relations, and that to mention it is *ipso facto* a declension from clear thinking. The philosophers' "I," "You" and "Other" have no dates of birth, and presumably no dates of death either. They are as ageless as they are sexless. *Homo ethicus* somewhat resembles his cousin *Homo economicus* in having parted company some time ago with the progeny of *Homo sapiens* that we meet on the street. They both lack a decisive feature of *Homo sapiens'* existence, which is constitution in time.

It is not merely that the human "is" in time, as everything else that is created is in time, nor even that the particular human takes time to emerge

---

10. C. S. Lewis, "As One Oldster to Another," in *Poems*, ed. W. H. Lewis (London: Bles, 1964), p. 41.

as what it is, as all living things take time to emerge. For humans it is a matter of existing *with the consciousness* of time, so the particular time determines *how* they emerge, knowing their own span of life as differently located in time from the span of other people. There are predecessors, who determined the actualities and possibilities of their time, and there are successors, whose experiences of time they will not share. Every member of the species who has achieved self-awareness (i.e., excluding small children and those incapable of self-understanding) can and must come to acknowledge temporal determination in this way. We cannot acknowledge it in the same way from each successive point in life, but when we acknowledge it authentically, it is always as a span from beginning to end. Not, that is, "I am young, and have my life before me," or, "I am old, and my life is over"—two things that we may possibly say, but inauthentically, not accepting our temporality as it is. The authentic forms of acknowledgment are, "I am young, and must grow older," and "I have been young, and now am old." Not admissions of *contingencies*, as though we could say "I happen to be old," as we could say "I happen to be of Irish descent." It is perfectly possible for *Homo sapiens* not to have ancestors from Ireland, which is why Irish descent is merely a "happening." It is not possible for *Homo sapiens* to be neither young-and-looking-forward-to-age nor old-and-recollecting-youth. Being situated somewhere on the arc between youth and age is an essential feature of human existence.

Of the two positions one is acknowledged with anticipation, the other with experience. The young may look on the full span of human time and understand much about it, yet will look on it with a degree of wonder, as a mystery as yet unsounded by experience. That wonder may sometimes be fearful. The old, on the other hand, reflect on the span of human time as possessed, for better or worse, by experience. That reflection may sometimes be bitter and resentful. When fear prevails on the one side and bitterness on the other, the relation between the generations can become a struggle for mastery, each trying to suppress the memory of human temporality that the other's presence brings to mind. But if God has made time the theater of his action, and has opened a further end beyond the end imposed by time upon human beings, then the acknowledgment of youth and old age is free to assume a different tone, as a *service of assistance* offered by old to young and young to old in charity. The relation of the old to the young is taken into the "communion of saints," which is the contemporaneity of all human generations in the decisive redemptive action of God. In contemporaneity we may receive and give witness to God's acts from one generation to another. And among all the generations that receive and give to one another there must be, for each generation, *one* from which it receives in particular, and *one* to which it gives in particular, the one before and the one after, which it knows face to face. The general human task of tradition (which includes speaking across many generations through historical and literary records) assumes a distinctive urgency and importance in relation to two successive generations between whom there can be a dialogical exchange.

But the relation between the two is not reversible. The young have their hands full mastering their world, and it rests upon the old especially to ensure that these two generations, with their temporally consecutive locations in world-time, can communicate. To help the young live effectively, not to exploit them as spare hands and feet in a world that still circles around the old, not to try to live vicariously through their experiences, is a service that requires temporal contiguity, not by some kind of dismissal of the generation gap, but within the tension of the difference, by establishing sympathy. The proverb declares, "The glory of young men is their strength, the splendor of old men is their grey hair" (Prov. 20:29), a contrast which captures a mutual but non-interchangeable service: an energy in relation to a greater experience, an experience in relation to a greater energy. ("Energy" and "experience," not "power" and "wisdom"; it is a contrast of resources, not accomplishments. There are such things as an impotent youth that wastes its strength and a foolish old age that wastes its experience.) Perhaps our first reaction is to wonder what has become of middle age. It is excluded — perhaps because it is *not* part of a polar relation, and therefore offers no direct point of access to another generation of humanity. When all is said and done, middle age is a concept about which we may well harbor suspicions. The pretension of middle age, with its balance of energy and experience, is to rise above its own temporality by interpreting itself as neither old nor young, making both youth and age look like deficiencies.[11] An era that understands equality as interchangeability, treating all citizens as equally productive contributors to the commons and equally dependent claimants on them, will certainly make old and young disappear, as it makes male and female disappear, and with everyone in a synchronous and symmetrical relation with everyone else, it can hardly avoid thinking of everyone as middle-aged. Middle age then becomes the "neither-nor" of youth and age, a reduction to lookalike

---

11. As is all too evident in Karl Barth's discussion of the generations in *Die Kirkliche Dogmatik* III/4, §56.2 (Zürich: Evangelischer Verlag, 1957), pp. 697-710 (= *Church Dogmatics* III/4 [Edinburgh: T & T Clark, 1961], pp. 607-18), where there is a commanding role for "*das Reifsein . . . nicht mehr zu früh und noch nicht zu spät.*"

work and citizenship, in which doing things and participating in common responsibilities eliminate, or push into private corners, the differences that make human beings capable of expanding each other's horizons. In this perspective the old become assimilated to "vulnerable adults," or, if not evidently vulnerable, they are the "third age" of the retirement salesmen, who see them as a market for cruises, autumn holidays, golf with friends, football with grandchildren, devoted housing estates in the nicest parts of town, and cheap auto insurance for which others foot the bill.

The proverb's assertion of an asymmetrical polarity between young and old, by contrast, promises to give back something of our humanity that was suppressed in the hegemony of middle age. What, it seems to ask, if the polarity of young and old is the *real* truth of our common humanity, and the neither-nor of the intervening years is simply a reduction? Non-interchangeability of youth and age does not mean, of course, that the two generations cannot experience mutual sympathy and appreciation. Between them they embody the historicity of the human race on its incessant passage from the depths of the past to the remotest future, and the dynamic of their relation is a context in which certain kinds of wisdom can be won on either side. Each generation represents to the other a truth of its own human being: the truth of human generations who were here in the world before us, and of human generations who will be here in the world after us. The tone of the relation is still wondering, but a wonder open to the appreciation of those who are simply different and not in competition. For the old it is an opportunity to recall their youth, for the young an opportunity to expand their horizons. Yet this exchange of gifts is accomplished *in the relation* of the two, not by mutual imitation but simply by enjoying the other's presence. To imitate is to be ridiculous, assuming the pompous dignity of years with inappropriate haste or aping the dress or speech of youth when it is no longer becoming, like an unseemly parody. Youth and age are mutually accessible in correspondence, not in assimilation.

To be sure, the distinctive conditions of being old are never *all* the conditions of anyone's life. One is never merely old, just as one is never merely young, merely a man, merely a woman. (Or merely middle-aged, a state of life which assumes a greater interest if we think of it as being *both* young *and* old, rather than *neither* young *nor* old.) We live as an older version of the particular human being we have been and are, carrying with us the gifts and vocation, the accomplishments and failures, which have given our life its character, and, to the end, our responsibility as agents for conducting ourselves. The most general description of the human calling is still what it was when we were young: living and acting in faithfulness before God in the world. Old age confronts that same calling in different circumstances: learning to be patient with the caregiver, as once we had to be patient with the secretary; apologizing when we forget things we should have remembered; answering letters kindly written to us, though it takes longer to do; not taking our family and familiars for granted; being interested in other people's experiences and not talking about ourselves all the time; noticing when someone needs a word of comfort, and so on. The terrain of old age, moreover, is extensive and differentiated, and the road that each of us takes across it will be an individual one. It is dangerous to take one example of a successful old age and make it a kind of ideal.

Old age bears on its face the burden that time imposes upon us. When common sense looks at old age, it thinks first of the fact that "our outer nature is wasting away" (2 Cor. 4:16). Age suffers losses and limitations to its mental and physical capacities; even in the absence of illness the body demands more attention, the mind demands more time to think things out. Old age can thus appear simply as a preliminary to dying. And though we may object to this that the wasting away of the outer nature, to which Paul refers, is not an eventuality that affects us only at a certain phase of life, but an eschatological reality with which we live consciously from the moment of our baptism, it remains true, to borrow an appropriate phrase from Barth, that "it is suggested in a particular way" in old age. The shadow of death is constantly represented there. When the shadow falls on youth, it is likely to be lightened by the prospect of getting better, or at least by the hope of compensating for what is lost, recovering a sense of normality, and so on. In older years these hopes have to face the persistent question of whether, and to what degree, they are fitting. We continue to seek cures for our ailments; we take up new pursuits to replace those we can no longer pursue; but we do so in the knowledge that the scope for such assertions of life is slowly shrinking. Longer-term practical dispositions become more speculative; realism begins to argue against making them.

On the physical ills of old age little needs to be said, as there is a great literature on them. Not only illness and physical dependence, which may be experienced in youth, too, but the slower performance of body and mind, and the greater attention they demand of us to ensure their routine functions. And with the physical changes of old age come new temptations, different from but no less challenging than those of youth and maturity: once cheerful, we may find ourselves often depressed; once outward-looking, we may become self-preoccupied. How the changes will affect us, how we may need to marshal our spiritual resources to confront them, will be up to us to discern, and what is involved in our struggles may not always be evident even to near observers. Reducing horizons and ambitions give old age its mood of melancholy; loss of strength and slower movement and thought contribute to its generalized anxiety; both are among the characteristic temptations it has to overcome.

To these we must add ills of a social and cognitive character. The old will be out of tune with the world of the young. They will be dismayed to find that the work the young do and the perspectives they bring to it are very different from their own, that their practices, their skills, and their understandings are different, too. The old are quite naturally perplexed at how the young arrange their business, at the compromises they make and the compromises they refuse to make. The young offend them morally, and, to their astonishment, they sometimes find that the young are morally offended by them. We may disagree about important things with anyone, not only with those of an earlier or later generation. But focusing these disagreements through the polarity of the generations makes them more intractable and painful. It suggests that moral and cultural affirmations which have been fundamental to society as we have known it should be seen as merely relative and perspectival fashions, now falling behind the times, which adds the greatest imaginable insult to the initial sense of injury. It is a paradox: differences are matters of generational perspective, to be somehow transcended, while at the same time they concern matters of fundamental human importance, worth spending our last breath to fight for. There is, after all, a certain inevitable justice in the typical perception of the old that the world is getting worse all around them. The goods they learned to know and love, the world as it was given to them to inhabit, are close to disappearing, and so they merit grief. It is a one-sided view, to be sure, but not illusory. The goods they valued were visible peculiarly to their generation, and are threatened with invisibility to the next. The way the world talked, the way it dressed, the way it channeled its affections socially, the way its communications conveyed understanding, its practices achieved ends and its failures were exposed to criticism, all encouraged the living of human life. If now that world is giving way to another, those whose life was enabled by it cannot pretend to say that another world may be just as good. To say that, and to mean it (for it is likely to be no more than a rhetorical flourish), would mean that they never *engaged* with the world they were given. Not to care for its passing would be not to care for the life they have lived.

Again we recall that there are not ultimately two "worlds," only one, but two aspects from which that one world may be viewed: in its objectivity, as God created it, and in its subjective appropriation as it has been received and imagined in the context of living life. The world for whose passing we necessarily grieve is "our" world, the ensemble of particular recognitions that have mediated God's created order to us. Making a cognitive home in the world is for the young, and its satisfactions properly belong with the burdens of the young, such as care for a family and pursuit of useful work. It is a seductive temptation for old age to try to take up home-building again as a delicious indulgence of work-free years: *now* I can live where I always wanted, and will never have to endure another harsh winter; *now* I can play golf every day and improve my handicap, etc., etc. We quickly discover that we no longer have the resources to inhabit the new homes we hope to build. Our cultural clothing was not tailored to outlast us, and it will increasingly be felt as a cognitive burden. Supremely, the friends on whom our love was lavished irrecoverably in the past are no longer on hand to occupy our worldly home with us. "They are all gone into the world of light! And I alone sit lingring here."[12] It is better for old age to accept moments when it feels itself "lingering," and recall the light that it once saw cast across its world, and is now withdrawn, than to imagine itself free to begin over again.

There is a third burden that time lays on old age, which is the burden of past experiences returning to haunt us. T. S. Eliot described it well as "the rending pain of re-enactment / Of all that you have done, and been."[13] To be haunted by experience is not the same as remembering it. Past experience returns not in recollection of a world coherent in its joys and sorrows, but as it were in free radicals of the memory that react with casual stimuli to produce chance deposits of shame and grief. Haunted by such dissociated recollections, we do not see youth's strength, only its inexperience and inadequacy. We were ignorant, foolish, insensitive, and reckless, or perhaps exposed and vulnerable, an object of pity or contempt. What is happening to us in these moments of vain regret? They are not repentance, to be sure, for repentance is always accompanied by faith, the conviction that God wills our lives to be restored as a whole, which strengthens us to search for a more coherent and balanced memory rather than brooding over disjointed recollections. We repent of what we did wrong by understanding how and why we went wrong, not by a fastidious distaste for what we were, which is

---

12. *The Works of Henry Vaughan*, ed. L. C. Martin (Oxford: Clarendon, 1914), p. 483.
13. T. S. Eliot, "Little Gidding," in *The Complete Poems and Plays* (London: Faber, 1969), p. 194.

too often a projection of distaste for what we are. There is necessarily a place for repenting in old age, as at every stage of life, and sometimes a place for repenting what was done long ago, but repentance needs objectivity. These fragmentary revenants of youth's shame are simply raw material for the work of an ordering memory; they need to be assigned to their proper place within a coherent narrative of the sanctifying grace of God. To be objective about the failures of youth, we must recall what it was like to be young, what we saw and heard and felt, what we attempted and failed or accomplished. And to recall is to be thankful—thankful that we were given strength, as now our children and grandchildren are given strength. Then we can be sober about our youth's mistakes. Otherwise we are caught up in an anguish that has little to do with acknowledging sin, but is merely a reflex product of the burden of time itself.

The ills of old age cannot be ignored. And yet the special proximity of old age to the shadow of death and the loss of its world is what allows it, in the light of the Gospel, to be the privileged witness to a temporality transformed by the conquest of death. The message of the resurrection, that God has given to life the last word over death, allows us to think of old age as living, rather than merely dying, and as witnessing to the accomplishment of life before those whose knowledge of life is only that of a possibility, opened up to them by the increase of their strength. In describing this service of charity as a witness, we intend that term in its full evangelical sense, as a testimony to the work of God in redeeming mankind from sin and death. It is, of course, by no means the whole of evangelical witness. It bears witness not to God's generic work of justifying mankind in Christ, of which the old are in no better position to speak to the young than the young to the old, but of a particular work of sanctification in remaking *these* lives in *this* generation, the experience of having lived and acted before God. It is a limited witness, but delivered, as it were, from the lip of the weir on time's stream, it can have its own powerful effect. *This* generation, the only one to which the young have direct personal access, was given grace to confront its tasks in *this* way. If the young are to form their world effectively, they need models. What they can learn from the old is how time may be endured with love, and they will learn that not by precepts but by observation—critical, no doubt, but not necessarily unsympathetic or uncomprehending.

The witness requires both flexibility and consistency. The old have neither to conform to the young, nor to resent them and stand at a distance, but to be themselves before the eyes of the young, to live and to die as they have lived up to this point, standing where they have stood on important matters, cheerfully adapting themselves, as best they can, in unimportant ones. That is what the young need of them. For the young have a task on their hands; they must by some means establish a cognitive and affective relation to the world in which their life is to be lived; they must come to recognize the sense and order of what God has given them. The conditions on which they have to do so are conditions which the old will be the first to recognize as difficult. When tempted to conceive the march of time as a march of invaders who take over their world, the old may draw on their experience to appreciate the extreme peril, the exposure to danger and temptation, in which the supposed invaders find themselves constantly placed. To grasp the meaning of time is to grasp that the young, too, are faced with the struggle of being in time, though without the resources the old were once given to encounter it. They deserve not envy, but compassion. "Like as a father pities his own children . . ." (Ps. 103:13).

And here we see how the paradox we encountered earlier may be resolved. The moral and theological truths to which we must be faithful in old age, as at any time, are not matters of *opinion* on which two people, or two generations, may simply differ in their views. They are truths demanding witness; they are a matter for communication, by which a certain grasp of truth attained by one is made available to another. They convey the very heart of the experience of being human. "I have been young, and now am old," remarks the Psalmist, "yet I have not seen . . ." (Ps. 37:25). And if the young are frankly incredulous at what the Psalmist claims not to have seen in all those years, "the righteous forsaken or his children begging bread," they may reflect that there is no final verdict on what has been seen and not seen until the point has been reached from which it can be looked back upon. Past experiences then become a vehicle for discovery of the most important matter for all human beings, namely, how God protects and upholds his righteousness in a world where righteousness is constantly contested. That witness, which may seem like a seed cast uselessly on the wayside, can take root in the imagination of those who follow, and grow to bear fruit there. But it will not do so by insisting that it should. Civilization does not march forward in straight lines, like a well-drilled column of infantry, following its generals' plans and predictions. Tradition is not handed on merely by being taught and learned, like lessons at school, but by being lived with conviction, so that it forms a backdrop to the struggles of later generations, offering a purchase for intelligence when and as the need for it is greatest. It is driven by a memory of a past which can provide it with an imaginative resource. The seed that flowers most prolifically today was sown generations back.

The contribution of the old to their successor generation is to make sure that what has been experienced shall be available, a living presence to transmit and to inspire as it is required.

So if the wasting away of the old nature is "specially suggested" in old age, so is the persistence of an active hope anchored in the promises of God. As old age heads towards the moment at which strength will not support work and memory will not support reflection, the task of hoping in God remains. "When you were young you girded yourself . . . but when you are old another shall gird you" (John 21:18). Jesus' words to Peter, as we have observed, may echo another proverbial comparison of youth and age, rather to the disadvantage of age.[14] But on his lips, as Saint John reflects on it, it is the occasion for Peter to "glorify God" in his dying. To glorify God is to bear him witness. And to glorify him in dying is to make the ultimate point of suffering the ultimate act of witness. If old age can be a slow and terrible stripping away of the world from the self, that is only in order that the new world of God's purposing may come more clearly into sight. The burden of time, which is the burden of old age, is not the burden of the past as such, but the burden of a witness to the future sustained beneath the weight of the past. And that, too, is something the young need, for the measure of *their* hope will be the horizon the old have been able to show them beyond the exactions of work and the limits of active endeavor.

In his famous anticipation of the gift of Pentecost the prophet Joel observed, "Your old men shall dream dreams and your young men shall see visions" (2:28). When the young see visions, their visions descend on them without warning and unprepared for. But the dreams of the old have been prepared for over a lifetime. They bring to them their witness to the good work of God in spreading his Kingdom, a witness to experience that is partial and conditioned by its own time, certainly, but with its own assigned place in the communion of saints. "I have been young and now am old, and have not seen. . . ." The Psalmist *has not* seen, perhaps, because now there is something of greater importance to see, which turns his eyes away from the immediate surfaces of life and its urgent practicalities to the horizon of the world, the end to which it is directed. The world re-envisaged in vision is not the world of tomorrow or the next day, any more than it is the world of the day before yesterday. It is the world of God's ultimate future, before which all generations find themselves contemporary. If the witness of the old can help the young, who have their own time and experience to interpret, it is

---

14. See *Finding and Seeking*, p. 162.

because their "dream" can make a connection with the "vision" of the young and offer it a substance that will sustain it over the years.

The Eternity of Love

"Love never fails," Saint Paul affirmed, and if that is true, it is because love has been able to relinquish a passing world that it has known, and rediscover reality in another, permanent world. It can follow the gaze of faith and hope into the future, and count on being at home in God's future, as it has been in this world's past. We have to ask what are the conditions that make this self-transcendence of love thinkable.

Love of the world has, of course, its own immanent capacities for self-transcendence. Love may, as we have said, reach out to the presuppositions of its object, interrogate the "givenness" of the object that is present to it, discerning on the rearward horizon of time a creating and preserving God who is open to be known and loved through the things that he has done. It may love God as the "secret of the world," in Jüngel's fine phrase. And in that self-transcending movement of love there may be either authenticity or inauthenticity. False claims to the love of God may be unmasked by failures of love to those who inhabit the world in our company. Love, as the apostle says, is "no new commandment, but an old commandment, which you had from the beginning" (1 John 2:7). Yet when we allow that the world we inhabit turns around a definite act of God to disclose himself within it, the matter becomes more complex: "It is a new command, which is true in him and in you because the darkness is passing away and the true light is already shining" (v. 8). If there were no passing away of the world in time, or if that passing away were merely a passing from darkness to greater darkness, the love of God would come to rest finally upon the brother, and the worldliness of the world would finally encompass us, making material care for one another all there was to shield us from the ultimate inscrutability of things. But it is not so. In the light of the Gospel the practice of love of the brother opens up towards a world that is promised and new.

At this point we must introduce an equation that lies deep in the Christian understanding of God: "God is love" (1 John 4:8). It is an equation of which Ethics can know nothing by itself, but only learn of from the evangelists and theologians, for the being of God is not a projection of practical reason. This proclamation is designed, indeed, to unsettle all our talk about loving God, turning what pious morality thinks of as the object of the verb into the subject. To speak of God as the further object that lies behind the world we love is easy enough, but what if God is also the subject of the love with which we come to love any thing? What if this verb, which we take to be the determining and all-encompassing description of our given relation with the world in which we live, has its own history prior to our relation with the world, prior to the world itself, a divine history that generated the story of our loves (with all their successes and disasters) since the dawn of time? The conclusion of that train of thought, if we take it seriously, can only be that "love," in its truest meaning, is not a known quantity in the world, a quantity that we could think of *extending*, as it were, to encompass God as the world's presupposition. It must itself be disclosed to us as God discloses himself to us. And that is the reason for the element of the ecstatic within Christian love: it is turned towards the future self-disclosure of God. A love capable of following hope beyond the horizon of the world is essentially, and not only occasionally, restless. John M. Rist has written persuasively of how the "passionate Augustinian view of union with God" was "overlaid by an Aristotelianizing account . . . more easily identifiable as the 'rational appetite' which for Aquinas is 'the will.'"[15] In accord with that judgment, and still following the lead of Saint Paul, we may name what has been lost sight of: eschatological disclosure. Love must be learned anew, as the one whose love underlies all love must be learned anew, at the climax of history. The disclosure of love, then, is at the center of eschatological disclosure.

Whatever we say about the being of God is eternally true, if it is true at all; that is as much the case with "God is love" as with anything else we may say about him. But though eternally true, it is not disclosed from eternity, but in history, and the disclosure points us to the conditions on which we can understand its truth and affirm it. These are that we should devote to the God who is love all the love that he inspires in us. The world that has been the chrysalis of our knowledge and love cannot remain as it has been, setting the horizon of our consciousness, but must fall away to allow a new-formed world to be constituted around the disclosed presence of God. "I saw no temple . . ." said the prophet. For the temple of our world is the love that simultaneously attests God and keeps God at bay. Our love for him in this world is mediated, passed through the prism of our love for the world. But he will not finally be kept at bay, but will be received as the totally absorbing presence he will offer, love present to itself in him and in us. So love must change its aspect, no longer diffused through the differentiated structures

---

15. Rist, *Augustine Deformed* (Cambridge: Cambridge University Press, 2014), p. 133.

and beings of the world, but focused upon itself as its source and end. We have named the love of the world, the acknowledgment of created good that leaves us still underdetermined for deliberation and action, "admiration." This love, on the other hand, enacts itself as it recognizes itself, so that the clarity of knowledge and the impulse of energy are wholly at one; we have named it "devotion."

Before this eschatological horizon we have to confront the stark alternative: friendship with the world is hostility to God. The God whom theological speculation pictured, stumblingly but not misleadingly, as by himself before the world was made, will never be, as speculation imagines, without his world. Love cannot be without its world; it must have its object. And so with the disclosure of God and of love we are told of a "new" world, a "new heaven and a new earth." About the newness of that world we have said enough to avoid the suggestion that it is simply *another* world, as a God who made one world and then replaced it with another would not be faithful to what he had made. But—and this is the point that Ethics, in particular, must hear from the eschatological proclamation—that world (both "new" and "restored") is not, or is not yet, *our* world, the construction of our love and knowledge. For that world to appear, the world constructed out of our common objects of our love must first be let disappear.

We may know things-in-the-world without loving them. There are things we know of but have no interest in, such as the football results. There are things that we hate, rather than love, and hatred is not possible for what we are perfectly ignorant of. It is simply not possible to imagine loving everything that may happen in the world equally—becoming a parent, traveling to the moon, dying of an attack by a crocodile. An attempt to sweep up the universe within the compass of our love always ends in some kind of indifference, which militates against deliberating, deciding, and acting. But while we "know" (to a degree) many things we do not love, we cannot know them without a love for the world as a whole. The only practical meaning we can give to living-in-the-world is love-of-the-world, since life clings to its own presuppositions. And when we order our loves—pursuing this, indifferent to that, avoiding the other, we affirm an order which we believe the world reveals—indifferent to the football results because they *don't count* among goods, hating the thought of a crocodile attack because it *cuts short* goods we know and love. Our order of love embodies a love of order, an organization of things in terms of their real significance.

"Our world" is an unstable construction, always subject to the judgment of "the real world," what God has *really* made and done. It cannot bring love to its goal, which is to rest in the reality of God's making and doing. It is the commonest of experiences to find that we have misvalued something or someone. What we thought didn't count turns out to count a great deal, and what we reckoned of great importance is shown up to be marginal, after all. "God chose what is low and despised in the world, even things that are not, to bring to nothing things that are" (1 Cor. 1:28). Our love of the world can end up in the bewilderment of contradiction. Erotic love, uniquely open to the quest of the self for expansion, continually leads us in directions that are destructive of our world and its relations, which is why it is a recurrent metaphor for the love of God. The logic of the seed that must die if it is to break out into new and fruitful growth is not only a logic of ourselves and our suffering, but of the world as our cognitive and affective object. Its destiny is to be the new heaven and new earth of God's kingdom, and to achieve that destiny it must die to us, as we must die to it.

But we, too, are our world, and in devotion to God we embrace him, also, as a consuming flame that engulfs us as it engulfs the stuff of which we are fashioned. The disclosure of God on the Day of Pentecost came as tongues of fire, "flames of incandescent terror" as T. S. Eliot described them, and confronts us with a choice:

> The only hope, or else despair
> Lies in the choice of pyre or pyre—
> To be redeemed from fire by fire.[16]

One way or the other we are to be burned, either by hope or by despair. That fire, we are told, is love. Love is fiery, because it is objective, or "unfamiliar." To our imaginations and wishes, our perceptions of ourselves and the world, it offers no compromise. It imposes the agonies of reflecting on reality. Yet at the same time, and again because it is objective, love is integrative and conciliatory, world-creating and not merely world-destroying.

Ethics after Pentecost, with which we have made our business in these three volumes, concerns what transpires between love and love, between reflection and reflection. There is a first reflection on the world and a second. The first takes in—with joy and fear, with disapproval or with triumph—all that the world displays to us of its meaning—its values, its order, its history, and its destiny, and perhaps its secret, the working of a creating and sustaining God behind it. The second takes that meaning in again, as a theater in

---

16. Eliot, "Little Gidding," p. 196.

which God has finally worked his purpose, and will disclose it fully, a scene on which our gaze may rest with praise and thanksgiving. In between the two we live in the tension of the eschatological difference; we put on what Eliot calls "the intolerable shirt of flame." We accept the flame of love within ourselves in the form of obedient action. And that is how the greatest of sufferings, the extinction of our world to us and of us to our world, can take form also as an act of faith and hope, through which love will finally prove itself sovereign.

Index of Names and Subjects

Acquisitiveness, 70
Addison, Joseph, 90
Aelred of Rievaulx, 142–43
Age: middle age, 217–18; old age, 37, 91, 212, 214–25; youth, 29, 35–37, 90–91, 111, 214–25
Ambrose of Milan, 24, 39–40, 141, 210–11
Anticipation, 25–26, 32–33, 37–40, 42–43, 57, 82, 131, 152–53, 183, 209, 216
Arendt, Hannah, 107–8, 110
Aristotle, 8, 16, 17, 45, 49, 89, 118, 140–41, 147, 226
Arnold, Matthew, 164
Augustine of Hippo, 4, 8, 9, 14, 24, 38, 40, 60–61, 64–65, 75, 88–89, 90, 105, 116, 134, 141, 182, 184, 188–91, 211
Austen, Jane, 169

Bacon, Francis, 104
Balthasar, Hans Urs von, 160, 180
Barth, Karl, 78, 105, 217, 219
Basil of Caesarea, 145
Benedict XVI, 63
Benedict of Myrsa, 130
Benjamin, Walter, 177
Berkouwer, G. C., 78, 84
Bernard of Clairvaux, 142
Beveridge Report, 121
Bewilderment, 200–207
Bianco da Siena, 21
Body, 48, 105–6, 146, 192, 196, 207, 208, 219
Bolcher, Henri, 75
Bolt, Robert, 181
Bonhoeffer, Dietrich, 86, 100
Book of Common Prayer, 84, 133
Brahms, Johannes, 2
Brown, Peter, 146
Brunner, Emil, 144
Burke, Edmund, 147
Butler, Judith, 179

Carroll, Lewis, 172
Chenu, M.-D., 107
Chesterton, G. K., 86
Christendom, 61, 93–101, 197–99
Chrysostom, John, 129
Church, ecclesiology, 2, 8, 15, 19, 22–23, 47, 58, 60–63, 74, 79, 82–84, 91, 93–95, 129, 132, 158–61, 180, 194–98
Cicero, Marcus Tullius, 24, 39, 109, 140–43
Collaboration, 115–16, 124–26, 131–32
Communication, 5, 8, 22, 23, 45–71, 102, 106–7, 111, 135, 137, 163–76, 179–80, 182–97, 223

Index of Names and Subjects

Community, 5, 8–9, 15, 19–20, 22, 45–59, 65, 76–77, 81–83, 101, 106, 125, 159, 160, 184, 188–90, 193–94, 198. *See also* Two cities
Competition, 150–52
Compromise, 63–65, 93, 97–98, 100–101, 195, 220
Conflict, 2, 11, 96, 101, 148, 150–51, 188
Conscience, 44; good and bad, 85, 140, 210; prospective, 42
Consequence, 24, 32, 36
Cosin, John, 84

Davidson, Andrew, 200
Davies, Oliver, 155
Deacon, *diakonia*, 129–30
Death, 28–30, 41, 43, 87, 128, 156, 158, 202, 207–14, 219, 222, 224, 228
Decision, 6, 23–24, 26–28, 45, 70, 83, 89, 136, 147, 182, 190, 206, 212
Deliberation, 1, 4, 12, 19, 21, 23, 25–28, 30, 41, 42, 119, 182, 209
Democracy, 96, 191
De Quincey, Thomas, 97–99, 129
Description, 73, 151, 166, 170–75, 179, 182–83, 197
Desire, 12–14, 26–27
Displacement, 124
Dogmatics, 40, 72–73, 76–77, 87, 102, 204
Donne, John, 61, 68, 161
Drama, 166, 180–82

Edwards, Jonathan, 3, 73
Eliot, T. S., 169, 221, 228–29
End: of action, 2–3, 5, 8, 14, 23–42, 45–46, 51–53, 56, 70, 119, 129, 135, 148, 152, 202, 207–9, 212; of all things, of time, 3, 37–40, 67, 96, 108, 112, 158, 180, 202, 211, 214, 224; cessation, close, 2, 28–29, 179, 202, 207–11, 214–16; and means, 31; ultimate, 9, 11, 33, 37–40, 45, 61, 129, 183, 216
Epicurus, 208

Faith, 1–2, 6–8, 12, 14–18, 21–22, 57, 70, 74, 75–78, 81–82, 88, 92, 127, 141, 156–57, 193, 200–203, 213, 221, 225, 229
Faithfulness: of description, 169–70, 191; of God, Christ, 85, 168, 207, 227; of human action, 88, 128, 180, 182–83, 219, 223
Falsehood, 57, 62, 69, 164, 178, 183–92
Ferguson, Adam, 123
Fernandez, Ramón, 9–10, 17
Fessard, Gaston, 55, 57
Forrester, Duncan, 103
Forster, E. M., 148–49
Frei, Hans, 177
Friendship, 135–62, 186, 197, 221; with Christ, 153–62; with God, 77, 153; political, 147, 150

Galbraith, J. K., 51
Gilleman, Gérard, 10–12, 15, 18
God, 6, 11, 18–19, 36–37, 52, 76, 83, 121, 137, 154, 164, 184, 227; as agent, 4, 7, 14, 19, 22–23, 46, 52–53, 72–85, 88, 92–100, 105–6, 114, 120–21, 128, 131, 133, 164, 175, 182, 192, 193, 197–98, 216, 222, 225; as good, 7, 52; as holy, 66, 72, 74, 79, 91; as love, 8, 12, 18, 85, 225–26. *See also* Judgment
Goethe, J. W. von, 166, 171, 204
Good(s), 3, 13, 40, 48, 50–53, 59, 63, 79, 124, 135, 189, 203, 220, 227; common, 53–59, 61
Gosse, Edmund, 49
Gregory, Eric, 97
Gregory of Nazianzus, 145
Gregory of Nyssa, 130
Griffiths, Paul, 188
Grotius, Hugo, 18, 75
Growth, 90–93, 126, 142–43, 152, 154

Habit, 9, 89–90, 99, 109–10
Happiness, 20, 39–40, 129
Hauerwas, Stanley, 176
Hegel, G. W. F., 8, 30, 107, 171
Heidegger, Martin, 15, 209–10
Henry VIII, 166, 181
Herbert, George, 111–12, 119, 121

INDEX OF NAMES AND SUBJECTS

Herodotus, 33
Hobbes, Thomas, 136, 152
Höffner, Joseph, 54
Holbein, Hans, 166
Holiness, 72–74, 84–85, 91
Holy Spirit, 7–9, 72, 75, 79, 82–83, 89, 153, 155, 158–59, 193, 204
Hooker, Richard, 18
Hope, 1–9, 15, 19, 57, 69–70, 78, 92, 183, 200–202, 209–10, 213–14, 224–26
Hostility, 147–52
Housman, A. E., 213
Hume, David, 16

Interest, 5, 20, 47–56
Irenaeus of Lyons, 6

James VI/I, 99
Jesus Christ, 7, 17, 44, 72–77, 82–84, 93, 118, 128–29, 153–62, 207, 213–14; teaching of, 49–50, 69, 80, 88, 133–34, 146, 176, 206
John of Salisbury, 54
John Paul II, 108, 111, 117
Jones, David Albert, 211
Judgment, 36–37, 40–44, 62–63, 85, 87, 89, 99, 143, 152, 195, 199, 205, 210–11, 226–27
Jüngel, Eberhard, 225
Justification, 18, 35, 45–46, 74–75, 77, 88, 126–28, 134, 143, 157, 192–93, 222

Kant, Immanuel, 8
Kierkegaard, Søren, 15, 36, 155–56
Kilmer, Joyce, 168
Kingdom of God/Heaven, 3–5, 8, 18, 38–40, 44, 60–61, 83, 94, 171, 211, 214, 227–29

Lacoste, Jean-Yves, 136–38, 163, 168, 184, 210
Language, 163, 167, 170, 172–73, 185
Levinas, Emmanuel, 163
Lewis, C. S., 90–91, 215
Livy, Titus, 174
Locke, John, 16

Love, 1–19, 22, 70, 77–78, 81–82, 92, 134–35, 144, 153–55, 184–85, 200–203, 214, 222, 225–29; *agapē*, 5–6, 132, 155; charity, 6, 10, 19, 142, 200–201; devotion, 14, 227–29; *eros*, 4, 12, 27, 140, 166, 228; for God, 8, 10, 67, 81, 153, 225; of money, 67, 69–70; of self, 67, 69; and truth, 2, 17, 190–91; of the world, 6, 81, 120, 203, 225, 227–28
Luther, Martin, 15, 17–18, 98, 196
Lying. *See* Falsehood

Management, 20, 115–17, 125–26
Mann, Thomas, 203
Marriage, 63, 74, 104, 140, 142, 144–46
Marsilius of Padua, 62
Martensen, H., 8
Marx, Karl, 107, 122
Meaning, 4, 27–28, 33, 48–49, 52–53, 80, 106–7, 110, 126–28, 135, 158, 163–99, 204–5, 228
Milbank, John, 15–19
Milton, John, 203, 206–7
Moralism, 196
More, Thomas, 181
Motive, 13–14
Murdoch, Iris, 41, 210

Narrative, 23, 66, 73, 170–83
Natural law, 63–64, 121
Newman, J. H., 15–18
Nicene Council, 94
Nietzsche, Friedrich, 130
Nygren, Anders, 12

O'Connor, Frank, 149–50, 166
Origen of Alexandria, 76, 168

Pain, 203–4
Pascal, Blaise, 15
Paulinus of Nola, 146
Peter (apostle), 160, 224
Philadelphia, 159–60
Philo of Alexandria, 67, 153
Pieper, Josef, 118
Pietism, 213

Index of Names and Subjects

Plato, 13, 140, 187, 209
Plutarch, 140, 159
Polycarp of Smyrna, 69
Postmodernism, 15, 169–70, 172
Pride, 65–70
Promise, 3, 12, 19, 38–40, 57, 128, 136–39, 152, 179–80, 183, 214, 224
Property, 49–50, 58–59, 130
Providence, 93, 96, 169

Qoheleth. *See in Index of Scripture References under* Ecclesiastes

Rahner, Karl, 77
Ramsey, Paul, 3, 103–4
Reflection, 2, 8, 21, 40–43, 80–82, 92, 120, 164, 166, 216, 228
Rest, 3, 6, 14, 19, 30, 38, 41–44, 70, 88, 109–10, 120–21, 134, 144, 214
Rist, John M., 153, 226
Rougemont, Denis de, 213

Sanctification, 65, 72–102, 105–7, 127–34, 153, 159–62, 192–93, 197, 202, 214, 222
Sauter, Gerhard, 175–77
Scofield, Paul, 181
Secularity, 15, 61, 93–95
Shakespeare, William, 68
Simon, Yves, 107
Socrates, 209
Stevenson, Robert Louis, 29
Suffering, 128, 201–8; distinct from sorrow, 201–3

Teilhard de Chardin, Pierre, 107, 112–13

Thanksgiving, 73, 78–86, 88, 222
Thiselton, Anthony C., 1
Thomas Aquinas, 9, 49
Time, 3, 7–8, 18–19, 35–37, 57, 70–71, 80, 91, 104, 113–14, 148, 152, 171, 174, 201, 208–9, 211, 214–17, 222–24
Truth, 17, 59, 63–64, 98, 144, 165, 172, 183–92, 194
Two cities, 59–65

Ulrich, Hans, 102–3, 177

Vanhoozer, Kevin, 180, 195
Vatican Council II, 54
Vaughan, Henry, 221
Vocation, 78
Volf, Miroslav, 113

Webster, John, 84, 177
Weeks, Stuart, 34
Wesley, Charles, 73, 84, 87, 93
Wesley, John, 73, 87
Whittier, John Greenleaf, 156–57
Wilberforce, William, 99
Work, 107–34
World, 4, 8, 13, 17, 23, 33, 42–43, 52, 68–69, 95–97, 108–14, 119–20, 137, 154, 165, 166, 174, 179, 192–93, 201–5, 213–14, 220–21, 224–29
Wright, N. T., 171
Wrong, 121–27, 147–52, 183–92
Wyclif, John, 52

Yeats, William Butler, 143

Index of Scripture References

OLD TESTAMENT

Genesis
1:1–2:4	171
1:31	120, 164
2:15	108
2:18	135
2:19	109
3:1–15	66
9:25	121
18	177

Deuteronomy
18:18–22	183

Judges
9:36	187, 189

1 Samuel
3	195

Job 44, 204
38:4–7	64

Psalms
30:9	201
35:19	147, 150
37:25	214, 216, 223
41:9	147, 152
49	34
55:20	147
65:1–2	80
66:16–19	88
69:4	147, 150
90:17	128
103:13	223
116:15	210
119	167–68
122:1	9

Proverbs 34, 37
20:29	217

Ecclesiastes (Qoheleth) 33–37, 113, 171
1:2–11	35
1:12–2:26	35
3:1–9	35
3:10–15	36, 37
3:22	109
4:13–16	36
8:5	36
9:16	36
11:9	36
12:11–12	34
12:14	36

Isaiah
14:12–15	66
64:6	44

Jeremiah
4:23–26	39, 137–38
6:14	101

Ezekiel
36:26	92

Joel
2:28	224

Amos
5:18–20	38

INTERTESTAMENTAL LITERATURE

Sirach
10:12–13	66

Wisdom
14:12	66

Index of Scripture References

NEW TESTAMENT

Matthew

5:16	127
6:4	83
6:9	83
6:10	80–81
6:13	81
10:8	39
10:34	63
11:25–27	80
18:20	150
20:1–16	118, 133
25:14–30	118
28:20	158, 162, 192

Mark

1:15	3, 87
3:29	204
8:34	206
13:14	66
15:34	83
16:8	157
16:20	128

Luke

10:21–22	80
10:41–42	134
11:33	159
12:10	204
12:16–21	50, 69
12:48	88
15:11–32	178–79
16:21	48–49
18:9–14	88
19:11–27	118
22:27	129
24:31–32	157
24:36–43	157

John

4:34	128
5:36	128
8:44	184
10:4	17
12:24	199
13:1–30	153
13:31–35	153, 154
14:6	183
14:15–31	153
15:1–25	153
15:26–16:15	153
17	153
17:4	128
17:17	74
17:21	83
19:30	128
20:13–16	157
20:17	192
20:19–20	157
20:22–23	82
21:6–7	157
21:15–17	155
21:18	224

Acts

1:3	153
1:24–25	83
2:33	77
4:32	58
6	130
20:32	74
20:35	49
23:1	85
24:16	85
26:18	74

Romans

3:28	127
4:24	75, 192
5:1–11	6–8
6:19	74
6:22	74
12:1	21
12:3	21
12:9–10	22, 159
15:16	74
15:26	47
15:30	132
16:3	131
16:9	131
16:21	131

1 Corinthians

1:2	74
1:28	228
1:30	74
2:6	89
3:9	131
3:16	74
4:4	85
6:11	74
7:34	74
10:12	88
12:31	5, 132
13:3	5
13:4–6	2
13:7–8	202, 225
13:13	1, 6, 19
16:16	131

2 Corinthians

1:22	90
1:24	131
3:3	119
4:7	160
4:16	219
5:5	90
5:20–6:1	131
7:1	74
8:23	131
13:13	5, 47

Galatians

5:1	20
5:6	7, 17, 77
6:14	214

Ephesians

1:14	90
5:26–27	74
6:6	130

Philippians

1:6	79
1:27	132
2:2–5	5, 20
2:25	131
4:3	132

235

INDEX OF SCRIPTURE REFERENCES

Colossians
1:7 — 131
1:22 — 74
3:1 — 177
3:12–17 — 81
3:22 — 130
3:23 — 129
4:7 — 131
4:11 — 131

1 Thessalonians
2:10 — 74
3:2 — 131
3:13 — 74
4 — 74
4:9 — 159
5:23 — 74, 105, 193

2 Thessalonians
2:3 — 66
2:13 — 74

1 Timothy
1:5 — 85, 194
1:19 — 85
2:15 — 74
3:2 — 195
3:9 — 85
3:15 — 194
4:2 — 85
6:10 — 69
6:17–18 — 69–70

2 Timothy
1:6–14 — 194–95
1:7 — 193–94
2:5 — 151
2:13 — 85
2:20–21 — 85–86
2:24 — 195
3:1–5 — 67–69
4:2 — 195

Titus
1:8 — 74

Philemon
1 — 131
2 — 131
24 — 131

Hebrews — 74
5:14 — 89
9:14 — 85
9:27 — 43
10:22 — 85
12:6 — 85
12:10 — 74
12:14 — 74, 88
13:1 — 159
13:18 — 85

James
1:27 — 160
2:22–23 — 77
3:1 — 195
4:1 — 69
4:4 — 153
5:14–15 — 160

1 Peter
1:2 — 74
1:15–16 — 74
1:22 — 74, 159
2:9 — 192
3:16 — 85
3:21 — 85
4:17 — 85

2 Peter
1:4–8 — 12, 92
3:18 — 90

1 John
1:1 — 175
2:7–8 — 4, 225
3:3 — 74, 79
3:16 — 154
4:8 — 18, 225

3 John
8 — 132

Revelation
2:2 — 89
2:17 — 128
5:5–6 — 47
3:19 — 85
6:9–11 — 80, 131
13 — 66
14:6–8 — 93
14:13 — 128
15:3 — 82
15:4 — 82
21:1 — 228
21:1–22:5 — 171
21:9–10 — 46–47
21:22 — 226
21:25–27 — 60